SETTING THE STAGE

MONTREAL THEATRE
1920–1949

SETTING THE STAGE

HERBERT WHITTAKER

Edited by Jonathan Rittenhouse

McGILL-QUEEN'S UNIVERSITY PRESS
Montreal & Kingston · London · Ithaca

© McGill-Queen's University Press 1999
ISBN 0-7735-2002-3
Legal deposit fourth quarter 1999
Bibliothèque nationale du Québec

Printed in Canada on acid-free paper

This book has been published with the help of grants from
the Samuel and Saidye Bronfman Family Foundation,
the McLean Foundation, and David Webster.

Canadä

McGill-Queen's University Press acknowledges
the financial support of the Government of Canada through
the Book Publishing Industry Development Program
(BPIDP) for its activities. We also acknowledge
the support of the Canada Council for the Arts for
our publishing program.

Canadian Cataloguing in Publication Data

Whittaker, Herbert, 1910–
Setting the stage : Montreal theatre, 1920–1949
Includes bibliographical references and index.
ISBN 0-7735-2002-3
1. Theater – Quebec (Province) – Montreal – History.
1. Rittenhouse, Jonathan, 1953–   . II. Title.
PN2306.M6W45 1999   792'.09714'28   C99-900744-0

"The Story So Far" and chapters 1–9 are a revised,
expanded, and corrected version of "Whittaker's Montreal:
A Theatrical Autobiography, 1910–1949," edited and with
an introduction by Rota Herzberg Lister, which appeared
in *Canadian Drama* 12 (Fall 1986).

Designed by David Drummond

CONTENTS

FOREWORD

Christopher Plummer

I was just sixteen when Herbert Whittaker made me a "star." So miasmal was the mist I floated through, I can barely remember the year. I think it was 1946. Why the distinguished drama critic of the *Gazette* had stooped to review a mere school production at Montreal High (from which I was nearly expelled twice), I had not a clue – but there I was in print, larger than life; and there they were – those golden words of praise for all to see. Of course, my head was instantly turned and I became even more arrogant and insufferable than the creature I was attempting to portray – the proud, disdainful Mr Darcy from Jane Austen's *Pride and Prejudice*. Grossly overblown by Mr Whittaker's flattering prose, I was convinced that I alone had not only helped Montreal to reach new artistic heights but that the whole of Canada itself had benefitted and taken several substantial steps up its cultural ladder. Not content with leaving me in this heady state of euphoria, Mr Whittaker further indulged my bloated ego by enrolling me in the Montreal Repertory Theatre, the MRT – the city's top English-speaking amateur stage company. No autographs! Please don't touch me! I'd arrived and, as was to be expected, had grown utterly prejudiced in my own favour. There was no turning back now! No, sir! Whittaker, whittingly or no, had sent me down the long path of destruction that was to be my life. I think he has a lot to answer for.

We were both Montrealers, Herbie and I, enjoying in our separate ways the glory years of the thirties and forties when that unique bilingual metropolis could, with a lascivious wink, smugly boast that it never closed, that it had almost as many nightclubs, casinos, and whorehouses as there were days of the year, and that jaded New Yorkers who had run out of trouble could more than easily be replenished by simply staggering across the border to our colourfully corrupt, persistently bad, and wide-open city of sin.

Besides trouble, there were big bands galore, non-stop jazz, superb cabarets, and that genius of strip, Lili St Cyr. Visiting theatrical, ballet, and opera companies from Europe and the U.S. with their attendant "stars" bustled in and arrived on our doorstep. You could easily ignore the cold, dreary winters, for every day was like an international festival. Somewhere, quietly in the background, however, the locals were getting restless. The French-Canadian artistic scene was showing signs of emerging importantly, our symphony orchestra was getting pretty good, Maynard Ferguson was blowing some cool trumpet in our school band, and young Oscar Peterson, tickling the ivories at the Alberta Lounge, was at the foot of his rainbow. But all this was barely noticeable amidst the hoopla, the imported glamour, the frenetic wild nights, for Montreal had fallen in love with itself as an original, multilingual, vital melting pot of activity which left the rest of Canada far behind.

As a journalist on the spot, Herbie covered everything there was to cover, except possibly the waterfront. Amateur theatre both French and English, films, ballet, and nightclub shows were his beat. He never went to bed – he was a creature of the night. When the famous visiting celebrities he had critiqued and interviewed waved him goodbye and vanished from our shores, Herbie's address book looked like a theatrical who's who. Many became his lifelong friends – rare for someone as threatening as a critic. But one day when the ballyhoo had subsided, the final curtain lowered on the last great touring company, and a mournful drumbeat ushered in the imminent death of jazz – the dream was over, and he plainly saw, now more than ever, that his fellow citizens, his very own brothers and sisters, hungry to express themselves in something other than hockey, were crying in the wilderness. So, taking every spirit to its full height, he vowed to do something about it.

Without once forsaking his pen, Herbert became a "straddler." He boldly climbed over the footlights, and before you could say "George Spelvin" had established himself as a first-class director and one of the best set designers in the country. He traveled across Canada between stints, seeking out talent old and young. He was involved in many a Dominion Drama Festival and directed and designed new Canadian plays, including Robertson Davies' *A Jig for the Gypsy*, which launched the Crest Theatre in Toronto for its first full season. By 1949 he had left Montreal to become the major drama critic at Toronto's *Globe and Mail*. Still he persisted in wearing his many hats and continued to create in the theatre, designing and directing a host of productions everywhere, among them Samuel Beckett's *Endgame* and, as early as 1951, Brecht's *Galileo*. He whipped up sets and costumes for three *King Lears* (Christopher Ellis's, John Colicos', and William Hutt's – the latter a daringly imaginative Inuit version that the Canadian Players toured cross-country). Co-sponsored by the *Globe and Mail*, he and Michael Langham established the Canadian Play Contest to encourage potential playwrights. For his tireless efforts he at last began to be recognized nationally and the awards and honours started to come his way – honorary degrees from York University and McGill University, the Order of Canada, honorary member of Canadian Actors' Equity, and countless more, but never enough to pay proper homage to his priceless contributions. When the Stratford, Ontario Festival was launched, he helped by ceaselessly promoting it in the press and he has served on the advisory board of the Shaw Festival at Niagara-on-the-Lake. Long since retired from the *Globe and Mail*, Herbie remains our senior critic – the Critic Emeritus of Canada – a devoted duty he has performed far beyond the horizon of its requirements. For all of us young writers and actors he helped lay the ground rules; he was there when we needed him.

It is well known that critics often achieve extra prominence through the causes they champion. Bernard Shaw allied himself with the new wave of modernism

by standing firmly behind Ibsen; ditto Kenneth Tynan when he sang out for
the "kitchen sink" and Arden, Wesker, and Osborne. In America, Eric Bentley
brazenly bored for Brecht. But Whittaker had nothing tangible to endorse when
he began. He had to get behind a whole country largely Calvinist in its indifference to things artistic and convince it that within its own boundaries such a
thing as art actually could exist; that its own talents hiding in amateur workshops
and church basements across the land would only come out of the closet if
someone had the guts to pay them. He didn't bully – he didn't push – through
his words he slowly but surely nursed a nation into realizing that what they had
at home was as good as anybody else had anywhere in the world. Other critics
(just as sincere perhaps) echoed his sentiments but their style was lofty and
remote, their knowledge limited, more cerebral than practical, and they lacked
his constancy and commitment. Herbie's conviction was deep-rooted and personal, it was his life; and his voice was the only really human voice we could
listen to. And we listened not just because he was firm, tolerant, and wise, but
because we saw that he loved and served the theatre and the arts as passionately
as we aspired to – that he had come over to our side and proved himself a
friend. I don't think there is anyone who has done more to free our country
of its old prejudices toward home-grown talent than Herbert Whittaker and it
was back in the good ol' bad ol' days in the Montreal he writes about, when
there was such a profusion of life imitating art, that his dream and mission
became one and the same.

Herbie is as young now as he ever was. In fact, he looks just about the same
as he did forty years ago. He walks everywhere, at great speed; he travels the
world catching up with old friends and new, and still sees everything there is
to see. His energy never falters. On a face that proudly reveals nary a line nor
a crease, there still remains an expression of innocence, surprise, joy, and curiosity – a look untarnished by time that I find most sinister in its implications

and which is slowly driving me quite mad with jealousy and rage. As I toss and turn and wrestle with my straight-jacket, I swear, on my very own grave, there has to be *some* grizzly portrait in *some* attic, *some*where that he is keeping from us in his customary devious underhanded way or my name isn't Mr Darcy of "Pemberley" county Derbyshire with ten thousand pounds a year!

ACKNOWLEDGMENTS

I owe so much gratitude, even for the period covered herewith, that my declaration would delay publication unbearably for me. Let me, then, make a few specific thanks, doing so chronologically, which should please my enormously contributing editor, Jonathan Rittenhouse.

My earliest genuflection goes to Professor Rota Herzberg-Lister of the University of Waterloo, who edited an earlier venture into memoir for *Canadian Drama* in 1986. Then to Jack McLelland for his early encouragement of the project. Next to Richard Horenblas who converted my typewritten manuscript to electronic format and to John Hobday and the Samuel and Saidye Bronfman Family Foundation for funding this process. To John Hobday himself who, with the collaboration of my dear friend Eric McLean (music critic of the *Montreal Daily Star* and the *Gazette*) drew this manuscript to the attention of the McGill-Queen's University Press, which took seriously its historical value.

So my gratitude reaches its peak at *Setting the Stage*'s present glorious incarnation, achieved under the guidance of Professor Rittenhouse with the assistance of Professor Rebecca Harries, also of Bishop's University, and Lisa Gaskell, student research assistant.

Aurèle Parisien, as editor for McGill-Queen's University Press, heads the valiant team of publishing experts responsible for the final product, having persuaded Professor Rittenhouse to undertake his monumental labour of love. The Samuel and Saidye Bronfman Family Foundation was joined by both the McLean Foundation and David Webster in generously supporting publication.

Being grateful to Jon Rittenhouse is second nature as he compiled a tribute and chronology for *Theatre History in Canada* 3 (Spring 1982), which turned me into a historical figure from being previously just an old friend of his family.

And I still have thanks left over for Christopher Plummer's witty and imaginative foreword, which I advise you to read if you have not already done so. Part of the Plummer distinction in theatre is the gift of remembering the good reviews, not just the bad ones. For that unique ability, my whole Canadian Theatre Critics Association thanks him also.

Space for a few other personal attributions: Nini Dagenais, for her francophone help in particular; Kate Barris, easing me into the computer century; Jeniva Berger, sharing the concerns of the Canadian Theatre Critics Association, which I thank for naming a national award after me; Margaret McBurney, its president, and the Arts and Letters Club in general; and finally, my beloved nephew, Jeffrey, and all the Western Whittakers, to whom this early memoir is affectionately dedicated.

Herbert Whittaker

INTRODUCTION

Jonathan Rittenhouse

The stage Herbert Whittaker sets for us is developmental and not strictly chronological. A short historical introduction – a Whittaker-eye view of things theatrical and cultural in his hometown – combined with a sketch of his family and early upbringing prepare us for the personal assessment of Whittaker's Montreal that is to come. He begins, then, by sketching in his openness to and love of the possibilities of the stage as a precocious and avid theatre-watcher, a child of the twenties seeing American movies and British and American performers, mostly unaware of locally produced fare – either English or French.

In the traditional way of most Montrealers of his era, he involved himself in theatre during the 1930s through connection to a church – the Church of the Messiah and the annual productions of its Everyman Players – and to a school – West Hill High and its productions of Shakespeare, in which he worked with my father. In these amateur arenas, as he so carefully details in chapter 2, he found his creative footing and inspiration. And he also found mentors and friends, people like Montreal musician and Everyman Players' producer George Brewer and his daughter Marjorie, and a special friend in my father. As he reminds us in his next chapter, "Finding a Role," he had yet to find the fullest opportunity to express his overwhelming sense that what he was doing was neither marginal nor insubstantial but, rather, vital to his own Everyman quest for self-identity and cultural confidence. However, becoming a newspaper professional at the *Gazette* would provide the careful watcher and neophyte practitioner with just such a tribune. Guided and helped by another good friend, his colleague Tom Archer, Whittaker experienced an unhurried but expanding apprenticeship to eventually become an astute theatre and entertainment critic and observer of Montreal's passing show.

While the prologue and first three chapters of *Setting the Stage* fully cover the chronological period of 1920–49, and so trace Whittaker's personal and professional evolution in Montreal, they do not tell the whole story. Focusing on Montreal's premier English-language producing company, the amateur Montreal Repertory Theatre, in chapters 4 and 5 Whittaker provides an insider's view and appreciation of Montreal's successful and influential amateur theatre through the thirties and forties. Many names are noted in these chapters but Martha Allan's name and influence on the little theatre movement in Montreal is given top billing.

As the memoir continues, chapter 6 offers an evocative assessment and paean to summer theatre ventures in Lachine and further east in Knowlton, Quebec, where Montreal theatre artists could play at theatre and dream of possible professional careers. And the next chapter further provides its readers with snapshots of the lively and varied theatrical fare produced by the many English-speaking communities that made up Montreal and details Whittaker's involvement with the YM-YWHA Players, the Negro Theatre Guild, the Canadian Art Theatre, and other amateur groups.

As he became more involved in theatre reviewing at *The Gazette*, Whittaker highlights for us in chapter 8 some of the more memorable shows he saw and admired from his vast storehouse of local viewing and precious visits to New York. Yet as his knowledge of theatre grew, the limitations in Montreal that would make it difficult for him to continue to evolve as either theatre practitioner or critic convince him, when opportunity knocks, to take up a job offer from Toronto's *Globe and Mail*.

In the final chapter, however, Whittaker provides one last survey of his hometown's theatre, this time concentrating on the great flourishing of French-language theatre at the dawn of the local professional stage. In particular he celebrates the many and complementary achievements of the classically oriented and spiritually influenced père Émile Legault and his company les Compagnons de Saint-Laurent, the populist Gratien Gélinas with his *Fridolinades* revues and spectacularly successful play *Tit-Coq,* and the intensely secular and contemporary Pierre Dagenais in the work of his company l'Équipe.

One last memory supplies the book's Epilogue – a 1953 one-night only extravaganza on top of Mount Royal of *King Lear.* Let me take the opportunity to conclude this brief introduction (a contextual afterword, chronology, and bibliography follow Whittaker's text) with one personal anecdote of my own. As a student beginning my doctoral studies at the Graduate Centre for the Study of Drama at the University of Toronto in fall 1975, I found myself in the somewhat difficult circumstances of having accommodation in a rooming house that I found less than congenial. Fortunately "Uncle Herbie" saved me by offering up his sofa to me for as long as I needed it. I stayed the year. In that year, however, both of us underwent those life experiences that mark one's life. Uncle Herbie retired from the *Globe and Mail* after decades of meeting deadlines and living the rhythm of the theatrical life. What was to come? And I received a telephone call in early December from my father telling me that Mom had passed away sooner than anyone had expected from her long battle with cancer. I remember feeling guilty that I had not been there at the end. But I do remember that as I immediately got ready to go home and looked around at Uncle Herbie's apartment, filled with the books, papers, posters, and memorabilia of theatre life that helped preserve his memories, I felt somehow cushioned from the blow I had received. What was to come? I did not know but the space I was in at that bleak moment provided solace that memories of my mother, Kathleen Marsh Rittenhouse, would live on. I thank Herbie for that.

SETTING THE STAGE

THE STORY SO FAR

In any country, no matter how thinly populated, no matter how widely scattered across a continent, people must eventually produce their own theatre, as objects on a landscape must produce their own shadows. The period when I arrived on the scene – I was born 20 September 1910 in Montreal – was an impoverished one, but it provided its own compensations. They were at first spontaneous, naive, perhaps a little absurd. There were concerts, recitations, and playlets; pageants, university and school theatricals; and much activity in church basements.

I should admit that when I started my Montreal theatre-going a decade or so later I didn't know what important indigenous theatre was stirring – what Martha Allan and the Community Players in Montreal, and all of those others from coast to coast, rallying slowly under the new banner of the little theatre movement, were working towards.[1] I had never even heard of Earl Grey's Musical and Dramatic competitions, which were held to encourage Canadian artists. They were the true begetters of the Dominion Drama Festival instituted by the Earl of Bessborough, Earl Grey's successor as Governor General of Canada, which was to become such a wonderful bridge to Canada's own theatre and a great stepping-stone for young theatre people like myself.[2]

Yet theatrical activity there was, as there had been in this country since its very beginnings, in many and varied forms. In fact, before I was born the Ice Palace behind my mother and father's flat on Pine Avenue had offered a form of theatre, especially when snowshoers paraded in their blanket coats, brandishing torches. And there were costume balls, some of them on ice, and winter carnivals.[3] The *Gazette*, the first paper I served, once editorially implored the great English tragedian Edmund Kean to visit Montreal. He did so twice in 1826: the first time he was received gloriously, the second time under a dark cloud because of romantic scandals and his drunkenness. The story is that Kean was so aware of the audience's censure for the latter that he left the theatre during the performance – at which point, insulted, the audience started to break up the building![4]

The crowded – and occasionally rough and squalid – theatres that welcomed Kean had been created in part by the officers and men of the British garrisons. They had numbered acting among their prized social accomplishments since the great David Garrick fever in the mid-1700s. In pursuing this peacetime activity, officers and men were only following the tradition of those military men in the winter of 1693–94 who had attempted a production of Molière's *Le tartuffe* in Governor General Frontenac's day and were stopped abruptly by the Church.

Frontenac's court had been entertained with socially successful presentations of Corneille's biblical drama *Nicomède* and Racine's classic *Mithridate*. Mazo de la Roche, in her 1944 book *Quebec, Historic Seaport*, imagined them as New World echoes of Versailles, "the thrill of enthusiasm stirring their hearts when, one winter, officers and ladies in striking costumes took part in these performances at the Chateau."[5] Such gaiety alarmed the clergy to the point of public condemnation and pastoral letters were written denouncing such dangerous frivolity. But when Frontenac was persuaded to allow Molière's scandalous 1664 comedy *Le tartuffe*, he faced more direct opposition. Meeting Frontenac on the street, Monsignor de Saint-Vallier, the Bishop of Quebec, bought him off that project for the sum of 100 pistoles. To do him justice, it must be reported that the Governor General accepted the bribe but turned it over to the hospital the following day.[6]

A position had thus been taken by the Catholic Church, and accepted, that was to have a long and persistent effect on the development of theatre in the province. (So strongly was the control established that it lasted well into the regime of Premier Maurice Duplessis, with his support.) Quebec had to wait another hundred years, until 1774, for the first performances of Molière – given in Montreal by British officers. Accomplished actors, they played *Le bourgeois gentilhomme* and *Le médecin malgré lui* – in the original language, no less.[7]

It has been estimated that at one time the garrison was responsible for one-third of Montreal's theatre. It was this same healthy garrison theatre that welcomed Charles Dickens on his much-publicized visit to Montreal in 1842. On one evening the stage-struck novelist starred in Thomas Morton's *A Roland for an Oliver*, the interlude *Two O'clock in the Morning*, and Poole's farce *Deaf as a Post* with Sir Charles Bagot in the audience. "A splendid scene … and didn't I come the Macready over them!" boasted Dickens. "The pains I have taken with them and the perspiration I have expended during the last 10 days exceed in amount anything you can imagine," he wrote to his life-long friend John Forster. A Montreal stage carpenter was impressed, conceding that Dickens was "a loss to the profession when he took up writing."[8]

Did these early days of drama feature only imported plays? They would have been excused if they had done so, more so than we can be today. But those redoubtable garrison actors were occasionally capable of original work, albeit in the field of burlesques or satires. One of my prized programmes is for the last of a series of "amateur private theatricals" at the Theatre Royal in 1865. Inasmuch as one can judge a performance by its programme, *Dolorsolatio*, the show in question, must have provided a great finale to the season.[9] Described as "a serio-tragical-comical-political-allegorical extravaganza," *Dolorsolatio* was presented under the patronage of Lt. Gen. Sir Fenwick Williams, Bart., KCB, Commander of the British Forces in North America. The cast was headed by Col. Lord Russell, RB, who played Grandpapa Canada himself, his older son being played by Lt. Col. Wolseley. Garnet Joseph Wolseley had been sent to Canada as Assistant Quartermaster General in 1861; he commanded the Red

River Expedition against the first Riel uprising in 1870. It would be interesting to know how good his acting was.

I write at such length about the gentlemen amateurs of the garrison because I have never underestimated the importance of the non-professional in establishing a national culture. Which was more representative of that emerging culture in 1865: the boisterous efforts of the officers and men making fun of Montreal life and the struggle for Confederation in *Dolorsolatio* or the desperate efforts of the growing number of needy theatre managers of the era to reproduce the popular fare imported from London?

Montreal's theatre-minded publics, French and English, encouraged the building of a series of edifices over the years and important new visitors graced these stages. In the year 1880 came the Divine Sarah Bernhardt, the most universally popular of French stars. Mgr Edouard Fabre, Bishop of Montreal, forbade his parishioners to attend immoral works such as the Bernhardt staple *Adrienne Lecouvreur*; but this only encouraged the Montrealers who flocked to Scribe and Legouvé's play as well as to Meilhac and Halevy's *Frou-Frou*, Dumas' fils *La dame aux camélias* (matinee only), and *Hernani* by Hugo. The receipts were described by a delighted Sarah as "fabulous"; in appreciation, she sent along a contribution to the Bishop.[10]

I loved to discover such old glories of Montreal's theatre. Indeed, when I fell heir to a drama group, the Sixteen-Thirty Club, I invited Janet Alexandra McPhee to write a play based on Sarah's 1880 visit to the old Academy of Music. My suggestion for the title was *Divinity in Montreal*. I can't resist repeating one extra note to the Sarah story, told about Bernhardt's 1917 visit, her last, by a devoted friend of the theatre, Louis Mulligan, to one of Montreal's most dedicated historians, Edgar Andrew Collard. Louis had gone to the stage door of the new His Majesty's Theatre to see Bernhardt come out. "There was a car waiting for her and she appeared sitting on a Louis XVI chair with poles on either side and was carried away by two men, as she was minus a leg. She hopped into the car and when seated turned to us and bowed graciously. She wore a leopard-skin coat, a brilliant sequinned pillbox perched on her fuzzy mop of bright red hair, and was heavily made up. The people cried, 'Au revoir, Madam, revenez-vous!'" But she never did.[11]

A city grows in stature with the visits of such world figures. Talent, even if briefly passing through, enhances and enriches communities, and with such histrionic inspiration Canadians could not help but aspire to act. When the Depression years did not allow them to do so at home, the more ambitious of them went abroad. There were, of course, many who stayed home and satisfied themselves with roles in community productions, including this stage-struck but non-actor youth of Outremont.

How came I, a small Anglican in Outremont, unaware that he was living in the second largest French city in the world and having just crossed Park Avenue before attending Sunday school at the Church of the Ascension, to stand in awe of a poster of Cardinal Richelieu pronouncing "the curse of Rome" as delivered by Walter Hampden in Bulwer-Lytton's *Richelieu*, coming to His Majesty's next week?[12]

I was stage-struck. I had been even as a child. Taken to London as a baby to be exhibited to my mother's family, I was caught by the outbreak of World War I. Despite German air raid and burning zeppelin, I was exposed to English theatre and was hooked. What theatre? First, pantomime, where I complained loudly when the gates of Fairyland flew up for the big transformation scene: "Gates don't fly up! They open in the middle!" "Shush, Bertie."

I was happier when I discovered that the Venus de Milo, in a music hall tableau of living statues, was achieved by a lady in a white leotard wearing an uneven pair of black gloves in front of a black curtain. And I was reduced to hilarity when the fascinating American star Elsie Janis popped out of a YMCA hamper to explain to Maurice Chevalier that YMCA meant "You May Come Across." That 1918 revue, *Hello, America!,* remarked upon the entry of the United States into the war, then called the Great War.

What I wasn't so aware of was that this exposure to the glorious London theatre was being enjoyed at the expense of an average family life. My parents, George and Eleanor (Trappitt) Whittaker, had split. He reestablished himself in Westmount, with a new spouse and another son. My mother settled back in Outremont (where I had been born) with my brother George and myself, living in comparative poverty in a series of flats. But George, being older, said our mother's decision to return to Canada after the war was the best thing that ever happened to us. I guess he was right because he, a military man, got to be administrative head of two major military hospitals – St Mary's and Sunnybrook – and I, non-military, became drama critic of two major newspapers – the *Gazette* and the *Globe and Mail.*

The Church of the Ascension on Park Avenue was a way station enroute to downtown Montreal. There, in the church hall, I performed the Toff in Lord Dunsany's little thriller *The Idol's Eye.* That was the peak of my performance career, although I did act as conductor to my school choir sometime later at Strathcona Academy, being very conscious that my jacket was showing where my mother had mended it. I was too shy by then to face the audience. In fact, I had started to write speeches for other people to recite in the school competition. But my name appeared as art director on the school newspaper, not so jokingly called *The Bankrupt* in those advancing Depression years.

I didn't stay at Strathcona Academy beyond tenth grade. The rents on de l'Épée, Champagneur, Davaar, Bloomfield, Bernard, and Bloomfield again were the swords of Damocles for we three Whittakers. I had to help out. Luckily my mother's friend Madame Bernier managed to get me into the Canadian Pacific Railway as a junior clerk, in the tallest tower of the imposing Windsor Station. So I left Outremont behind and the rest of my childhood there: the little woods

The program cover of André Obey's *Noah*, which Whittaker saw in London (summer 1935).

near Guy Drummond School, the Big Woods up on Van Horne Avenue, favoured for playing Robin Hood and collecting trilliums and jack-in-the-pulpits. And Outremont Park, where I skated dismally on my ankles in the bitter winter twilight.

I'm afraid I cheated the CPR, for I eventually discovered that by going down to the stacks to search out invoices, I could find time to design costumes for church plays. And that I could get a pass to take my first holidays in New York, staying at the YMCA on 34th Street and eating at Neddick's, a quick-and-easy counter specializing in orange juice. In New York I saw such great Broadway fare as Lillian Gish in Sean O'Casey's *Within the Gates*; the Theatre Guild's lavish production of Molière's *The School for Wives*; Clifford Odets' *Gold Eagle Guy* (and discovered backstage how it staged the San Francisco earthquake); and the glorious revue *As Thousands Cheer*, with Marilyn Miller imitating Lynn Fontanne, Clifford Webb being Gandhi, Ethel Waters singing "Heat Wave," and Irving Berlin's "Easter Parade" as a rotogravure come to life.[13]

Such excursions and treats in theatre finally encouraged me to quit my CPR job in 1935 (if I needed any such encouragement) when mother offered me the chance to return to London. She had received a legacy from her brother Alf, the only one in the family who had stayed in the traditional family business of goldsmith, the legend being that the Trappitt family had a shop on London Bridge before it burned. So in that year I saw more great theatre: Russian ballet in Covent Garden Opera House, *A Midsummer Night's Dream* in Regent's Park, and, best of all, John Geilgud playing André Obey's *Noah*, directed by Michel Saint-Denis (with Alec Guinness playing the Wolf). I now suspect my mother knew then that I would find my vocation in theatre. After all she was a Londoner, and two of her brothers were actors. Why not? And she herself had made sure that theatre was part of my introduction to the great life.

Chapter One

BEGINNINGS:
HAMLET LAUNCHES THREE CAREERS

> Let four captains
> Bear Hamlet like a soldier to the stage,
> For he was likely, had he been put on,
> To have proved most royally; and for his passage,
> The soldiers' music and the rites of war
> Speak loudly for him.
> Take up the body. Such a sight as this
> Becomes the field, but here shows much amiss.
> Go, bid the soldiers shoot.   (V,ii)

Four tall soldiers bear the figure of the Prince upstage to the shallow platform backed by low parapets against a high red sky. As they raise him slowly, the stricken court drops as slowly to its knees. This double action signals the first of the cannon's boomings. On the second booming, the front curtain of His Majesty's Theatre in Montreal begins to descend. As the curtain hits the floor of the stage, I think my heart will burst!

These were the final moments of my first *Hamlet*, performed by Sir John Martin-Harvey and company on 2 January 1924, and following the scenic principles of his fellow member in Henry Irving's Lyceum Theatre Company Edward Gordon Craig. Overwhelmed as I was, I took note of how superbly Martin-Harvey had timed and planned that ending. The director within was stirring.

The Craig-like designs had yet another lasting impact. The great cyclorama and the low parapet were essential to the play's action. Embellishments were

A rendition of a famous moment in the Sir John Martin-Harvey production of *Hamlet*. This same production toured Canada in 1924.

added sparsely when necessary, including some ancient monuments for the graveyard and thrones for the court, backed by sweeping purple curtains emblazoned with shields, all against that huge stage sky – the tallest I have ever seen, I think. Returning home, I made maquettes of those designs, colouring them with pastels. I treasured them, and they must have been what inspired me to design so ambitiously for the stage.

But was the future critic absent that day? No, for much as I was willing and able to accept the sixty-year-old Sir John as the young prince, I had strong reservations about his wife, Miss Nina de Silva, and her realization of Ophelia. I remember her considerable bulk in a green robe and her voice quavering, "There's rosemary, that's for remembrance" across the century, and still hold them against her. I was later startled and somewhat ashamed of myself to find my kindly friend Robertson Davies putting in such a good word for her fictional counterpart in his splendid evocation of the Martin-Harveys in his *World of Wonders*.[1] A critic must learn to forgive.

As I look back across most of a century, I am less surprised that one *Hamlet* should inspire me in three different directions in the theatre than that I was later able to work in all of them. The opportunities in Canada in the 1920s presented few hopes for a career in the theatre. But I was fortunate in having encouragement at home, as many Canadians of my generation did not. Since my parents were former Londoners, accustomed to the theatre of a great city, it was taken for granted that theatre would be part of my life. I used to work hard at school to achieve the reward of a weekend visit to a theatre from my mother, bless her.

Montreal was still a good theatre city in the years after World War I. The old Gayety was a burlesque house, so that was ruled out for schoolboy visits with mother. But that still left His Majesty's, the Princess, and the Orpheum, the latter best known as a stock company theatre. That there were, of course, many other theatres in Montreal that favoured another language did not occur to me, as my family did not speak French. It was some years before I ventured to the Saint-Denis or the Monument-National.

My appreciation of Martin-Harvey as Hamlet was matched by that for his utter nobility as Sydney Carton in *The Only Way*, his sad charm as Tom Robertson's David Garrick, and the exciting stagecraft of his production of *The Lyons Mail*.[2] In that Charles Reade romance he made his exit as the good merchant and passed outside a row of inn windows, vanishing stage right at the exact moment he re-entered as the wicked highwayman through the inn door at stage left! That doubles' trick was repeated at the end of the melodrama. What a treat and what an exercise for the young theatre-goer who had to learn to be moved simultaneously but never exclusively – both by the performance and by the technique of the performance! That has to be credited to the critic's side of my ledger.

So does Martin-Harvey's revival of Irving's great success in Lewis's *The Bells* at His Majesty's in 1932. This play was one of Henry Irving's greatest Victorian triumphs. "This is proof indeed of the great Irving personality, for the play is the weakest peg to hang great acting on, containing as it does not one well-rounded characterization besides the central one." I quote myself from pencil notes on a yellowed programme. Obviously Martin-Harvey's performance of the Burgomaster, Mathias, did not convince me that he could rival Irving's magic and I wished I had seen him in Maeterlinck's play as that other Burgo-master, he of Stilemonde.

After so many years, I am still envious that it was my brother who was taken, from Lower Canada College, to see Martin-Harvey's celebrated production of Sophocles' *Oedipus Rex*, originally staged for him in 1912 by Max Reinhardt. Later, my editor at the *Globe and Mail*, Richard Doyle, was amused by my need to see any notable productions that my readers might have seen. But I was baffled, I admit, by what the veteran theatre critic of the *Montreal Daily Star*, S. Morgan-Powell, once said to me: "Until you have seen Johnston Forbes-Robertson play Hamlet, you have not seen *Hamlet*!" He thus doomed me forever since Forbes-Robertson was already dead. But I still boast of Martin-Harvey's Prince.

Martin-Harvey was not my only Shakespearean actor in those early Montreal days. In time, I was taken to see Robert Bruce Mantell play King Lear.[3] I regarded Mantell with some incredulity when he entered, his hands splayed under the large bottom of Genevieve Hamper's Cordelia, who was carried by two stronger men, crying "Howl, howl, howl!" I can hardly believe that Mr Mantell also played Gloucester, yet he did. I somehow think that I saw Miss Hamper double Cordelia with the Fool, a practice that carries one back to Shakespeare's original all-male company.

I had learned to spot talent in supporting casts by then. I particularly enjoyed Kenneth Wicksteed in the title role in a production of *Julius Caesar* by the Stratford-upon-Avon Festival Company of the Shakespeare Memorial Theatre at the Princess. I far preferred him to Wilfred Walter's Marcus Antonius, Eric Maxon's Marcus Brutus, or Dorothy Massingham's lisping Calpurnia when that company came my way in 1928, performing six plays in one week. I managed to see *Julius Caesar* and *The Merchant of Venice*, which had George Hayes playing Shylock.[4]

Back in those early Montreal years, I was generally attracted by those stars whose achievements were made more exciting by stage direction that favoured and flattered them. I had been saddened with the rest of the world when the greatest of them all, Sarah Bernhardt, died in 1923. From a local newspaper, I clipped out a rough reproduction of her as Phaedra with her arms outstretched – something I still have. Yet my sense of loss was sharper when Eleonora Duse perished of the cold in Pittsburgh one year later, for Montreal was on her schedule and I had been promised I would see her.

The star I recall most sharply was George Arliss, a dapper Englishman who had marked gifts as a high comedian, which suited the new performance style then beginning to prevail. I remember him most vividly at the Princess in April 1928 as Shylock in Winthrop Ames' company, which also included Peggy Wood as Portia and Spring Byington as Nerissa. Arliss's Venetian Jew was a highly British individual – urbane, cynical, smiling – smacking his lips over the bargain he was making. His extravagant exit from the courtroom, falling as he went, was topped for me by a curtain call that was the epitome of stage modesty. He was summoned, by public demand, after all the other players had taken their bows and departed the stage. His air of surprise, mingled with pleasure, was most touching. And when the stage manager slyly lifted the curtain again to catch him before he got over the bridge supplied by Winthrop Ames' production, we were all delighted at his further astonishment. Later, a more perceptive playgoer, William Graham, a devoted Ontario theatre-buff, pointed out that the entire Belmont setting of the last act had had to be changed back to Venice for this effect!

Over the years I had admired Arliss as the Rajah in William Archer's *The Green Goddess* (January 1923) even before the talking-film version of 1930, and I needed no film to help me appreciate him as the Galsworthy hero who eats himself to death in silence in *Old English* (May 1926). How we all sat rapt in the balcony of the Princess Theatre as he silently savoured each forbidden delicacy! Arliss's later rash of historical films also suited my taste for costume drama. The other day, I came across a letter he wrote in 1932 from Maida Hill, London, to this particular young fan in Outremont, acknowledging his obligation to me for a suggestion: "I have often considered Richelieu, and some day perhaps I may do a version, with the Cardinal as the central figure. Yours truly, George Arliss." In 1935 Arliss did add Richelieu to his historical roles on film, which included Wellington, Alexander Hamilton, a Rothschild, Voltaire, and Disraeli, all of whom happened to closely resemble this dapper Englishman.

The highly identifiable Arliss was a favourite with professional impersonators long after he departed the scene. The brilliant actor Alec McCowen came to lunch at my flat on Chestnut Park Road in Toronto in 1979 when touring his unique one-man show *St. Mark's Gospel*. To my delight, McCowen transformed himself into a most recognizable Arliss, complete with a large coin as a monocle. I had had this parlour impersonation in my repertory long before he had, but I had to admit he was closer to the mark than I had been back in my Outremont youth.

I also retain a persistent memory of Arliss's one-time co-star Minnie Maddern Fiske and her formidable chin line in Ibsen's *Ghosts*, performed at His Majesty's in May 1927. When people such as my friend Charles Rittenhouse got to boasting about having seen the Russian Alla Nazimova in *Ghosts*, I have had occasion to say, "Ah yes, but did you ever see Mrs Fiske play Mrs Alving?"

What my mother (who took me to a performance) thought the play was about, I do not know. But it wasn't about ghosts as this schoolboy knew them.

Were there no Barrymores left to tour? My childhood favourite, John, had plainly succumbed to Hollywood, as had his craggier brother, Lionel. Sister Ethel had resisted and I saw her at His Majesty's in May 1932, rather mature to be passing herself off as the young Lady Teazle when she toured in Sheridan's *The School for Scandal*. From our elevated point of view in the upper reaches of His Majesty's Theatre, we watched her plumes shake behind the famous screen, as if she were taking a little nip. Was that celebrated husky voice of hers a whisky baritone, speculated the knowing youngsters up in the gods?

Not all of my early Montreal theatre-going was as classic or as heavy. Indeed, some of the most memorable trips downtown were to see such joyous fare as Donnelly and Romberg's *The Student Prince* or Hammerstein and Friml's *Rose-Marie*. Then Noel Coward's revue *This Year of Grace*, originally staged by C.B. Cochran at the London Pavilion in 1928 and opening in New York in November of that year, arrived to open up for me a whole world of wit and sophistication, undreamed of previously in Outremont. By the time it reached Montreal in May 1929, *This Year of Grace* had shed such famous stars as Jessie Matthews and Anna Neagle. But the production still had Beatrice Lillie, and that was enough for me.

I had known nothing so wittily sung and danced in my life before, and the casual high mockery of Coward certainly was a revelation. Miss Lillie, carrying all the roles once shared with Jessie Matthews, was undoubtedly the high spirit of the occasion. That eccentric presence, bright and knowing rather than beautiful, was now responsible for several songs – "Mad about the Boy," "Dance, Dance, Dance Little Lady," and "A Room with a View." To learn later that Beatrice Lillie was a native of Toronto (or maybe Huntsville or Cobourg, which she variously claimed) startled me and made me proud, just as I was proud to learn that Mary Pickford, Marie Dressler, and, later, Walter Huston and Raymond

A caricature of Beatrice Lillie
by Whittaker.

Massey were Canadians. I date my appreciation of such Canadian talent back
to *This Year of Grace.*

There was, unfortunately, little homegrown Canadian theatre to influence me
during this period of the twenties and early thirties. Though the stock companies
of the day produced remarkable natives such as Mary Pickford and Jane Mallett,
both performers and plays were essentially extensions of New York theatre. At
its best, the stock company had charm and familiarity, with special favourites to
draw a weekly public. One of these Montreal favourites was Mildred Mitchell,
a versatile player later married to William Wray, whose family ran the best-
known undertaking business in town. She was to make many contributions to
the local little theatre as actress and director, but such links were rare.

Among the hordes of acrobats, musical clowns, condescending stage stars, comedians, jugglers, singers, dancers, and the performers of miniature farces that rotated on the great Keith/Albee and other vaudeville circuits, appearing in each town for from one day to one week a year, there were some figures who particularly entranced me.[5] For instance, Bransby Williams, Cissie Loftus, and other impersonators of the international great fitted my vaudeville bills most satisfyingly.

Perhaps I had even seen the ubiquitous Scottish comedian Sir Harry Lauder, but I am not sure because the others all imitated him. I was thrilled when Cissie Loftus turned up on the circuit. Had she not been the young actress who had once replaced the great Ellen Terry on tour with Irving? Did she "do" Terry or Duse or Bernhardt? My only memory of her is doing – or "taking-off" as my mother would have it – the celebrated French *diseuse* Yvette Guilbert singing "Les Cloches." "Imitation is the sincerest form of Cicelia Loftus," was George Arliss's knowing tribute.

Best of all was Bransby Williams, a great impersonator of Dickens' characters long before Emlyn Williams. This Williams was a one-man novel, so full of characters was he, walking out through the door as Peggotty in *David Copperfield* to re-enter as Micawber.[6] To this day I believe that impersonation, once a respected skill of the consummate actor, has been downgraded. I revered Bransby and Emlyn Williams as well as George Arliss on stage or in films.

Sometimes high hopes can be raised in early youth that are not to be ever quite matched. When I was eighteen, the American Opera Company, led by one Vladimir Rosing, a man with revolutionary ideas on opera, arrived at the Princess. He and his music director, Frank St. Leger, insisted that opera become more like music drama, though not in the Wagnerian sense.[7] With strong stage direction, distinguished design, and a group of willing if unknown singers, the American Opera Company staged Puccini's *Madame Butterfly* in a complete Japanese paper house, Bizet's *Carmen* with clashing Futurist settings, a black and silver *Marriage of Figaro, I Pagliacci* by Leoncovallo done on a modern midway, and *Faust* made beautiful by the bold designs of Robert Edmond Jones. Because I was oriented more visually than aurally, I retained more joy from Jones' creations than I did even from Gounod's final trio.

Unfortunately, my next bout of opera came from the San Carlo Company, which reduced me to rude laughter with its production of Wagner's *Lohengrin*.[8] I remember how the row of seats in which I sat shook as I tried not to burst out laughing at the sight of its pitiful "Wedding March" or the tiny knight being manœuvred around the stage by the big bossy Elsa. Although I later experienced such rare operatic achievements as Strauss's *Die Fledermaus* in Vienna's Redoutensaal or Tchaikovsky's *Eugene Onegin* at the Bolshoi in Moscow, I can still hark back wistfully to those days of the American Opera Company.

Certainly the magic of Robert Edmond Jones' *Faust* stayed with me, if not that of the singers – Patrick Kilkenny, Clifford Newdall, and the sisters Hall. Jones' settings, with their vivid contrast of light and shadow, were patently more realizable than Edward Gordon Craig's soaring projections, although no less poetic. Jones' design work for Max Reinhardt and Harley Granville-Barker, the Diaghilev-Nijinsky ballet of Strauss's *Til Eulenspeigel* at the Metropolitan Opera, and his contrasting work for the new plays of Eugene O'Neill were often reproduced in *Theatre Arts* magazine, so is it any wonder that this neophyte designer in Montreal was mightily impressed? Jones won for the stage designer the position of major collaborator in production. That advance was to filter down to the outer shores of theatre (namely Montreal) by the thirties, when I slipped into my first career in theatre.

Chapter Two

THE CHURCH AND THE STAGE MEET

In the summers of my youth I sometimes played tennis just off Côte Ste Catherine – generally with the Hodgson boys, Maurice and Frank, schoolmates at Strathcona Academy. Unlike me, they were Unitarians. Their father, Harold, sang bass for George Brewer at the Church of the Messiah downtown on Sherbrooke Street. Brewer was not only a well-known organist but also an associate and examiner of the Dominion College of Music.[1] So much respected was he, I learned, that his parishioners had installed a Casavant organ for him – no small gesture in those days of economic hardship. I also discovered that Brewer, in gratitude, had decided to do something to help with the payments. He decided to present, in the Church of the Messiah, performances of Hugo von Hofmannsthal's *Jedermann*, which his daughter Marjorie and he had seen recently at the Domplatz in Salzburg. It was a decision of some daring – and it was to affect me deeply.

As this production was to become so important to me, I talked to Marjorie about it in 1977, at her home in Monte Picayo, Valencia. She remembered it this way: "We went to Europe on a three-month visit when I was eighteen as a result of an insurance policy falling due. We went to Salzburg for the Mozart Festival. Daddy had seen the Reinhardt production of *Jedermann* before and had the idea that a presentation of it at our church would be possible. I recall the voices as impressive, the costumes gorgeous, but it was in German. Daddy responded with his usual enthusiasm. He spoke again of putting it on in the church, even of repeating the difficult effect of Riches appearing from the

The first production of *Everyman* by the Everyman Players at the Church of
the Messiah (April 1933). Everyman (played by George Brewer) is surrounded by
the Debtor's Wife and her children, the Guard, the Debtor, Fellowship, Back,
the doctor, and his two acolytes.

church pulpit." When her father expressed doubts about staging this production, Marjorie reassured him.

In Montreal in September of 1932 production plans were formulated for
an early spring performance in English of *Everyman*. The minister's daughter
had submitted design sketches, but Maurice Hodgson suggested that my ideas
would be more acceptable. They were, save by one participant, who rejected
the colour of her costume for the Courtesan because it was "goddamned
French-Canadian pink!" She insisted on wearing green. Because it was agreed
that the name "Courtesan" was unsuitable for a church, her role was referred to
as "Ladye." I'm afraid I enjoyed the fact that the green costume she wore
turned mud-coloured in the amber of the floodlights. These were suspended

on the first chandelier to illuminate the chancel where the action was to take place.

Our lighting was primitive but imaginative. There was a yellow light when Riches emerged from the lidded pulpit dripping gold and a green spotlight to shoot Death's shadow up high when he appeared at the memorial door to the west of the pulpit. I still remember how upset I was as designer when the actor playing Death insisted on wearing a small pair of black sateen knickers over his black tights. George Brewer smoothed matters out, as he did again when another actor wanted to wear a full suit of armour as Lohengrin in the next play, George Brewer's own work, *The Holy Grail*.

In addition to the other aspects of theatre that I was experiencing, Brewer was also introducing me to the craft of drama's essential contributor, the playwright. I was to wage many a battle on behalf of his numerous successors – Canadian playwrights, the true champions of our country's place in theatre. His own two plays were intelligent, and quite forceful, with strong dramatic lines and workable confrontations. Brewer had picked up some knowledge of the craft from his old friend "Billy" Tremayne, the Broadway playwright who been a director and mainstay of one of Montreal's oldest amateur theatre groups, the Trinity Players. He might well have discussed the construction of drama with "Mr Tremayne" – which was how Marjorie Brewer always referred to him – embarking on his two remarkably effective religious dramas, *The Holy Grail* and *The Spanish Miracle*.

Perhaps these discussions were shared with Basil Donn, who in time succeeded Tremayne as director of the Trinity Players. From the theatre historian Murray Edwards one gathers that Tremayne had been a working playwright since the end of the nineteenth century and had written for my first Lear, Robert Bruce Mantell, when a member of his company. He wrote on demand for other actor-managers and later contributed early film scripts as well as radio plays for Rupert Caplan. Charles Rittenhouse told Edwards that Tremayne's last

George Brewer's *The Holy Grail* as staged by the Everyman Players in the Church of the Messiah (April 1934). Whittaker's design.

days had been rather desperate, with his friends supporting him. When the playwright died in 1939, one of those friends, Walter Wakefield, came across a trunkful of decayed manuscripts. He burned them, but a few of the plays by "Canada's most prolific playwright" have survived as samples of the kind of work expected of a working dramatist at the turn of the twentieth century.[2]

Brewer was an uncommon combination of mystic and practical business-man. A Rosicrucian, a classical musician, an organist of note, and a shrewd investor, he had a most aesthetic countenance – wiry greying hair parted in the middle, piercing eyes, and a jutting nose and chin. (The sculptor Marc-Aurèle de Foy Suzor-Côté did a bronze bust of him, which I always coveted.) When Brewer wrote *The Holy Grail*, he discussed scenes with me. I responded by suggesting a character, that of the Forest god. I also found in the Brewer's pantry cupboard an alabaster vase that we converted into a most acceptable grail. Lit from inside, it floated heavenward to conclude Brewer's studious compilation of many legends about the Grail, accompanied by appropriate Wagnerian music on the Casavant.

Brewer followed through the next year with a play about the Spanish mystic Ramon Lull – a fine role for himself. In preparing this religious drama, he took me and Marguerite Dorken, who translated the costumes from my rather vague sketches, on a private visit to the Sir William Van Horne art collection because I wanted to design the whole production in the manner of El Greco. Van Horne was an amazing man, a considerable artist himself and a discerning collector.[3] The quiet gloom of his mansion on Sherbrooke Street was illuminated by the glowing presence of two El Grecos: *Holy Family with a Dish of Figs* and *Head of St. Maurice*. I had known this fascinating Greek painter only through sepia prints, so his colour was a revelation to me, as much as what we interpreted as the "astigmatic" elongation of his figures had been.

The Spanish Miracle emerged resplendent in April 1935, filled with elongated figures of infantas, acolytes, cardinals, and gypsies. By then the Everyman Players, the group formed for these annual productions from members of the congregation, had caught the public eye, largely due to very flattering reviews by both of Montreal's leading critics, Thomas Archer and S. Morgan-Powell.[4] We went on to repeat *Everyman* on a larger scale and to stage Eliot's *Murder in the Cathedral,* Shaw's *Saint Joan*, Paul Claudel's *The Tidings Brought to Mary*, and, finally, in 1940, Marlowe's *Dr Faustus*, each one conceived more artistically than the last – although I do believe the 1938 *Saint Joan* was our best. What an opportunity for a journeyman, nay a novice, stage artist!

From 1936 on the members of the congregation had been replaced in major roles by more talented actors from outside. To remain as a guiding member of the Everyman Players, I had been asked to join the Unitarian Church. I did so willingly, for a church that understood its link with the theatre was one with which I could easily identify. The thespian newcomers included Tom McBride, Doug Peterson, Agnes McKillop, John McLeish, and Charles Rittenhouse.

They were also to become the nucleus of the junior acting company derived from the Everyman Players, the Sixteen-Thirty Club. Others added later included Ivor Francis, the versatile Robert Goodier, and at least one senior performer, Maud Aston, whose somewhat broad interpretation of Lechery in *Dr Faustus* remains memorable.

As designer for the Everyman Players, I was by now in charge of the whole look of a production, deciding what platforms were needed, where the various scenes were to be played, and how they were to be lit and grouped. In the lighting of them, which became subtler yearly, I had the vigorous support of Jan Raven, who gave me whatever I wanted – from a celestial spot to a grey light – and infinitely gradual dimmings. He even allowed me to work the latter when he built a switchboard up in the organ loft.

If George Brewer was the spiritual centre of the Everyman Players, Marjorie contributed the acting talent that set the standard for others. That she was an actress of true quality became evident in that first production of *Everyman* when she was Good Deeds. Subsequently, she played Salomé and Kundrie in *The Holy Grail*, the gypsy Blanquerna in *The Spanish Miracle*, a leader of the Women of Canterbury in T.S. Eliot's *Murder in the Cathedral*, Helen of Troy in *Dr Faustus* and, most memorably, a very moving Joan in Shaw's history play. The mighty Montreal Repertory Theatre itself used her in the title roles of Hsuing's *Lady Precious Stream* (November 1935), and, later, in Maxwell Anderson's *Mary of Scotland* (November 1940) and *Joan of Lorraine* (May 1947).

Incidentally, the dynamic founder of the Montreal Repertory Theatre, Martha Allan, sent pictures of Marjorie to Morris Gest, who was to produce *Lady Precious Stream* on Broadway but whose production was delayed because (so Marjorie says) he had "to be carted off to the loony bin occasionally." "I had visions of Broadway," Marjorie admitted much later, "but Gest never replied." Certainly her talent was enough to project our own ambitions beyond the big annual church play. The younger members soon turned the

Sixteen-Thirty Club into a theatrical troupe that matched the senior group in ambition.

I still have some of those first designs created for the Everyman Players, which so altered the course of my life. But I am distressed that they now seem so paltry. However, as the productions rolled along yearly, the colour, concept, and execution of my drawings showed a marked improvement. Obviously experience and my classes at l'École des beaux-arts had some effect. Charles Rittenhouse, writing in 1949 to Margaret Ness of *Saturday Night*, reviewed the Everyman Players and my part in them very favourably: "Most popular was *Everyman* itself, which gave its name to the group and in which I played Good Fellowship, a role that I like to remember in connection with my relationship with Herb. The productions were most spectacular, with much pageantry. Undoubtedly, the person most responsible for the great success of the Everyman Players was Herbert, whose costume designs became increasingly imaginative and spectacular." A good friend, Charles.[5]

If the Everyman Players provided the creative opportunities for me to test my designing talents, it was Charles who pushed me hardest to improve and hone my skills. Our working relationship began early in 1934 when, near the corner of St Catherine Street and Atwater one lucky day, I greeted Charles Rittenhouse, just barely an acquaintance, with the resounding salutation, "How now, proud Rittenhouse?" To which he snapped back without hesitation, "How would you like to design *A Midsummer Night's Dream* for me?" He was, it turned out, planning such a production for West Hill High School. Naturally, I accepted on the spot. Such offers were rare. Still are. That was my second year after *Everyman*, which he must have seen. Thus began a partnership of great satisfaction. More than a partnership – a long and close friendship, with the two of us egging each other on to further achievement in theatre.

Charles was volatile and saturnine, I rather pale and dreamy, but we managed to achieve many productive collaborations, particularly in our work on

Shakespeare. In 1934 my settings for *A Midsummer Night's Dream* were in the simplest and least expensive mode – two tall pillars that doubled as Athens and the trees beyond its walls, with modest backcloths behind them. The "rude mechanicals" played in front of a small screen and against a forest plainly inspired by Rousseau (le Douanier), still a favourite of mine.

The next year Charles managed without me at West Hill with his production of *As You Like It*, but he returned to inspire me to a much less facile setting for *Romeo and Juliet*, a considerable achievement by both of us. It was on my return from England in fall 1935 that Charles gleefully accepted my designs for this production of *Romeo and Juliet*. I had envisioned a set of great flexibility, with a slender tower centre to serve as balcony, flanked by platform and steps, with more steps leading down to the stage. The little tower held a statue of the Virgin Mary, which was helpful in identifying Friar Laurence's cell. The costumes were bold but simple.

On reflection, though, I have to admit that Charles' gift for spotting likely talent and handling it with enthusiasm were the primary reasons our *Romeo and Juliet* got such favourable attention, particularly in the *Gazette* from Thomas Archer (who was ecstatic about an accidental lighting effect) and even from Toronto's *Saturday Night*.[6] Betty Taylor, a remarkably instinctive young actress, was delicate and moving as Juliet, while Ivor Francis was a strong and intelligent player opposite her. Charles used them well and gave his production pace and fire. He was also very firm about his students' speech, which helped greatly.

We followed up that splendid success with a large-scale production of *The Taming of the Shrew* in March 1937, again staged at West Hill High School. I had progressed farther along my own William Poel path by creating a permanent setting[7] – ostensibly bright Italian buildings with the far landscape behind, somewhat obscured by the travelling players' portable stage and its cut-out scenery.

Charles excelled himself as director. The introduction of comic business was his delight and, by retaining Christopher Sly as part of the continuing action, he was at his most inventive. Charles saw Sly as a comical/pathetical Everyman – "Man is Lord for but a brief day": broadly comic when, for instance, the bare arm of an actress beckoned him backstage, sad when laying aside his gaudy robes and poppy wreath, a Charlie Chaplin waving the players down the aisle at the end. In young Ivor Francis, who had played Romeo earlier, Charles discovered a comedian who could handle both aspects well. The young nobleman, Romeo, became a poor tinker and was enriched in the process.

My own work did not go unnoticed. In his *Gazette* review of the *Shrew* (5 March) Tom Archer referred again to *Romeo and Juliet*, so "terribly touching," for him "a model performance, a thing of beauty the like of which we may never see again." Heward Stikeman, however, was alert to the advances made by the production of the *Shrew*, comparing it favourably in the *McGill Daily* with that season's production in Stratford-on-Avon. "The teamwork onstage and the balance of the mise-en-scène defy description," he wrote, finding that the reintroduction into the action of Sly had "a miraculous effect." There were kind words for me also in his 1937 review: "Herbert Whittaker's set was a revelation in its freshness of colouring and compositional balance. In a slightly stylized form he managed to blend the traditional with the ultra-modern."

Stikeman spoke of the synchronization of setting and costume with the stage action as being "almost too perfect." But, principally, he recognized the success of the Rittenhouse aim "to recapture something of the spirit of Thames-side clowning and the vigour of improvisation in Commedia dell'Arte."[8] When Charles went off to the Yale School of Drama, his analysis of *The Taming of the Shrew* and his scheme for its production won him invitations to dinner from the great British scholar Allardyce Nicoll and from Tucker Brooke, editor of the *Yale Shakespeare Series*.

Charles and I argued a lot and he pushed me hard, later declaring procrastination to be my great fault. "I have had, on occasion, to sit at his elbow, practically gun in hand, while Herbert finished off some design for which the stage or costume crews were yelling" is the way he remembered it. "His lack of technical training would keep him from becoming a professional designer for, say, the New York stage," he added; "he couldn't pass the necessary apprenticeship in mechanical drawing."

Charles, who remained Good Fellowship in our long association, was not the Everyman Players' first actor in the role – Harold Hodgson was. But from the second revival of *Everyman* on, Charles was closely involved with the Players. I remember how drastically he cut *Saint Joan* for us so that we could retain the Epilogue. He was also part of the younger production group, the Sixteen-Thirty Club, and in winter 1936 joined Marjorie Brewer, Jan Raven and me, Doug Peterson, Tom McBride, and our good friend Margaret Sutherland to stage a one-act play by J. William Rogers called *Judge Lynch* on the tiny stage of Channing Hall, behind the Church of the Messiah. I designed the small Southern-Gothic shack required and was part of the Sixteen-Thirty committee. The performance went well enough to be entered into the local competition of the three-year-old Dominion Drama Festival (DDF) and, to our glee, merited an invitation to Ottawa for the finals, along with the prestigious Montreal Repertory Theatre. In those early years the festival was made up of one-act plays and single scenes that made it possible for the small fry to compete with the established contestants.

Alan Wade was the local adjudicator. The adjudicator at the DDF finals of 1936 was none other than Harley Granville-Barker, the legendary figure of British theatre. Not only had Granville-Barker created Shaw's Marchbanks (*Candida*) and John Tanner (*Man and Superman*) but he had also been co-producer with Shaw at the Royal Court Theatre. In addition he was an important playwright in his own right who had also written those enlightening "Prefaces" to Shakespeare's plays. Lacking money, we piled our scenery and ourselves into Jan Raven's second-hand truck and headed up to Ottawa. On our arrival we were taken under the wing of Mrs Dorothy White, who treated us as if we were the Montreal Repertory Theatre itself.

Granville-Barker treated us even better. We won top approval for our setting, which, under much-improved lighting, looked infinitely superior on the larger stage of the Ottawa Little Theatre. Charles' celebrated brother-in-law — the artist Edwin Holgate — had approved our setting before we left home and even suggested the addition of a small strut to support the carefully sagging roof. Yousuf Karsh, who used the DDF ladder to achieve attention for his art with the camera, photographed us and one of these pictures appeared in Toronto's *Saturday Night*. Heady stuff, this!

Happily Granville-Barker picked a Canadian play, *Twenty-Five Cents*, as winner of the Festival's top award, the Bessborough Trophy. This kitchen drama by Eric Harris of Sarnia, directed by Catherine "Kizzie" Brickenden for the London Little Theatre, launched the DDF along its path of encouraging Canadian writers as well as actors, directors, and scene designers.

When I read Betty Lee's 1973 account of the Dominion Drama Festival, *Love and Whisky*, I marvelled at how she had traced every eccentric political phase of the DDF's rise and decline. But I found one aspect missing — the sense of wonderment and delight we all felt as part of a great national movement. Even in its earlier primitive days the festival offered that joyous challenge. Ringed around by high protocol as it was, it was still open to non-establishment competitors, as we discovered. Having outranked the mighty Montreal Repertory Theatre itself in the opinion of no less an expert than Harley Granville-Barker, we returned to our hometown with a better opinion of ourselves. And others recognized our claim.

That victory in the highest Canadian court of drama encouraged Charles to go ahead with his academic plans and within the year he had applied to and was accepted by the Yale School of Drama. In the fall of 1937, then, we were bereft of our director. We had a talented knot of players, a genius of a practical boss in Jan Raven, but no director. As I was the only other member of the Sixteen-Thirty Club who couldn't act, it seemed logical that I should take over Charles' position. I took on the new responsibilities nervously, although I knew it was my chance to put some of my ideas into practice.

In Oliver Sayler's 1922 book *The Russian Theatre* – Morris Gest's own copy, which I picked up in a second-hand bookstore on my first visit to New York – I read about Pushkin's adaptation of a longer English original, Wilson's *City of the Plague*, presented in the Studio of the Moscow Art Theatre under the title *Festival in Time of Plague.* The scene – London under the Black Death – and its characters – a group of young people defying, in revelry, the overhanging doom – seemed eminently suited to the Sixteen-Thirty Club and its new director. Were we aware how pertinent the Pushkin poem was? A group of young people in a playful vein, staving off the world catastrophe growing beyond our church hall walls? I suspect not, at least not consciously.

What if there was no English translation? I discovered a Pushkin Club in Montreal and they supplied a translator – a most charming young Russian named Irena Groten of just the right age to fit into our group. I had already announced the name of the entry of the Sixteen-Thirty Club to the Western Quebec Regional Festival. It was startling, therefore, when Irena produced her translation as more poem than play. We converted it into a play as the Studio of the Moscow Art Theatre had done, with new music by George Brewer for the songs that Pushkin had inserted.

Tom McBride (who played leader of the little group), Ivor Francis, Marjorie Brewer, and Betty Taylor gathered around my old oak table, inherited from the Hon. James McGill. I designed the costumes and the setting. When we produced the play nobody in the audience seemed to notice that Doug Peterson, as the monk who admonished their unseemly revelry, made his entrance over the rooftops, because the bay window through which the death-carts were

Pushkin's *Festival in Time of Plague*, translated by Irena Groten and directed and designed by Whittaker for the Sixteen-Thirty Club (March 1938). Seen are Betty Taylor, Marjorie Brewer, Ivor Francis, Tom McBride, and (with back to camera) Sylvia Gordon (née Somers) and Gordon McLachlin.

observed so graphically on the streets below placed the action in an upper room. But the proper entrance of a threatening black-and-white cleric was surely at the top of a flight of stairs.

This was the lowering spring of 1938. Undaunted by world threats of disaster beyond our walls, *Festival in Time of Plague* had five performances: in our own Channing Hall, at the Western Quebec Regional Festival in the Sun Life Auditorium (where it was a winner), and at a repeat performance to raise travelling money in Tudor Hall at Ogilvy's department store. We appeared next in Winnipeg's historic Walker Theatre, when the DDF held its first finals away

Marjorie Brewer on the train to Winnipeg to play in the Sixteen-Thirty Club production of *Festival in Time of Plague* for the Dominion Drama Festival final in 1938. This was the first time the finals were held outside Ottawa.

from Ottawa, and there Marjorie Brewer was declared the country's best actress for those few startling moments in which she recounted the death-carts' terrible message. Upon our return we showed Montreal our prize-winning play once again, this time in the more elegant church hall of the Erskine and American Church just a few streets over from Channing Hall. That victory was almost overlooked in the excitement of the wedding of our "best actress" to Jan Raven. I was their second-best man.

It was then that I boldly commissioned a pair of new writing friends, Douglas and Janet McPhee, to recreate for the stage the famous 1880 visit of Sarah Bernhardt to Montreal as recounted in her *Memoirs*. This book was another prize discovered in a second-hand bookstore in New York in 1934. Sarah faced bitter chill, a great welcome, an escaped criminal, a promotional whale, the wrath of the bishop of Montreal, rapturous audiences, and a visit to the Iroquois.[9] And in a highly workable one-act play by Janet alone, we again won a DDF award in 1939 and, for Marjorie, another acting award as Sarah.

The calibre of the players I was working with in my first directorial attempts was obviously high, a fact borne out by DDF approval. However, while Marjorie's Sarah had won an award in Montreal, adjudicator S.R. Littlewood gave the

Marjorie Brewer as Sarah Bernhardt in *Divinity in Montreal* by Janet McPhee, directed and designed by Whittaker for the Sixteen-Thirty Club (March 1939).

best actress award not to her but to Betty Taylor, playing her sister, Jeanne, when we took our original play to the finals in Ottawa that year. Littlewood rejected our view of Sarah because he had once met Bernhardt when she was on tour while he was a young sheep farmer in South Africa. She was really quite a different kind of woman, one interested in sheep farming, he explained rather naively to the audience at the DDF finals![10]

Marjorie and Betty were both on his short list for best actress. Janet, on the other hand, won the Sir Barry Jackson Challenge Trophy for the best Canadian play hands down, which gave the Sixteen-Thirty Club and Janet much new prestige. For Janet, it was the beginning of her career as a writer. In 1940 she wrote an original one-act play, *Bus to Nowhere*, for us, which allowed us to experiment with theatre-in-the-round, placing chairs in formation in the middle of Channing Hall and dramatising a bus trip. We could no longer simply prepare annual entries for competitions. The Sixteen-Thirty Club was now much more ambitious than that − or I for it. We plunged precipitously into full-length dramas in the winter season of 1939–40, audaciously presenting Shaw's Russian-influenced *Heartbreak House* and Chekhov's *The Seagull*.

What nerve, and on the Channing Hall stage − the size of a postage stamp! For *The Seagull*, a silver-painted flat from a previous production of Shaw's *The Dark Lady of the Sonnets*, tilted to catch the light, became our lake, reflecting through some black cut-out trees. On one side a bold white trellis declared Madame Arkadina's territory, advanced after the play-scene to trace out the confines of her garden. Dressed in yellow, Marjorie appeared like an exotic parakeet as the Russian actress, perched on a little gilt chair.

Betty was again a match for her as an entirely instinctive Nina, with Doug Peterson, also instinctive, as the baffled Constantin and Tom McBride immensely world-weary as Trigorin. Irena Groten, our new and genuinely Russian recruit, was Polina opposite Leslie Johnston's schoolmaster (he taught at Lower Canada College, my brother's old school). Agnes McKillop was another strong talent as Masha. Sam Vatcher and Chester Lemaistre, two MRT stalwarts borrowed for Sorin and Medvedenko, were both great assets.

I still have the notes for my scenic plan for *The Seagull*, staged in that small space. Perhaps they bear recalling: "Scene One: The dark trees frame the scene and the view of the lake. But the lake, shimmering like silver between them, is not to be seen at the moment, where the little framework stage, with its white curtains, hides it. On the opposite side, though, it can be glimpsed behind the latticework of a garden trellis. Soon the chattering members of the household who gather to watch Constantin's play will group themselves against this framework like birds in a cage. This framework is opposed by the little stage … as the ideas and aims of the young playwright oppose those of his mother and her Trigorin.

"Scene Two: Now is the rule of the birdcage triumphant. It stretches its white trellis across the full width of the stage. Behind the movement of two croquet players, we may see Arkadina and her followers. In the big chair is Sorin, the childless patriarch. Next to him on a little gilt chair sits Arkadina, a nurse by his bedside, her feet, so smartly shod, displayed on a footstool. On a bench facing them are the others: Polina embroidering, Masha sitting idly … Dorn leans easily over the back of the bench. In this birdcage it is Arkadina, in her yellow dress with a touch of green and a wide-brimmed straw hat, who is the parakeet, the others being magpies and sparrows. Shamrayeff is the intruder who comes to pick a fight with Madame. It is Madame who exits with him, arm in arm, at the end of the act to proclaim an undoubted victory.

"Scene Three: The living room retains much of the birdcage as its white-framed windows stretch across the back of the room. Here is Arkadina's little gold chair with its fellows. Here the graceful sofa, the low upholstered bench. A birdcage hangs in one window. Beyond the windows, the lake still gleams. The trellis cleverly becomes windows, suitably draped, of course. Indeed, Nina was an outsider in Arkadina's birdcage."

Despite my success with *Festival in Time of Plague*, or perhaps because of it, McBride resented my elevation to directorial status. He sauntered through my suggested moves with visible disdain, but this didn't destroy his contribution to the overall result. Loving one's director doesn't necessarily produce better performances than does a healthy conflict. Too many directors mistakenly expect deep trust and devotion from their temporary charges. It is a way to bring their talents under control, but sometimes it works differently, I found. McBride was a very good actor and that was the important element, not the group harmony and the beloved director.

Our production of *The Seagull* was very Russian, for we emphasized the difference between Chekhov's characters and our Canadian counterparts. The translation by Constance Garnett helped. I must also mention that, in addition to choosing, designing, and directing the production, I was allowed to review it for the *Gazette*, where I was by then second-string critic. While commending

A production photo of the Montreal Repertory Theatre production of
Jupiter in Retreat, a play written by Janet McPhee and Whittaker, designed by
Whittaker, directed by Charles Rittenhouse, with Ena Gillespie, Chester Lemaistre,
Madeleine Sherwood, and Tom McBride as Gilbert Stewart (April 1942).

the play fervently, I didn't say anything about its director/designer. I think this
was the only time I combined all my theatrical interests in one production.

Heartbreak House, the other epic to grace our tiny stage, required even more
ingenuity. In particular, the moment when the cast of seven rushes upstairs to
discover the Burglar was nerve-racking because I had placed the staircase centre

stage. But all our actors knew how to accomplish miracles without excess stage movement, and they pulled off the surprise introduction of the intruder. Marjorie was Mrs Hushabye, and I persuaded her to adopt a Lynn Fontanne drawl. Unfortunately the susceptible Betty Taylor also adopted it, and I had to appeal to Marjorie to discover another rhythm for the contrast – something more brittle.

The two leading ladies of the Sixteen-Thirty Club vanished too soon. Betty Taylor, a high-school Juliet and Nina in *The Seagull*, died young. A slender strawberry blonde, she was the most naturally gifted of performers that Charles had discovered in his West Hill High days. I must pay special tribute to her performance of the leading role in a melodrama that Janet McPhee and I wrote in 1942. Playing opposite Tom McBride as the oppressive novelist, Betty brought great delicacy of shading to her portrayal of the terrified employee and made the Montreal Repertory Theatre production of *Jupiter in Retreat*, our rather formulaic mystery drama, seem much better than it was.

Marjorie Raven (née Brewer) was an equally rare talent. She had a truly beautiful voice, rather deep, a small shapely figure, and a heart-shaped face. Most important, she possessed a gift of evocation, intellectual as well as emotional, which meant she could encompass wit and humour as well as passion. I admired her more than any other actress and in a wider variety of roles. She had established standards for the Everyman Players, crowning her outstanding contributions with a Saint Joan that was both high-spirited and highly spiritual. For me, she was a properly theatrical Madame Arkadina and a dazzling Mrs Hushabye, as well as Shaw's Queen Elizabeth, Pushkin's Louisa, and our own Sarah Bernhardt, all memorable creations. But then she and husband Jan launched into an adventurous career following his special talent as an industrial trouble-shooter on an international scale. The role of Joan of Lorraine brought her back to MRT one last time in 1947 before the couple finally settled in Andorra. Marjorie never acted again.

The high severe structure of the Church of the Messiah allowed me as a designer to explore my understanding of William Poel's reforms of the playing space, offering an open platform with formal exits, though I was fond of using the central aisle, too. It also allowed me to follow the lofty tenets of such other innovators as Gordon Craig and Adolphe Appia. When Tyrone Guthrie came to Canada in 1952 with his plan for a Shakespearean stage at Stratford, Ontario, I was already receptive and appreciative as a drama critic. How fortunate for me that, going to and from playing tennis in Outremont, I had become friends with those two Strathcona Academy schoolmates whose father sang bass in the First Unitarian Church in Montreal.

POSTSCRIPT

The Church of the Messiah was in itself a work of art as well as a citadel of reasoned devotion. When Montreal's first Unitarian church burned down, the parishioners determined to replace it with something "artistically rich, an expression of the most poetic and devotional spirit" – in the words of Wilfred "Bill" Barnes, the Everyman Player whose grandfather, William, had been the church's first minister in 1865. And that's what the new Church of the Messiah was – a serious art-nouveau creation, the work of Edward and W.S. Maxwell, the architects also responsible for the classic Museum of Fine Arts and the baronial Windsor Station.[11] (Both buildings had an important part to play in my Montreal beginnings.)

This architectural masterpiece enhanced Sherbrooke Street from 1906 to 1987 when it too burned down. Or rather was burned down under circumstances tragic and terrible to the high-purposed Unitarians. They had welcomed as organist a fine musician but a troubled soul. Named Wilheima Tiemersma following a sex-change, she was diagnosed as manic-depressive and given to suicide attempts. But her devotion to the fine Casavant organ, which she had named "George" in memory of Mr Brewer, was believed to have a calming influence on her. In fact, her playing for services and after was much admired. Then madness claimed her again on the night of 26 May 1987 when she was driven to set fire to her organ music, leaving it to burn. Unfortunately guilt struck her too late. When she called the fire department, the blaze was already uncontrollable.

Two Montreal firemen died in their attempt to save the doomed building. By morning, the Church of the Messiah was a charred ruin. Its memorial window to George Brewer, with its grateful reference to *Everyman*, had melted along with other superb examples of stained glass. Only Channing Hall remained. There it was that the memorial service to my old friend, Fraser Macorquodale, took place on 23 February 1994 and his role in Everyman Players was recalled. He'd been the Dauphin in that long-ago *Saint Joan*, amongst other intelligent contributions as actor and member of our company of church players. "To have known a thoroughly good man like Fraser Macorquodale in those days," I began my tribute at his memorial service, "is indeed something to be treasured." I went on to recount our times together, particularly those related to this same hall and to the destroyed church. At the end of my words, one voice broke out. It was "Bill" Barnes, linking those two eras and areas as few others could do. Later, I learned that repairs to Channing Hall would force the sale of the church property and thus put an end to any hope of restoring that truly inspirational structure. By June of 1996 the congregation of the Church of the Messiah had moved to another home in Westmount.

Chapter Three

SEARCHING FOR A ROLE

Sir John Martin-Harvey, my first great star in the theatre, made his last appearance in Montreal in 1932, taking with him the echoes of the great Victorian actor-managers. The succeeding era was heralded that same season by the arrival of Sir Barry Jackson's Birmingham Repertory Theatre, playing Rudolph Besier's *The Barretts of Wimpole Street*.[1] That it was not a star theatre is illustrated for me by the fact that though I admired Daphne Heard as Elizabeth and Julian D'Albie as Mr Barrett, I completely overlooked the Browning in my notes. He was played by Donald Wolfit, who was to carry on the old actor-manager tradition for years after. But in this play he was simply part of the company. The critic inside me stirring, I scribbled "Miss Sophie Stewart made too much of Bella's final exit" and I found designer Paul Shelving too frivolous in his costume colours. Incidentally, from *The Barretts of Wimpole Street* programme I notice that the prices of admission were $0.50, $1.00, $1.50, and $2.00, emphasizing the least expensive. When the order of prices was reversed years later, I realized that the Depression was over at last.

What did I read in those days save *Theatre Arts* and *Stage Magazine*? Certainly plays. Young designers are too often satisfied with scripts as launching pads for their own thrusting creativity. The passion for murder mysteries and detective stories had not hit its peak then. Sherlock Holmes satisfied that interest. Nor had paperbacks made their appearance. So what to read after leaving Robert Louis Stevenson behind and Mallory's *King Arthur* and the Stalky yarns of Kipling?

Lewis Carroll came late and lingered on. Then it was time for John Galsworthy and Hugh Walpole and discovering the Saki stories of H.H. Munro.

When I rose to the distinction of directing plays, I was necessarily more attentive to reading scripts, beginning with Shaw and Chekhov. But at the age when I should have been through Dickens and on to Dostoyevsky and Tolstoy, my weak eyesight was discovered. "No small print," warned the fierce ophthalmologist of Dorchester Street. And in those days, all classics were writ small.

It was about this time that I started to haunt second-hand bookstores such as the Classic on St Catherine Street and others, including Drama Books and Eaton's. The latter replaced Goodwin's, which had brought my father to Montreal from Toronto, as the major department store on St Catherine Street. Eaton's sometimes came up with discards of books for 49¢, a favourite price of mine. As a former youth of the Depression, I have always sought out cheap books. I'm afraid this has had a discouraging influence on my literary tastes.

I had also started to read up on theatrical criticism, favouring the British – such as the prolific James Agate, whose *Ego* volumes I devoured second-hand. William Hazlitt, Max Beerbohm, and the great Shaw himself were taken into account as well as my favourite of the Americans, Brooks Atkinson, the gentle man from the *New York Times*, bolstered by the inspired caricatures of Al Hirschfeld. And about this time I discovered the *New Yorker*. My mother encouraged my passion for this smartest of magazines by giving me my first subscription. Its wit and elegant style countered, I hope, some of the influence of those cheap books.

In the fall of 1935 I was without a job, without money, but very high in hopes. I had recognized by then, through my early work at the Church of the Messiah, West Hill High School, and the Montreal Repertory Theatre Studio, that my life had to be linked closely with the theatre on a full-time basis. But the theatre that was developing in Canada at that time was still comfortably amateur. Where was I to find a professional life in the theatre without leaving the country? It was a dilemma that was to plague Canadians for several more decades. My own solution strikes me today as something close to the absurd – I became a director/designer/critic.

Edwin Fancott's coffee house on Union Avenue was a gathering place for those of us who were out of work and determined to stay that way until something worthy of our artistic talents came along. I did some inventive little settings, hoping to interest the art director at Eaton's into hiring me as a window designer. But I got so nervous waiting for him outside his office that, when his secretary said I could go in, I left, saying I was sorry but I had another appointment. Rather like Stephen Leacock's "My Financial Career," my career in commercial art seemed doomed by my very self.

By the way, Leacock was then teaching economics at McGill University and swerved briefly into my view when he contributed his pen and person to one of McGill's *Red and White Revues.* I recall his crumpled appreciation of his own jokes, which I shared. Our great humourist also contributed burlesques and satires to the *Montreal Standard* on a weekly basis. One that I recall was on Greek tragedy and another on the reading of "whodunits," both of which I thought deliriously comic.

The most conspicuously talented of those frequenting the coffee house was undoubtedly John Ployart McLeish. He looked like a young John Barrymore and painted like a young Kokoschka, but he eventually went off to Hollywood to do animation for Walt Disney. John Barber, tall and delightfully vague, was another gifted artist and so, I remember, was Alan Harrison, one Montreal artist who remained in Canada. In time they all became involved in the lively little theatre movement through the Montreal Repertory Theatre, the Everyman Players, or the Sixteen-Thirty Club.

I was delighted when Fancott decided to restore an old house in the heart of Old Montreal with the intention of turning it into a restaurant. How we all scraped and scrubbed away the dirt of centuries! The Old House, as he called it, did not thrive as a restaurant for long, but I came to understand the great labour and application demanded by such restoration. Fancott was a man before his time. A visionary. Another of my colleagues, Eric McLean, started restoring the Maison Papineau soon afterwards, and he launched the move to revive Old Montreal. I watched Eric go through the same process of scraping and scrubbing and cheered his eventual triumph.[2]

Between classes at l'École des beaux-arts and designing for various little theatre groups – which included my first attempt at the George Kaufman and Edna Ferber comedy *The Royal Family*, using a space concept with silver paper windows to suggest the glittering Manhattan skyline and staged at Victoria Hall[3] – I came downtown daily to look for work. One welcome distraction from this search came on Fridays when Tom Archer, reviewing for the *Gazette*, would ask me to accompany him on his rounds of seeing new movies. I had come to know Tom through the Montreal Repertory Theatre, particularly his own play *Three Characters in Search of a Plot* (a December 1933 Studio production of the MRT). Our acquaintance was further encouraged into friendship by his generous critical appreciation of my design work for the Church of the Messiah and West Hill High School. I enjoyed my free movies and paid for them with knowing chatter, being more of a film fan than was Tom, whose burning passion was music.

Knowing that I was supposed to be looking for work, Tom suggested I apply for a job at the *Gazette* in 1937 when that paper daringly launched a once-a-week radio page, hoping to attract advertising dollars away from the rival medium. For the *Gazette* to have a special page for radio listings every Friday, somebody would have to assist Tom. This somebody would have to collect the listings, prepare them for type, help edit and fill the daily theatre page, and supply material for the Saturday theatre pages. I went to be interviewed by Charles Peters, who as editor-in-chief was the grave but kindly representative of the White publishing family, and he agreed to give me a trial. Luckily he forgot to ask me if I could type – and I couldn't!

Whittaker on the radio beat – Gratien Gélinas and
American comic Joe E. Brown share a laugh.

With my assignment to the radio page, the Music and Drama Department
of the *Gazette* swelled to two. Covering radio had first call on my services, and
often I stopped off at the CBC offices in the King's Hall building on St Catherine Street to put together the radio listings. A pioneer, I was the only customer
and knew just what I wanted. I was also to be available on occasion to do
general reporting. I can't say I was a great hit with the city desk, however.
When sent to cover funerals, I went to the wrong church; when I hit the right
one, I had to have help from veteran reporters at the *Montreal Daily Star* and
the *Herald* to bring back enough names. Names of those attending were published in those days. One time I became indignant when a presumptuous
secretary phoned me to say her boss couldn't attend a particular funeral but
would like his name added to the list. This practice, all too customary, struck
me as shockingly deceitful.

A photo from Whittaker's radio page for *The Gazette*. Seen are Eleanor Stuart as Martha Trent, Bobby O'Reilly, Betty Taylor, and Ivor Francis doing a scene from the CBC studio in Montreal of Joseph Eaton McDougal's serial, "Miss Trent's Children."

I couldn't have been as disastrous a reporter as I remember today. Recently Bill Weintraub, a qualified *Gazette* reporter and a chronicler of Montreal's heyday era in his *City Unique*, sent me a clipping proving that within two years I had won a byline on the news side. Dated 27 July 1939, there was the story (with three-column photo) headed "Police Dog Nursing Baby Kitten / Despite Repute as a Cat-Killer" and it is signed by Herbert W. Whittaker! Let me quote the first unbelievable paragraph. "Thwarted mother-love has led Teddy, a two-year-old police dog, to adopt and nurse Mickey, a few-weeks-old kitten. Both dog and cat of this touching relationship between traditional enemies of the domestic animal world belong to Victor Stone, 3478 St. Famille St." That is the first of eight paragraphs. At the very least it proves that by then I had learned to type.

The resistance to me as a member of the *Gazette* staff diminished as I learned to type quickly with two fingers. In fact, I became quite smart-alecky.

I blush when I examine the files in later years. But between the period wisecracking there are glimpses of the beginnings of a lifelong campaign to draw audiences into the theatre. Even filmgoers. How I got away with the following article (1 January 1944) herewith only slightly edited, I know not. But I did.

What Shows Are Worth $5?

"Have you ever noticed how the brightest parts of a party so often take place in the kitchen?" [I started out, then purported to record one example.] "What shows would you gladly pay for – say, the price of a Broadway show?" "Shaw's *Saint Joan*," ventured a man looking for beer in the icebox. "*Oklahoma!*" was the second contribution. "You'd be lucky to get a seat for five bucks. I couldn't," said a man of experience. "But you'd be glad to pay it if you could." Sniffed a charming young Russian, "I'd choose *The Cherry Orchard.*" When somebody countered with *You Can't Take It With You*, there was general approval, some even claiming they'd pay five bucks to see it again.

"Shakespeare," flatly announced a bystander who had already found the beer some time ago. "Fi' bucks for Shakespeare." Then the Russian charmer asked rather scornfully, "What Shakespeare?" There were several suggestions all around, but the consensus was *Othello* with Paul Robeson. I mentioned *King Lear*, but the feminine contingent declared for "*Othello* – that big black man and the beautiful blonde." Whereupon they all left to ask if the host had any recordings by Paul Robeson, Shakespearean or otherwise.

"Five bucks is a lot of cash for a show," someone brooded. "Not in New York, it isn't," said the travelled one. "So how many shows did you see?" He was put to the test. "Only one. That's all I had time for." "And what was that?" a doubter inquired. "*Paul Othello?*" The answer came back: "No, *One Touch of Venus*. That Mary Martin has certainly got something."

At that time I knew that the films I reviewed were clever shadows that didn't compare with "the real thing" of the stage, which had caught my devotion first. I found I could mock film performers, whereas I had to treat live players with respect. My generation, however, had witnessed the squawking birth of the talkies and were overcome with American novelty. Back in 1929 when Montreal cinemas were re-equipped for the "Pictures That Talk Like Living People," as the Vitagraph ads claimed, we exited dancing from *The Broadway Melody*. But when I came to the junior critic's estate for the *Gazette* almost a decade later that novelty had worn off somewhat, and it didn't seem to matter if one poked a little fun at some of the absurdities in the B-films (Tom Archer still handling the majors). Nobody took them seriously after all. Except perhaps the exhibitors, Consolidated Theatres. My mockery or disrespect enraged Mr Hirsch, head of this all-powerful film house chain, and he threatened to withdraw the advertising for his major film houses in Montreal from the *Gazette*. The paper knuckled under – what else could it do? – and I was dismissed. However, I was invited to stay on until I found another job, meanwhile training my successor. When that successor learned how much work I was undertaking, he decided the army would be easier on him and left. Since nothing more was said about my leaving, I just stayed on. And I did take my job seriously enough to attend Film Society showings, usually held in basements with pauses to change the reels. There I recognized the ancient art of mime, as practised in the motion picture's silent days, and was awed by *The Battleship Potemkin*, Emil Jannings's *Faust*, and Conrad Veidt in *The Cabinet of Dr Caligari*.

I became accepted as a newspaperman of sorts by the genuine articles, somewhat under the wing of the star reporter, John Rhodes Sturdy. He and his fiancée, Roma, allowed me to arbitrate their premarital arguments when we repaired to the Samovar, a local bar. Other *Gazette* men of note – tall Kenneth Wright, wise Myer Negru, Ian Ogilvie, Bill Weintraub, Al Miller, and Jack

Gazette staff members at one of Montreal's favourite nightspots, The Samovar, amongst them Donald C. MacDonald, Ken Olgivie, Ken Wright, Jack Masters, Tim the barman, and Whittaker.

Marsters – took me on face value, although I suspect the desk men who handled my news copy still had their doubts.

Did I let slip the name of the Samovar? That particularly picturesque nightclub, or rather cabaret, was introduced to me as the after-work oasis of *Gazette* reporters. They had probably been led to it by the fiery John Rhodes Sturdy, after the previous oasis, Mother Martin's, had fired a favourite waiter. Up the hill marched the *Gazette* newsmen to Peel Street just above St Catherine to this more exotic nightspot.

Exotic it was, with Byzantine murals executed by one Shabayev, whom I had already encountered teaching pottery to Westmount ladies at Edwin Fancott's "commercial" art studio behind his coffee shop. I remember Shabayev prowling around the tables where students potted in their colourful smocks and pretty little aprons like a particularly revolutionary wolf. I also remember the table I acquired there – an old oak once belonging to James McGill himself, its dowelled top somewhat brutalized to fit into an alcove. It has graced all my residences since and made more public appearances in plays by Ghéon, Pushkin, and Shaw. Can one have partnerships with inanimate objects of furniture? If so, I've certainly enjoyed one with this McGill refectory table.

The Gazetteers confined themselves mostly to the Samovar bar where they could drink and argue until three o'clock in the morning. When last call was sounded, they would order their final rounds. Afterwards, the more insistent drinkers repaired to a speakeasy around the corner. By then, I had cautiously wound my way home.

When Tom became deeply engrossed in his biography of Richard Strauss, I inherited the nightclub beat. I could then legitimately pass the watchdog we knew as Madame Goodbosum to enter the Samovar's dining room and secure a good table to review the entertainment which, I may say, was of the highest quality. Its suave entrepreneur and master of ceremonies, Carol Grauer, could summon attractions such as the triple-octave songstress Ima Sumac, or the zany Broadway clown Imogene Coca, or that popular songstress Irene Hilda. Or even a teenaged evacuee from England who became the pet of Royal Air Force trainees, famous later in life as stage, film, and television personality Angela Lansbury. Entertainment was provided regularly by the Kraft Sisters, oriental specialists (Beatrice taught me Javanese head-movement), and the Van Gronas, a top European dance team. Yes, the Samovar was easily my favourite night-beat chore.

Other newspaper people in Montreal frequented other nightspots for it is of nature a gregarious profession, the city being a night-town (as it still is). The noontime *Herald* crowd hung out at Slitkin's and Slotkin's, the pseudonymns adopted by owners Lou Wyman and Jack Rogers of this bar and restaurant on Dorchester near Mountain. It had the added appeal of a gangster clientele, which coloured nightlife after purges in Chicago drove its darker denizens to

Montreal. The weekly *Standard* lot stayed on at Mother Martin's, though some of them – such as Bob Duffy, Kit Shaw, and Mavis Gallant – may have preferred the Marine Bar at the Ritz-Carlton.

Nobody I knew "frequented" the Normandie Roof, despite the fact that the Press Club was located in the basement of its Mount Royal Hotel. The acts presented there, always from out of town, were superior. We reviewers were honoured when performers came to sit at our press table: the young dark pianist with hopes of playing Gershwin in the film *Rhapsody in Blue* (though Liberace didn't get the job), the famously French chanteuse Hildegarde, and David Brooks, the up-and-coming singer who was to star in Broadway's *The Bloomer Girl* and *Brigadoon* and to become a good New York friend. All class acts.

So I became part of Montreal's nightlife in a particularly golden period enriched by trainees from abroad. I can't pretend to have delved into its wickeder bypaths, as the writer of my preface, young Christopher Plummer, did. That noted actor was a boy around town even before he played at the Montreal Repertory Theatre. Rockhead's Paradise was never on my beat, as it was on his and Joy McGibbon's (later Lafleur), then our debutante of the year.

I do remember Joy at the Samovar, though, one night at the bar. She had been flicking ashes over an anonymous woman nearby, who became enraged. Putting her martini carefully inside her handbag, Joy defended herself. The rest of the people in the bar stood by entranced. Tim, the bartender, had to separate the scratching ladies. Whereat Joy retrieved her martini from her purse, looked into its mirror and wailed, "And I was to have my screen test at Metro-Goldwyn-Mayer tomorrow!" She might have too; a real dazzler was Joy Lafleur – charming, wilful, and fascinating. A good actress too.

Over the years, the *Gazette* employee whom I was closest to was dear Tom Archer, who had suggested me in the first place and was already my friend. We spent long hours together, usually discussing the remarkable talents of Richard Strauss. Gradually I became fully attached to the Music and Drama Department (this designation preceding that of "entertainment" in newspapers). There I brought my energies to bear on the expansion of our music and drama coverage. I reported on all minor theatre groups, determined that no theatrical achievement would go unheralded or unreported in the *Gazette*. This was by no means unique – every good newspaper depends on employees who become so dedicated to their "beat" that the readers are given more and more extensive information about the subject.

When the 1940s burst upon us I was able to test my wings as a theatrical critic. I went to Moyse Hall to see the McGill Players' Club perform Keith Winter's English domestic comedy *The Shining Hour*. In *Stage Magazine* I had read Hiram Motherwell's vivid account of the production that Raymond Massey and Gladys Cooper had brought to Broadway back in 1934 – a piece of original theatrical reporting that still impresses me. So I knew what was to be expected from the student actors. The McGill Players' Club obviously fell short of Massey and Cooper, and I recognized this fact in a notice that put the Players' Club in its place, firmly and scornfully.

Happily for thousands of later players across the country, I had Adam Marshall as city editor on that occasion. Adam was a wise man and, when he saw what I had written, he suggested that I had brought rather heavy guns to bear on what was, after all, an undergraduate effort. I snatched the review back and conceded a milder version. Over the following months, and years later, I came across the rejected copy and reread it. Each time I did so, I was able to recognize it more sharply for what it really was: a document of youthful arrogance proclaiming the little I knew as evidence that others knew less. That humbling recognition was to guide my future career as a professional critic. Thanks to Adam Marshall, I had made the first important step along that path.

When, in 1945, I started to review major dramatic attractions, *The Herald*, a formidable noon competitor to the *Star* and the *Gazette*, offered me the post of theatre and film critic. When I told this to Charles Peters, he came up with

Herbert Whittaker at his
desk at *The Gazette*.

a counter-offer of the same post. I was pleased but much concerned about how
Tom would take this news. After all, it was his kindness that had won me my
position at the *Gazette*. But Tom took it generously, after a week of coolness,
and so with his approval I could attend opening nights at His Majesty's Theatre
and then make the dash to St Antoine Street to rush my reactions into print.
As his gesture of acceptance Tom presented me with his whole bound collection
of the plays of Eugene O'Neill and concentrated his library on the works of
Richard Strauss. His biography, *Richard Strauss: The Man and His Muse*, completed and accepted for publication, was withdrawn from production during
wartime and then forgotten. Tom never recovered from the blow.

It had been a long apprenticeship. I had earned the advantage I held for
many years afterwards, that of being the first critical notice available on the
street. The speed this required to meet deadlines also saved me from the dreadful
temptation of brooding about what I was going to write, searching for quota-

A press conference for a visit by Greer Garson to Montreal. Whittaker is leaning over her and *Gazette* illustrator Grant MacDonald is to his right. Kneeling are Roy Kerwin and Burt Hall. *Gazette* columnist "Fitz" Fitzgerald is above, centre.

tions, or seeking some special way of putting down honest responses. I certainly learned to pay attention all through the performance and to trust my memory of it. With the continual advances of computer technology, this frantic skill is no longer needed. Nor does being first on the street seem so important. But back in those days being first was much prized and very exciting for me.

I gradually came to know the most senior and experienced of my fellow drama critics, the legendary S. Morgan-Powell of the *Montreal Daily Star*, who long ago helped launch the Montreal Repertory Theatre. Morgan, as we were allowed to address him, was "the authority" in every aspect of his career. In the theatre he had the advantage of touching greatness or of having been touched by it. Once, summoned to join a supper-party at the Windsor Hotel by Sarah Bernhardt herself, he arrived late. With no thought that drama critics worked when the artist's work was finished, she showed her anger: when he offered her a bouquet of roses, she snatched them up and beat him with them! As I remember the scene from Morgan's account, the blow was followed by an embrace.[4]

Understandably, Morgan–Powell refused to move with the times. He refused to recognize the place of the director in the theatre, preferring to credit the actor-manager. He wrote fluently and richly of the theatre of the day as if it were unchanged since those great days of Bernhardt, Ellen Terry, and Henry Irving. When I left the *Gazette* in 1949 to continue my critical role in Toronto, he spoke well of me and my contribution in his column in the *Star*.[5] Later, when I visited him with Sydney Johnson – who had had to wait such a long time to succeed Morgan as the *Star's* critic – he signed his prophetic book *Memories That Live* to "my friend Herbert Whittaker, who has upheld through his career of drama critic the highest standards of constructive criticism." That meant something, coming from Morgan.

Chapter Four

THE MONTREAL REPERTORY THEATRE

By the early thirties the national community or little theatre movement was recognized as "the tributary theatre" by two important magazines: *Theatre Arts*, the American publication devoted to serious theatre since 1916, and the more Broadway-oriented *Stage Magazine*. Recognition from the latter meant that the movement was being accepted more widely, if a shade reluctantly and condescendingly. So was the underlying premise that artists within any community had the right to establish their own kind of theatre. In 1922, George Kelly had mocked the movement in a hilarious farce called *The Torchbearers*, but even he could not laugh it out of existence. By 1930 the commercial managements, with their slick devotion to Broadway fashions and their blurred reproductions of them for the road, were being resolutely challenged by this homegrown theatre.

Of course, such theatre-peddlers had been opposed on their own theatre ground as far back as 1919. That's when the four-year-old Washington Square Players, having not quite survived the Great War, re-emerged as the New York Theatre Guild, that powerful champion of a meaningful theatre in a commercial world. One of Broadway's luminous new stars, Katharine Cornell, came up through the little theatre movement in Buffalo, New York – one of the first to come that way, making her New York entrance with the Washington Square Players.[1]

Downtown on MacDougall Street, pointing to the off-Broadway trend of the far future, the Provincetown Players moved into Manhattan from Cape Cod, where Eugene O'Neill, Robert Edmond Jones, and Kenneth Macgowan had rallied to the cause in 1915. Two years later Jacques Copeau brought his Théâtre du Vieux-Colombier from Paris to visit New York and took up residence at the Garrick Theatre. The new American movement reflected the startling advance of the European art theatres after World War I.[2]

These little theatres were serious, not just targets for comic authors such as Kelly. They attracted the educated members of any community, who could otherwise only read classic dramas. After the old actor-managers relinquished their handful of familiar great roles, the Broadway managements had set their sights on the lowest common denominator of the day's theatre for touring from coast to coast. These were plays that would not challenge anybody: Anne Nichols' *Abie's Irish Rose*, Collison and Hopwood's *Getting Gertie's Garter*, *Peg O' My Heart* by J. Hartley Manners, and such.[3]

That little theatres rallied against such fare from coast to coast justified a Boston publisher's 1920 printing of three volumes of plays boldly labelled *Little Theatre Classics*. This alternative repertory looked to the past, dredging up English satire, Jacobean tragedy, and even Japanese drama for ambitious non-professionals. Universities combined forces in the rebellion against the Broadway carpetbaggers, with Harvard and Yale making significant contributions in the United States while Toronto, McGill, and Queen's universities followed in Canada. In fact, Montreal's most successful and influential little theatre company, the Montreal Repertory Theatre (MRT), began its life under the wing of McGill University and performed its earliest productions on campus in Moyse Hall.

The little theatre campaign, thus encouraged, spread across the continent like a grass fire after battle. Eventually it reached different parts of Canada, a country by no means ahead of its day. Macgowan, general manager of the Provincetown Players and a valuable recorder of post-war theatre, was able to list a number of Canadian institutions in his book *Footlights Across America*, published in 1929: the Vancouver Little Theatre, the Winnipeg Community Players, the University of Toronto's Hart House, the Ottawa Little Theatre, and others.[4]

If you belonged to one of those big little theatres back then, you knew you were sharing the hopes of the serious theatrical world. All of your feverish activity – the scrounging, the improvising and the devising, the stretching of imaginations and talents, the feeling of being part of democratic action by dedicated folk – was pretty heady stuff. I know that's how I found it in the 1930s when I was in my twenties.

I think it was Marjorie Brewer who first told me about the Montreal Repertory Theatre, although I do remember a poster for Chiarelli's *The Mask and the Face* by a new group calling itself MRT coming into focus across St Catherine Street when I was trying on a new pair of glasses. However, I soon discovered the MRT, tucked behind Henry Morgan's superior department store at 1461 Union Avenue, an address also occupied by Morgan's real estate division. Two parts of the building – a rather grand downstairs office on two levels and a chilly loft on the top floor – had been lent by F. Cleveland Morgan to house the new theatre venture. The upstairs, with its tall studio windows, was often cold and always draughty, but the downstairs office had an imposing entrance and a fireplace. That entry was intimidating enough to overawe a somewhat threadbare art student who was also earning his living in the early thirties as a very junior clerk for the Canadian Pacific Railway. It would have been over-powering had it not been for May Linton, a friendly presence who was the MRT secretary and who smiled, chatted, and let me look at the copies of *Stage Magazine* and *Theatre Arts* in the office.

Most of the successful little theatres were led by women – strong and independent, backed by social power. The MRT was no exception. The commanding presence of the MRT, its initiator and founder, was Martha Marguerite Allan. Perfectly bilingual (she liked to call herself Marthe at times) she was a close-cropped blonde, slim of figure, and always very well-tailored. She was also overpowering and very abrupt, though friendly enough in manner, and used all the influence at her command as the daughter of Sir Montagu, head of the Allan Steamship Line, and Lady Allan of Ravenscrag on Pine Avenue.[5]

Educated in Montreal, London, and Paris, Martha was in London when World War I broke out. She returned to Canada for the necessary training and then went back to France as an ambulance driver, where she suffered a shrapnel wound that was to plague her for the rest of her life. The Allans lost two other daughters when the Lusitania sank, as well as a son, Hugh, when his plane went down during the war. When Martha came back from France, it was not to rejoin the old social round but to study at the pioneering Pasadena Playhouse in California. Once back in Montreal she moved out of the grandeur of the family mansion and into Ravenscrag's coach house, and from there launched her own Canadian little theatre.[6]

The Montreal Repertory Theatre was formally announced on 23 November 1929 at Victoria Hall, Westmount. At a public meeting, Martha, as founder, had assembled several notables, among them Sir Barry Jackson (the principal speaker), a notable champion of the English repertory movement, and that greatest of Canadian-born actresses, Margaret Anglin. Also on hand, their notebooks ready, were the *Montreal Daily Star's* Samuel Morgan-Powell and the *Gazette's* Thomas Archer. Both were highly supportive of Martha from the beginning. Indeed, Morgan-Powell later lectured MRT members on the aims and duties of repertory theatre.

MRT started out quite cautiously in March 1930 with A.A. Milne's *The Perfect Alibi* as its test production. To get her new venture launched properly, Martha chose to stage Shaw's *Candida*, in modern dress and furnishings, *La souriante Mme Beaudet* by Denys Amiel and André Obey, and Somerset Maugham's *The Constant Wife*. In all of these plays she carried the leading roles, although she had enjoyed playing men's roles back in her old days with the Community Players. This first full MRT season, 1930–31, also included Karel Capek's expressionistic *R.U.R.* and John Galsworthy's *The Roof.*

By 1931–32 MRT was confident enough to stage a *teatro grottesco* epic, *The Mask and The Face*, written by Luigi Chiarelli in 1916 and later translated by C.B. Fernald, as well as Fernald's Chinese adaptation *The Cat and the Cherub,* and another A.A. Milne work, somewhat more biting, *The Truth about Blayds*. In the early years MRT had a nice balance of art theatre and refined popular offerings in its public programme. Later, with the creation of its Studio Theatre on Union Avenue, more avant-garde plays were shown. The Studio Theatre served the higher artistic aims admirably and economically, while recent West End, as opposed to Broadway, hits gave pleasure to larger audiences at a variety of more spacious rented auditoriums such as Westmount's Victoria Hall and McGill's Moyse Hall.

Montrealers, aware of the decline of the British and American touring companies, were also in a mood to welcome classical fare from MRT. Shakespeare's *Hamlet* (1932), *Romeo and Juliet* (1933), *Twelfth Night* (1933), and *The Merry Wives of Windsor* (1935) were given reasonably respectable productions. MRT audiences also enjoyed contemporary dramas such as J.B. Priestley's "daring" *Dangerous Corner* and Sidney Howard's *The Late Christopher Bean*, which was acceptably advanced in its advocacy of modern art. Audiences admired European classics such as Ibsen's *Hedda Gabler*, Gogol's *The Inspector General*, and, for those who spoke French, Obey's *Noé*. They were entertained by George S. Kaufman's *Dulcy* with Martha in the lead, although she was not as well suited to that as she was to Hedda. Ashley Duke's more sophisticated *The Man with a Load of Mischief*, produced in November 1934, preceded broader fare such as the mock-heroic *Young England* by Walter Reynolds and the Aiken/Thomas dramatic adaptation of *Uncle Tom's Cabin*, played as old melodrama. Quite respectable fare in the context of that Depression era, eh?

But it was in the Studio offerings that MRT achieved real distinction. In their draughty space, once a miniature golf course, more venturesome choices were possible. Cecil West, Martha's right-hand man, solicited new one-act plays and got a dramatic version of Susie Frances Harrison's folk ballad *Rose Latulippe*, *Problems Have Their People* by Leslie Stone, *Between Two Worlds* by my new and clever friend Charles Rittenhouse, and Martha's entry, *All on a Summer's Day*. The latter won the 1934 Western Quebec Regional Drama Festival and went on to the Ottawa Dominion Drama Festival finals.

Cecil West is the unpublicized figure in the MRT story, for he realized that Martha had to be the star attraction to win the necessary support. An Englishman, whose wife Jean was also much involved backstage at MRT, he not only guided productions onto the boards but also influenced the programming, particularly at the experimental studio. Tall and quite distinguished, he also acted. He had McGill connections, enlisting some of its young supporters in MRT productions.

For Eugene O'Neill's *The Hairy Ape*, MRT found Reginald Genest to play its title role impressively while Clifford Odets' powerful protest play *Waiting for Lefty* suitably outraged some of Martha's elderly supporters.[7] There were also exotic offerings such as Henri Ghéon's *The Marvelous History of St Bernard* (the first Studio production that I saw), a Czech work, Frantisek Langer's *Periferie*, directed by Louis Mulligan, and even *An Evening of Grand Guignol*.

The MRT attracted the best actors in Montreal because Martha soon established it as the leading theatre in the city. Actors from the Trinity Players and the Little Theatre of the YM-YWHA – the older local dramatic societies – the McGill Players Club, St Lambert Players, and the Dickens Fellowship were honoured to be asked to perform at MRT. So were players from about forty church and community groups led by the previously described Everyman Players (and the Sixteen-Thirty Club) of the Church of the Messiah.[8]

Two stalwarts of that Sixteen-Thirty Club, one of whom had shown his passion for things Russian by exhuming a dramatic poem by Pushkin, were offered another play by another Russian, Anton Chekhov, as an MRT Studio experiment. The play was *Uncle Vanya* and Charles Rittenhouse was invited to direct it and I (the Pushkin one) was to design it. It was intended for the Union Avenue studio, as can plainly be seen from my designs, but wound up being played to the larger audience at Victoria Hall. Two Sixteen-Thirty Club actors, Rae Guess and the introspective Douglas Peterson, were recruited, while the Little Theatre of the YM-YWHA provided one of its best players in Pauline Trehub. None of the cast realized that we were giving *Uncle Vanya* its first production in Canada.[9] This in November 1938!

Under Martha's banner the best of Montreal's experienced amateurs were joined by others of even higher calibre. Eleanor Stuart and Mildred Mitchell (that darling of Montreal's Orpheum stock company) were both known professionals. Lorna Sheard came from Toronto's Hart House where she had played Shakespeare's Cleopatra and been seen opposite New York's Jacob Ben-Ami. Basil Dignam, Cyril and Cicely Hessey-White, and Whitfield and Maud Aston added British weight while Randolph Crowe, Somer Alberg, and Cecil West were other mature and experienced talents.

They mixed with bright local youngsters such as Richard Newton, Lionel Murton, John Pratt, Robert Goodier, Robert Watt, and Charles Rittenhouse. The younger actresses included Eileen Clifford, Gillian Hessey-White, Stella Sprowell, and our Marjorie Brewer. But the most glamorous of the latter group was undoubtedly Joy McGibbon, later Lafleur, whose professionalism took her to the Stratford Festival in 1957 playing Gertrude opposite her old Montreal playmate Christopher Plummer.

Had there existed a professional English-language theatre in Montreal, these people could have fairly laid claim to it. As it was, they were already learning to make money from their talents through the only professional market at their disposal: radio broadcasting.[10] Some of them, such as Eleanor Stuart and Eileen Clifford, came to depend on that outlet as a principal source of income while the next generation, youngsters such as Christopher Plummer, John Colicos, Richard Easton, William Shatner, and Richard Gilbert – first established their professionalism in broadcasting. Even such a partial Montreal listing shows the kind of talent that was available across the whole country but which congregated in one place only when the various individuals became involved in the once-a-year finals of the Dominion Drama Festival.

Since Montreal had been a way station on the road for American and British tours until the 1930s, the style of acting at MRT was something of a blend of the two schools. It must be remembered Stanislavsky's influence on American theatre, which evolved into the celebrated method acting, had only just been felt and had certainly not affected the touring companies or the stock actors. At that time American and British styles were not dissimilar, the English stage still maintaining its old influence on the New York style.

In Montreal this English influence was represented by players such as the Hessey-Whites, the Astons, and Basil Dignam. They were joined by Roberta Beatty, an American, as well as Madge and Filmore Sadler, who had an advantage in being teachers of the young MRT actors. With Martha Allan, who drew on her Pasadena training, they were responsible for the MRT's acting style, which was then characterized as "mid-Atlantic."

But it was a period of change in acting styles everywhere. The great old British actors and their American counterparts – Robert Bruce Mantell, Walter Hampden, E.A. Sothern, and Julia Marlowe – were fading from the North American scene. The most admired company in North America was Broadway's ambitious and cosmopolitan New York Theatre Guild. This company imported the best of European and British drama and backed its productions with stars such as Alfred Lunt and Lynn Fontanne, Helen Hayes, and Katherine Hepburn. But it also promoted such American dramatists as Eugene O'Neill, Maxwell Anderson, and Robert Sherwood. It was the marvel of the continent that it should prosper without condescension to the popular taste. No wonder the MRT hoped to repeat the Theatre Guild's success.

In its own way the MRT emulated the Theatre Guild while maintaining an affiliation with London's West End stage. In fact, MRT had started out as the Montreal Theatre Guild but had been forced to change its name because the New York group had copyrighted the name. In general the style adopted by MRT would now be seen as rather stagy, although it did not seem so then. The younger MRT players used to scorn old-English ham when the Astons, for example, pushed too hard; yet we always envied their resonance, confidence, and theatrical effectiveness. Actors still behaved like actors – not like you and I. Older actors, like the Astons, were ever aware of their audiences and the size of the theatre. Starting with radio, newer actors were aware that the microphone, and then the camera, was their audience, an eavesdropper, so they played more intimately, dropping the voice accordingly and thus reducing the vocal range needed for classic plays. The eye-lock with fellow actors was favoured, in performance as well as in rehearsal, and the awareness of audience in theatre diminished. As we moved step-by-step into an electronic age, acting styles followed suit. The Astons, however, remained, resolute and audible.

There was yet another abundant source of Montreal talent that Martha explored – she soon established contact with French Canada's more professional theatre. She saw to it that MRT had its French section, although it failed to flourish financially. Mario Duliani, who headed it, paid this special tribute to Martha in 1952 after a disastrous fire destroyed the MRT playhouse: "MRT was always open to French Canadians, thanks to Martha Allan." He then listed some of the French-speaking professionals who had gotten their start with her: Yvette Brind'Amour, later head of le Théâtre du Rideau Vert, Janine Sutto and Nini Durand of l'Équipe, run by Pierre Dagenais, Judith Jasmin, François Bertrand, and Gisèle Schmidt, all popular favourites later; and the extraordinary Gratien Gélinas, whom I first remember in 1935 as Dr Caius opposite Whitfield Aston's substantial Falstaff.[11]

Others of promise were involved seriously in matters of production. Young architects such as Hazen Sise, George How, and Richard Eve gathered under Cecil West's supervision to paint the walls of 1461 Union Avenue, transforming it into the Studio Theatre for Martha. Later they built scenery and served on stage crews under Martha's stage manager, Paddy Creagan, when her productions went elsewhere.

Of these young professionals recruited by Cecil West from McGill University, Hazen Sise is remembered as a particularly dazzling fellow. A banker's son and a trained architect, he went off to Spain to join that most impressive Montrealer Norman Bethune, then introducing revolutionary medical practices to the fight against General Franco. We respected Hazen for this, though some Montrealers I knew remained scornful of "pinkos."

I delicately put my toe in the mainstream of MRT when I ventured to submit designs for the competition it held to design for André Obey's *Noé*. I see now that my concept, lofty and Craig-like,[12] was totally unsuitable to Obey's modest masterpiece. Very properly the Kingston artist André Bieler, whose submission sensibly put the Biblical parable into a Québécois setting, was the designer MRT favoured. But I recall an incident about that *Noé* competition that excited me. Lord Bessborough came to inspect the drawings with Martha when I was there, so I hastily hid in the paint-cupboard under the stairs. He asked about my drawings, which I had entered rather pretentiously under the pseudonym of "Inigo," after the great Jacobean designer Inigo Jones. Martha, never at a loss, said they were by one of her most promising young designers, although she had no idea who "Inigo" was. I, of course, was dizzy with delight at her generous ad lib.

I encountered Martha in my next role as stagehand. That was perhaps at Salle du Gesù for *Noé*, perhaps at Moyse Hall when *Hamlet*, the joint production of the MRT and the Ottawa Drama League, opened in the Arts Building auditorium at McGill University in December 1932 for two evening performances

Montreal Repertory Theatre founder Martha Allan (1934).

and a matinee. The Earl of Bessborough was both producer and designer, his son, the Viscount Duncannon, was playing Hamlet, and Martha was the director, with Rupert Caplan assisting as well as doubling the role of the Ghost with Somer Alberg. Trumpets were sounding. I counted myself extremely lucky to be allowed to assist backstage on such a prestigious production. I could not have dreamt then that in a few more years I would have my chance to design three Shakespeare plays for this same McGill stage.

Eric Duncannon made an eager, handsome, and well-spoken Prince Hamlet. Mackenzie King, federal leader of the Liberal Party, wrote most appreciatively to him about his performance (a tribute that the Countess Bessborough, Eric's mother, treated scornfully as sycophantic). "It was like drinking at a stream of living water to see and hear again one of Shakespeare's plays by real artists, after having been parched in the barren theatrical lands of these times," wrote King from Laurier House. " I do hope that the [little theatre] movement, which has been given such a splendid impetus by last night's performance, may be the beginning of a new era in the reproduction of great plays and that the theatre may come again into its own."

The dowager Countess' scorn was raised by King's personal tribute, which followed: "Your youth, the inflections of your voice, the restraint of your enunciation, the artistic touch in everything and, above all, your splendid rendition of every line and of the character of Hamlet itself combined to leave an impression which was both vivid and profound, an impression of grace and power. It was truly remarkable." This rare example of a future prime minister as drama critic was signed "yours very sincerely, W.L. Mackenzie King" and dated 28 December 1932.

As I got to know Eric better in later years and to stay with him on occasion at Stansted, the family home, I was always ashamed to admit that I remember this 1932 *Hamlet* best for an incident that happened at its first night's final curtain. The solo spotlight fell not on the dying Prince but on the slain and prone Laertes. "Illuminating Laertes' derrière," was the way Martha put it bluntly. To hear a live lord curse an electrician was a fine thing, to be sure. To see Eric, Viscount Duncannon, chasing the hapless electrician, sword in hand, was heaven indeed! My delight was shared, I remember, by my fellow stage-hands, who included Fraser Macorquodale and Donald Wetmore. The latter enriched my library when he left to pioneer theatre in the Maritimes, dividing his theatre books between MRT's May Linton and myself. Fraser remained loyal to our church groups, while maintaining a highly successful life as a corporate lawyer.

I also remember the dress rehearsal for that *Hamlet*. It ran until three o'clock in the morning, by which time we were all exhausted and Gertrude was asleep on the piano. The streetcars had stopped running by then, so I faced a torrent of melting snow as I battled my way uphill across Fletcher's Field. I didn't feel at all sorry for myself because I had been part of the great world of Montreal – nay, of Canadian and even world – theatre.

But I soon emerged from being a mere stagehand when I did a design for a ballad play called *Fair Annie* directed by Marguerite Cleary. My drawing for three twisted Gothic arches was considered interesting enough but totally impossible to construct without money – a requisite ability in Studio productions. Instead, I had to fall back on the painted back wall of the Studio stage, one canvas pillar, and the curved steps Lord Bessborough had created for his imposing *Hamlet*. But I was finally associated with MRT as a designer of scenery.

After that, I did what any ambitious stage designer does if he hangs around a theatre long enough: I made masks for a French MRT production, *Thespis en panne*, and more for a Studio show … *We Mortals*, written by Martha Allan. I supplied the MRT School of Drama with no fewer than eleven expressionist settings for a capsule history of drama directed by Mada Gage Bolton, who went on to write her own dramas.[13] Because of my new acquaintance with Thomas Archer through the Everyman Players I was even offered a leading role

Whittaker's first setting for a Montreal Repertory Theatre production – Ashley Duke's *The Man with a Load of Mischief* (November 1934). Shown are Cyril (Teddy) Hessey-White and Lorna Sheard.

in his attempt at satire, *Three Characters in Search of a Plot*. Acute self-consciousness at the first reading decided me against an acting career. Tom took over the lead role himself, supported by more experienced actors such as John Pratt, later the star of *Meet the Navy*. I did a constructivist setting for it, as I was then fascinated by the word back from Russia.

When the MRT explored the possibility of using the ballroom of the Ritz-Carlton Hotel as a theatre, Cecil West asked me if I would like to submit a design for a temporary proscenium arch. The first production there, in November 1934, was to be Ashley Dukes' London hit of 1924, *The Man with a Load of Mischief.* This Regency play, set in a country inn, easily caught my fancy so, instead of concentrating on the temporary arch, I set out to create a timbered interior with staircase, a fireplace with settle, and an ingenious jog in the wall to fit everything in. When West, MRT's production chief, accepted my design, I was greatly elated. Not only was I moving into a major production but the Dukes' comedy was also to star the eminent Eleanor Stuart (then Nichol) opposite popular "Teddy" Hessey-White and Lorna Sheard. Stuart was definitely one of the people who had established the standard of MRT acting, both as a professional player and as a voice teacher of extraordinary perception.[14]

Eleanor Stuart Nichol was a pale classic beauty with a haunting voice who had abandoned a very promising career abroad to return home to Montreal. Roberta Beatty's story had it that, when she was understudying Spring Byington as Nerissa in the same Winthrop Ames production of *The Merchant of Venice* in which George Arliss had made such an impression on me, Miss Byington was fired – which would have given Eleanor her chance. But because she shared a dressing room with the actress, she took Miss Byington in hand, coaching her so successfully that the producer kept her on. Spring Byington went on to Broadway and Hollywood success, proof of Eleanor Stuart's teaching patience and her notable self-effacement.

To design a production starring Eleanor Stuart was an achievement already touched by distinction, to say nothing of the superior Ritz-Carlton location. I swelled with pride when I beheld my setting and my name on the theatre programme for which the notable artist, Edwin Holgate, had supplied the cover design.

But Eleanor Stuart was not the only figure from the professional stage to enhance MRT's life at that time. The celebrated Mrs Patrick Campbell once arrived as Martha's guest and took over rehearsals for Shaw's *How He Lied to Her Husband* with the authority of one who had created the playwright's Eliza Doolittle in *Pygmalion*. She included speeches from the latter in two readings she gave at the Ritz-Carlton. Another Hollywood-bound actor in similar circumstances was Alan Marshall. In New York, he had appeared in J.B. Priest-ley's *Dangerous Corner*, which was on the MRT schedule, and had asked Martha for a chance to audition. After playing for MRT he went on to Hollywood to act opposite Greer Garson and Ginger Rogers.

A more permanent contributor was Mildred Mitchell, she of Montreal's Orpheum stock company. Her sunny personality had won her a personal fol-lowing in the wide variety of roles demanded of a stock company actress. As Mrs William Wray, of Wray's Funeral Parlour in Montreal, she proceeded to lend her theatrical prestige as well as her talent to MRT, eventually succeeding Martha as producing director. Blonde, quiet and rather fussy, she was a gracious concerned director as well as an accomplished actress.

But for some of us Rupert Caplan brought even more prestige since he had actually been with the Provincetown Playhouse in New York, working with legendary pioneers such as Eugene O'Neill, Robert Edmond Jones, George Cram Cook, Susan Glaspell, and Jasper Deeter. I was particularly impressed when I discovered that he was The Pilot in *The Ancient Mariner*, Eugene O'Neill's 1924 adaptation of Coleridge's famous poem, directed by Robert Edmond Jones and James Light, two major Provincetown luminaries. Caplan, who had been involved earlier with Montreal's Community Players, had returned home to direct productions at the Young Men's Hebrew Association.

He was on hand for the opening of the Montreal Repertory Theatre and directed a number of its plays. But his great contribution was in the production of radio drama for CBC and in the number of actors to whom he gave employment in a series of continuing broadcasts. These epics included Frank L. Packard's *The Red Ledger*, biblical dramatizations for "The Way of the Spirit," and his own soap opera *Laura Ltd*. Caplan's contribution to Montreal's profes-sionalism was immense.[15]

Roberta Beatty made her appearance on the MRT scene in 1938, although I had met her earlier at Tom Archer's and was immediately fascinated by the poise of one who had played on Broadway. "I had come to Montreal in 1937," she later told me, "and after I'd been there a year, I was sitting beside Pauline Donalda, who by then had a famous voice studio, at dinner. She invited me to lunch at her house and she also invited a lady called Martha Allan. Pauline thought we might be compatible because I knew something about the Broadway theatre." Madame Donalda, later to be famous as a producer of opera in Montreal after her career as an opera singer ended, proved to be right. Although startling in physical contrast, Martha Allan and Roberta Beatty had a great deal in common, beginning with a mutual respect for theatre.

After her initial meeting with Roberta, Martha used to drop into Roberta and Julius Cohen's home in the Chateau Apartments on Sherbrooke Street, staying late into the night to talk theatre and to discuss her plans. "She was very pleased that I had come to town," Bobbie Beatty explained, "and had the idea of me playing Eleanor Stuart's sophisticated sister in John Van Druten's woman's play *The Distaff Side*, with herself playing the grandmother's role and Joy Lafleur as the wild daughter." Other Montreal notables in this January 1938 production included the Hessey-Whites (Pegs and Teddy, their nicknames used by everybody), Cedric Hands, and Brownie Evans, two of Martha's favourites, and Chester Lemaistre, surely one of the most resourceful of the local actors.

It was the only play in Montreal with Roberta listed as one of the actors, for Bobbie soon became one of the city's major directors. Not surprisingly, Martha brought that about. Bobbie had never directed a play, despite her varied professional career. Martha, however, storm-bound in Pasadena, sent her a wire asking her to take over as director of Frederick Lonsdale's *Aren't We All* (April 1939), knowing that Bobbie had played in it on Broadway opposite Cyril Maude and Leslie Howard. Martha thus enticed yet another major player onto her theatrical team.

Also from the United States came the Sadlers – Filmore and Marjorie – who had met and married as students at the Leland Power School of Theatre in Boston. Filmore was pure New England — a Yankee, breezy and outgoing; Marjorie ("Madge"), more retiring, came from Johannesburg. They landed in Montreal because Marjorie's mother, who didn't favour the marriage, had sent Madge to join another daughter already living in Montreal. Filmore followed. He tried managing a hotel in the Eastern Townships for awhile, then wound up making Martha's dream of a theatre school come true on Union Avenue. He returned to the Townships in 1936 to create an invaluable summer theatre and school — Brae Manor — in Knowlton.

The Sadlers soon became deeply involved in MRT productions as players and teaching staff. Martha's net was wide and the people she brought into it became lively contributors to the Montreal scene. These included Sir Andrew MacPhail, a notably plain man who became a very handsome benefactor of the MRT Studio. Other dignitaries who were members of Martha's committee, which had Howard Murray as chairman, were Sir Arthur Currie, principal of McGill University, E.W. Beatty, president of the Canadian Pacific Railway, Lt. Col. Molson, F.E. Meredith, KC; Edouard Montpetit, head of l'Université de Montréal, the Hon. Mr Justice Fabre Surveyor, and Frank M. Ross.

Sir Andrew, noting that the French citizenry of Montreal was importantly involved with the MRT, observed in *Theatre Arts* in 1932 that Martha Allan herself had early training "in the hard school of the Comédie-Française" and that her Québécois associates included René de Foure, Ernest Cormier, Marie Ouimet, and Adjutor Savard. To that list, I must add Pacifique Plante, busy in MRT before he concentrated on confronting Montreal's growing underworld, and Ferdinand Biondi. Active on the English-language side were Cecil and Jean West, Edwyn Wayte, Donald Wetmore, and the dedicated decorator Louis Mulligan.

There was also a great host of hangers-on, of whom I was one. I was shy, with no technical skills and only a small graphic gift, but the MRT opened up a world of theatrical imagination for me, as it did for other youngsters. I was learning about the world of Broadway from copies of the same *Theatre Arts* for which Sir Andrew wrote and the glossier *Stage Magazine*. I learned more from rare theatre books such as Oliver Sayler's *The Russian Theatre*, and from *The Provincetown* by Helen Deutsch and Stella Hanau.

When I say that I admired Martha Allan for encouraging all of us who had something to give, I do not overlook that she did so for her own cause. Arthur Carveth, whom Martha allowed to sleep on the premises of Union Avenue as watchman, office boy, and general dogsbody, says that she never really recognized the privations undergone by some of her supporters. "It was, in those so-called Depression years," he reminded me quite unnecessarily, "brutal for some of the more needy players." Adoring Martha as he did, Arthur had to admit that she never seemed to take into consideration the fact that several players had to walk to and from rehearsals because they had to save their carfare to get to daytime jobs.

Next to Martha, Bobbie Beatty was plainly the most dynamic influence on the MRT. A formidable presence, bracelets jangling ominously in rehearsals, she taught us a great deal through her highly professional reactions. "Entertain my ear!" she would command the inexperienced. She had no patience with the details of production, for in her theatre there had been experts to look after such matters. Hers was the Broadway of the Shuberts and Charles Dillingham, of the youthful Astaires, "Jerry" Kern, and Sigmund Romberg, for whom she had created the role of The Princess in *The Student Prince* back in 1924. Her career actually touched that of William Gillette, for she was with that distinguished American star personality on his last tour of *Sherlock Holmes*.[16]

How we all shivered with delight at her casual reference to these people and to the glamorous John Barrymore, into whose garden flat on 14th Street she moved after he left. As a young designer I was in awe that she knew the greatest of American scenic artists, Robert Edmond Jones. He had even stayed with her during the summer when he was working on his designs for O'Neill's

Mourning Becomes Electra! She also remembered her friends Stella and Edward Ballantine searching Greenwich Village for O'Neill while the playwright sat holed up in a room over Sheridan Square with a bottle.

It was through a friend – Saxe Cummings, the publisher – that she read the manuscript of O'Neill's *Mourning Becomes Electra* and attended its opening night, which had the great Broadway star Alla Nazimova as Christine Mannon. "I will never forget Nazimova," Bobbie recalled, "when her lover told her he would not go with her after she had murdered her husband. She aged fifteen years before my eyes, sitting there in the ship's cabin. A real tour-de-force!" Bobbie's great moments of theatre held us in awe: Alfred Lunt with his back turned in Sherwood's *There Shall Be No Night* as Montgomery Clift as his son told him that he was going to war, or John Barrymore expressing untold emotion with just one hand in Tolstoy's *Redemption*. Later I was to share one of these great moments with Bobbie when Laurette Taylor nagged her son to bring home a gentleman caller in Tennessee Williams' *The Glass Menagerie*. By then, 1945, I was visiting Broadway as the accredited drama critic for the *Gazette*.

Chapter Five

MRT TO GUY STREET AND MOYSE HALL

When Martha Allan died unexpectedly in the spring of 1942 in Victoria, British Columbia, word of her death rattled the whole theatre community of Montreal, French every bit as much as English. Everybody in Montreal theatre knew Martha and they called her that without further identification, as they did in the loftier circles of Ottawa and elsewhere. Never to her face, of course, for there was dignity due Montreal's "royalty."

Martha knew that the theatre must be full of surprises, as well as providing a direct link with the finest drama, which at that time was England's. She was our champion against shoddy, patronizing road shows coming up over the border. But she also knew the importance of audience. And she knew about patronage. Her family and friends, Montreal in excelsis, had to be brought onto her side when this indominatable scion launched her Montreal Repertory Theatre that day in Westmount. She talked them, man-to-man, into supporting her all the way. When Henry Morgan turned over that space on Union Avenue, behind his major department store, MRT was launched. Great location, lovely space, near St Catherine, blessed by the Anglican cathedral Christ Church, right across the road.

I was one of her minions there as a young part of the Union Avenue studio. Our relationship grew as I rose in the ranks of the *Gazette* and the Dominion Drama Festival though I can't say we were ever close. I only saw Martha's nerve shaken once and that when Hal Grindon's illness pushed her onstage in the title role of Brian Doherty's play, *Father Malachy's Miracle*, in London's Grand Theatre during Festival week. Back in a male role so many years after the Community

Players days! Backstage (I had an entry too) I caught that one moment of vulnerability in the remarkable woman who had made Montreal theatre a full-time, often-united activity of character and high standard. Canada owes much to such women of the theatre but none could match the dignity, effeciency, and respect that were Martha Allan's by right. A truly independent soul, she brought independence to Canada's theatre at a rare, bright period of its development.

After her death the MRT lost its downtown headquarters on Union Street, where it had started. Significantly, perhaps regrettably, it retreated in the direction of Westmount. Its new home at 550 Guy Street was just below Sherbrooke, that distinguished English avenue which balances the lively St Lawrence Main in the city's cultural topography. The new premises even had some faint theatrical past, having once been known as Norman Hall because a Professor Frank Norman had conducted his dancing academy there. But the address had a more curious, perhaps even symbolic, career behind it.

First known as the Simpson House, it had originally been built on McGregor Street, higher up the mountain at the top of Simpson Street, where it had been graced by the presence of Edward VII, then prince of Wales. For some inexplicable reason it had been relocated to Guy. With apartments installed above it and shops on either side of its doorway, it was no longer a desirable address. But the MRT, recognizing that its balconied ballroom could be turned into a charming 200-seat theatre, bought it. It is possible that even Martha Allan herself could not have rallied the town's tycoons to provide a larger, more profitable home for MRT. In 1942, under Louis Mulligan's supervision, MRT Guy Street was made most attractive. Light walls, dark carpets, a graceful brass chandelier, and a fine collection of old theatre prints and playbills lent an eighteenth-century air to the new home, reassuring MRT audiences by its charm.

To my delight, the Guy Street Playhouse now housed the Community Players' Library. The Players, originally founded by Professor Lloyd of McGill University, T.T. Stoker, and Brooke Claxton (later Canada's minister of

Proposed set design for André Obey's *Noé*,
produced by the French section of the
Montreal Repertory Theatre (March 1933).

Merlin — the old wary of his features is displayed on black velvet — surmounted by the seven stars

Costume design for George Brewer's *The Holy Grail*,
produced by the Everyman Players
at the Church of the Messiah (April 1934).

Set design for *Fair Annie*, a studio production
of the Montreal Repertory Theatre
(September 1934).

Costume design for George Brewer's *The Spanish Miracle*,
produced by the Everyman Players
at the Church of the Messiah (April 1935).

Costume design for George Brewer's *The Spanish Miracle*,
produced by the Everyman Players
at the Church of the Messiah (April 1935).

Costume design for the adaptation
of Pushkin's *Festival in Time of Plague*, produced by
the Sixteen-Thirty Club (March 1938).

Set design for Chekhov's *Uncle Vanya*,
a studio production of the Montreal Repertory Theatre
(November 1938).

Portrait of Charles Rittenhouse.

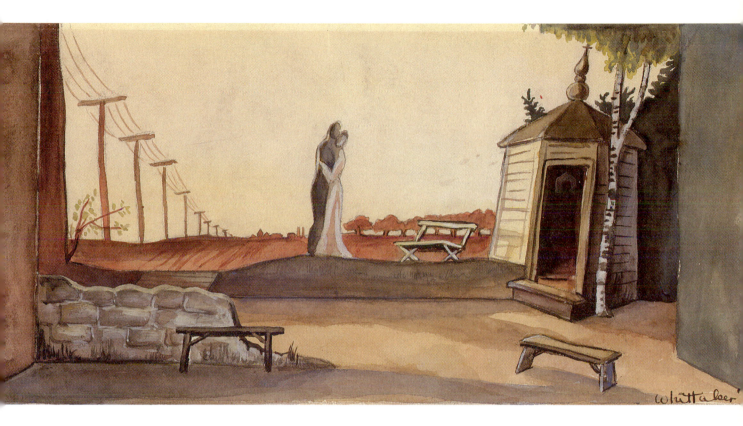

Set design for Chekhov's *The Cherry Orchard*,
produced by the YM-YWHA Players
(January 1945).

Costume design for Shakespeare's *Much Ado About Nothing*,
produced by the Shakespeare Society of Montreal
(May 1945).

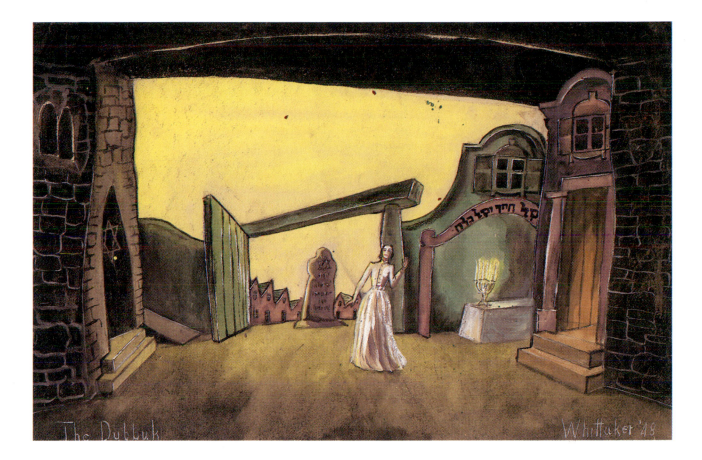

Set design for S. Ansky's *The Dybbuk*,
produced by the YM-YWHA Players
(November 1948).

Costume design for Shakespeare's *King Lear*,
produced for Les Festivals de Montreal
(August 1953).

Defence), had been dissolved in 1924 and their remaining funds allocated to establish a theatrical library. By the time MRT – under the supervision of Louis Mulligan, Rupert Caplan, and its librarian, Marie Stehele – inherited this library, it had been enriched by the Walker Collection of photography, prints, and playbills, which had been donated by C.P. Walker, one-time manager of Her Majesty's Theatre. Martha Allan's personal library also enriched the collection.[1]

These Walker items decorated the staircase at 550 Guy Street, while the second floor housed 5,000 volumes or more of books. Playbills dating back to 1824 could be perused between acts and a gloriously pop-eyed photo of Wilton Lackaye as Svengali invariably made one laugh. The international success of Quebec's first great opera singer, Emma Albani, was recalled by a programme printed on silk. In March 1952 fire was to consume all of these past glories – an irreplaceable loss indeed.

My old friend Filmore Sadler first stepped into the great gap left by Martha's death. First of a series of solid, if less spectacular, successors to the woman who had made the MRT her own personal creation, Filmore was succeeded by book-seller John Hoare (1943), Mildred Mitchell (1944), and then Doreen Lewis (1946), who proved the most admirable producing director. Doreen was closely supported by Virginia Watt, who had come to Montreal from Winnipeg by way of New York's Traphagen School of Fashion to be a designer for Malabar's, the costuming house. Doreen saw to it that the eighteenth-century atmosphere of the new premises did not extend to MRT's activity onstage.

The opening production at Guy Street in early 1943 was Lillian Hellman's highly topical drama *Watch on the Rhine*, first staged on Broadway in spring 1941. Hellman's strong warning against the Nazi threat may have been Sadler's first choice because he could direct it with one of MRT's strongest casts ever – one that included Betty Wilson, Bob Goodier, Pegs Hessey-White, and Charles Ritten-house, with Mimi and Claude Jutra (the fated film director-to-be) as the children.

After my first training in the MRT studios in the mid-1930s, I had done most of my designing and directing outside its walls. I presume it was my design work for the Church of the Messiah and West Hill High School that caused Filmore Sadler to invite me to design this first MRT production on the new stage. I remember being highly honoured. The stage was small, the effort great, but I already had much practice fitting large interiors into small spaces. It was exciting to be part of the revived ongoing MRT. I had fun experimenting with new designs, though I remember that Edwyn Wayte, directing Julian Thompson's *The Warrior's Husband,* had rejected my bright idea for it back in fall 1942. Edwyn hadn't liked my formal setting for a *Richard II* at the old Studio either. One had to learn not to tread on other people's toes stepping into the new market. But I was the designer when Filmore Sadler next directed one of my favourite plays, Sidney Howard's adaptation of *The Late Christopher Bean.* Its story of a small-town household coming to grips with an artist of talent has always delighted me. Another show that I designed that first season of the Guy Street Playhouse, Alexander Afinogenov's *Distant Point*, required a whole railway coach onstage.

The Montreal Repertory Theatre was very busy in its first full season in its new location, 1943–44, presenting, amongst others, John Hoare's *The Devil and All* and Philip Barry's *Hotel Universe*. The following season MRT staged J.B. Fagan's adaptation of Pepys's diary *And So To Bed*, *Guest in the House* by H. Wilde and D. Eunson, and Paul Osborn's *On Borrowed Time*, followed the next year by William Saroyan's *The Beautiful People* (March 1946), the latter under Charles Rittenhouse's direction and with a beautiful setting by Hans Berends. This new work, staged only a few years following its 1941 Broadway premiere, was very much attuned to the new post-war period and conveyed a feeling for the appeal of the small man after an era of conflict between big men.

In 1945 the Shakespeare Society of Montreal, an affiliate of the MRT, decided to produce a play on the stage of Moyse Hall in the Arts Building of McGill

University – a stage dominated by two huge classical columns. This was a hall hallowed for me as the first home of the MRT and for its viceregal productions of *Hamlet* and *Romeo and Juliet*. The Shakespeare Society of Montreal was a long-dormant cultural body that suddenly decided that the ultimate tribute to the Bard would be to produce his works. In its three-year existence (1945–47) it became a true extension of the fine Rittenhouse productions at West Hill High School a decade earlier. Shakespeare's best high comedy, *Much Ado about Nothing*, was chosen as the first production of the revived Shakespeare Society. Bobbie Beatty was asked to direct it and Charles was to serve as producer. I was to be the art director.

I was elated, for I could now explore further my convictions about the proper staging of Shakespeare and the classical dramatic writers. In all such work the structures of the existing stages of their times are implicit. William Poel's return to the shape of the Elizabethan platform had been appreciated mostly by scholars but Tyrone Guthrie and Tanya Moiseiwitsch were to be influenced by Poel in the design of the stage at the Stratford Festival in Ontario. Examples of stage designers' work, then being reproduced for the first time, show how many different visions Shakespeare could evoke: Gordon Craig's screens for *Hamlet* in 1912, Robert Edmond Jones' gothic distortions for *Macbeth* in 1921, or Norman Bel Geddes' multi-levelled *Hamlet* in 1931. But the designers overlooked what Poel knew – that Shakespeare's plays move most naturally and easily when one follows the floor plan of the Globe Theatre.

There is nothing profound about this now, any more than there would be if I said that the plays of Ibsen and Chekhov sit more comfortably on a proscenium stage with a curtain, or that the greatest Restoration comedies are happiest when the actors can address us from an Italian frame down by the footlights. The particular version of realism that a bold succession of Broadway playwrights offered us also demands a frame and a curtain, even if they now scorn the artifice of footlights and painted drops.

In Montreal in 1945 I was not advocating a replica of the Globe Theatre on Bankside any more than Guthrie was in 1953 when he shared his vision for the tent at Stratford, Ontario, with his great designer Tanya Moiseiwitsch.[2] I did want to give Shakespeare back his comfortable structure of upper and inner stage, of centre and side entrances and a balcony; but I didn't think that a comedy as high and Italianate as *Much Ado about Nothing* should have a backing of timbers, half or otherwise. A pale palace with ornate balustrades and an inner stage that could house a little baroque altar or a marble tomb better suited Don Pedro's sportive tricks with human lives.

That's what I gave Bobbie Beatty and her company of actors – George Alexander as the Pedro, John Dando and Cecily Howland, his principal victims, the young Dr Victor Goldbloom as Claudio, and all the MRT stalwarts. The Italian palace setting was formal in that it was framed by a black cyclorama and set off by the two huge pillars of Moyse Hall. Because I had not learned to provide my exact choice of balustrade, MRT's principal scenic artist and designer, Hans Berends, worked up some that were rather heavier than I liked; my design for the curtains with a muted pattern of the mask of comedy was most faithfully stencilled. The astute Tom Archer in his *Gazette* review put it succinctly, "This was Globe technique without being self-consciously historical about it."[3]

"Was it *Much Ado about Nothing* for which you designed a black and white set for the stage of Moyse Hall and was that an MRT production?" Sydney Johnson of *The Montreal Daily Star* asked me in a 1980 letter in which he discussed his most memorable Shakespearean productions over years of theatre-going. "That set has remained in my memory, though I remember nothing else about the production." It wasn't black and white, just pale against blackness, and it wasn't technically the MRT, but I appreciated being remembered in Sydney's list. I wrote to thank him and he replied: "I meant to mention the novelty of your permanent set for *Much Ado*. I was as much impressed by its Shakespearean quality as I was by its aesthetic appeal and have never forgotten it. I remember it as a very decorative black and white semi-circle. It must also have impressed some of the French theatre people here because, much later, I reviewed a French production of *The Merchant* with a somewhat similar basic background permanent set."

Costumes, too, were my department. I favoured the Elizabethan, but not slavishly. I was proud of my Dogberry design for stout Whitfield Aston, born to play the role, and I enjoyed putting Douglas Peterson, our Don John (surely the most laconic villain in the canon), into unexpected white from head to foot, made more important by a Conrade and Borachio in black. Perhaps that contrast stirred Sydney Johnson's memory about this particular *Much Ado.*

This whole extravagant creation amounted in cost to the dizzying sum of $4,000 – unheard of in those days of repainted flats and rented finery. We made a deal with Malabar's that, if they made the costumes according to my designs, they could keep them after our production was over. For years afterwards I would see my costumes reappearing in productions often far removed in character or period from their original intent.

While Charles Rittenhouse, as producer, made the major decisions that gave this first production by the Shakespeare Society of Montreal its scope and stature, Bobbie Beatty's direction achieved a combination of emotional truth, pace, and physical crispness. Although she had a wide experience from her New York days, her experience with this production of *Much Ado about Nothing* was her first attempt at Shakespeare. Yet it proved successful enough to allow us to mount a second major production the following year.

In growing awareness of Montreal's French-language theatre, the Shakespeare Society of Montreal invited Pierre Dagenais, inspired director of the influential theatre company l'Équipe, to direct its next production, *King Lear.* It was understood that Charles would be responsible for the text and much of the interpretation. Pierre and I worked long hours into the night over the visual concept. Here, my Elizabethan approach took some digression. For instance I

The final scene of the Shakespeare Society of Montreal's production of *King Lear* (May 1946) with Christopher Ellis as Lear, Adelaide Smith as Cordelia, Robert Goodier as Albany (with Lear), Leo Ciceri as Edgar (standing), Ken Culley as Kent (kneeling), and Ed Wilson as Old Man. Pierre Dagenais directed and Whittaker designed.

moved the balcony, or upper stage, to stage left to allow for a great jagged opening at centre stage, which could be closed off by a tall sliding panel. In this way various locations could also be characterized: pavilions for war scenes, oasthouses for the countryside, established by small set-pieces, and a great wind-driven tree for the heath.

I was delighted when a visiting designer from the Metropolitan Opera, Richard Rychtarik, took the trouble to write to me from New York: "I am glad that I had the opportunity to see your *King Lear*, which was very beautiful

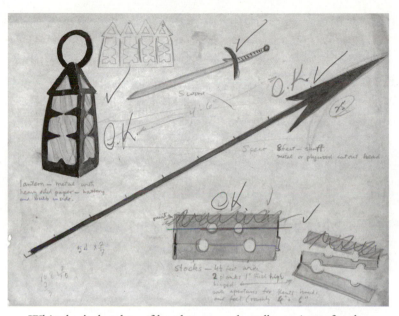

Whittaker's sketches of hand props and small set pieces for the
Shakespeare Society of Montreal production of *King Lear* (May 1946)

and served well to the evolving of the action," he wrote on 15 May 1946.
"Particularly the gallery to one side was a very clever device. I have only seen
the rehearsal, when some of the lights were harsh, which surely was improved
in actual presentation. I loved particularly the lovely tree in the wind, which in
design was the storm itself." The harsh lighting was improved, but Moyse Hall
did not supply electricity strong enough to correct our lighting problem completely. I had demanded a cyclorama of parachute silk to allow backlighting, but
our floodlights never completely cancelled out all of the harsh shadows.

For this *King Lear* Dagenais created extraordinary effects with his actors –
in particular a superb living chain for his storm scene. He was also able to stir
the English actors of Montreal to their utmost with his drive and passion. The

cast was an impressive one. For the title role, Christopher Ellis, the dominant English voice of CBC Radio, was a fine choice. Then there were Fran Malis, Rosanna Seaborn Todd, and Adelaide Smith as the three daughters, Robert Goodier and Rudy Stoeckel as the usurping husbands, Alfred Gallagher as Gloucester, and Leo Ciceri, the Edgar. Ivor Francis, Charles' Romeo and Sly from West Hill High, created an extraordinary Fool for us – a young possessed antic.

Following up on his success as producer, Charles felt encouraged to undertake the third, and what proved to be the last, Shakespeare play himself. He chose his old West Hill favourite, *Romeo and Juliet*, confident that Betty Taylor could repeat her much admired Juliet in an adult production; for the second time, I was called on to design this production for Charles. Or, to put it more accurately, with Charles, for he was an active participant in any design made for him, being as demanding as he was appreciative. It was a hard-driving collaboration and the more exciting because of it.

This second *Romeo and Juliet* in association with Charles had to be re-designed for the imposing stage of Moyse Hall. Again I used a central tower with a balcony in a central position. This balcony was flanked by two colonnades in diminishing perspective on either side of the stage, very useful for friars' cells, street scenes, and even ballrooms. Along with these three elements, the cyclorama could be used. Full stage curtains, painted with two diminishing perspectives of Verona streets, could be drawn behind the central tower, incorporating it within an exaggerated cityscape. I made sure it was a curtain too, hanging in folds, not a backdrop, to diminish any suggestion of realism. For the graveyard, tombstones tilted against the cyclorama. But I remember that the formal symmetry of this *Romeo and Juliet* rather bothered me at the time.

Charles, on the other hand, was delighted with our second Verona. Like the scenic scheme, my costume designs derived from the West Hill originals but were more lavish. The cast, of course, was now more mature. I remember

Betty Taylor and Maud Whitmore as Juliet and the Nurse in *Romeo and Juliet*, produced by the Shakespeare Society of Montreal (May 1947) and directed by Charles Rittenhouse.

affectionately Maud Whitmore's clucking comfortableness as the Nurse opposite Betty Taylor's slender strawberry blond Juliet. Alfred Gallagher was a most sympathetic Friar while the rising young Christopher Plummer played his first Shakespearean role as Paris. Our well-spoken Romeo, Kenneth Leigh-Smith, was self-conscious about having thin legs, I recall, so I gave him a long cloak with the same dark red lining as his tights. The Shakespeare Society's *Romeo and Juliet* matched the standard of its *Much Ado about Nothing* and *King Lear*. Not since MRT's *Twelfth Night* – and its *Hamlet* and *Romeo and Juliet* under the Earl of Bessborough's patronage – had Montreal seen any homegrown Shakespeare on this scale.

While I had been able to further develop my design concepts in these productions, I finally debuted as a director of a major MRT production in April 1946 with Rodney Ackland's play from Hugh Walpole's *The Old Ladies* – but

A production photo of *The Old Ladies* by Rodney Ackland – Whittaker's debut as a director for a mainstage production of the Montreal Repertory Theatre (April 1946).

my contribution, I realize, was still largely scenic. Master of the tiny space, I provided – with Hans Berends' technical expertise – a three-storey rooming house for the three old ladies, their three rooms visible even from the Guy Street balcony. (We did this by building a connecting staircase with four-inch risers suited to the elderly.) *The Old Ladies* was successful enough – although its rival that season was *The Corn Is Green* with Doreen Lewis so admirably cast as Emlyn Williams' staunch schoolteacher – to set me up as a regular MRT director.

In the next season MRT welcomed Pierre Dagenais as a new director. His production of François Mauriac's *Asmodée* impressed mightily – both with its cast, which included Christopher Plummer, Betty Wilson, Adelaide Smith, and Charles Rittenhouse, and with its single room setting. The latter was turned –

a different back wall seen each scene – as the action progressed. Bobbie Beatty was responsible for two shows that year, both blockbusters in Montreal terms. Her *Amphitryon 38*, which introduced me to Jean Giraudoux's work, was delightfully witty and glamorous, with John Dando in Alfred Lunt's role as Jupiter and Cecily Howland as Alkmena, with another comer, Leo Ciceri, as Mercury. The success of this production was enough to win it an invitation from Toronto's New Play Society, the first such invitation to my knowledge. It played the Royal Ontario Museum Theatre on a stage no larger than MRT's and with even less wing space, so it was quite at home. This production went on to the finals of the revived Dominion Drama Festival after winning the Western Quebec Regional for Bobbie.

The second Beatty blockbuster was Rudolph Besier's *The Barretts of Wimpole Street* with Eleanor Stuart as the poetess – "perfectly cast" according to Sydney Johnson in the *Star*. Its players included George Alexander as Moulton-Barrett, Charles Miller from CBC Radio as Browning, and a host of MRT stalwarts, among them my friends Adelaide Smith, John Colicos, and John Gibbon. Another important director, Malcolm Morley, handled MRT's last play of that happy 1946–47 season. First known to Canada as an adjudicator for the DDF, he returned as a founder of the Stage Society, later the Canadian Repertory Theatre in Ottawa, that important pioneer enterprise which was carried on later by Amelia Hall. Morley, like Bobbie, had an impressive background – even more varied than hers. Malcolm had managed at the prestigious Birmingham Repertory Theatre and produced at Stratford-on-Avon and the Oxford Playhouse. He was an actor, director, producer, manager, adjudicator, author, journalist, and playwright – Brae Manor Playhouse in Knowlton did one of his plays – as well as a very valuable, if forgotten, theatrical pioneer for Canada. Not only did he settle here at this time to give Ottawa a resident and professional playhouse when there was none in the land, but he also directed for MRT. He produced Shakespeare for Rosanna Seaborn Todd's Open-Air Playhouse on

Mount Royal after the Shakespeare Society folded. A remarkable contributor, a loveable bear of a man when I came to know him.

For MRT's 1946–47 season Malcolm was invited to direct Maxwell Anderson's *Joan of Lorraine*, a play I had been very keen to direct because my favourite actress, Marjorie Raven, was back from Texas and available to play its Joan. She was fascinating as Anderson's histrionic saint, as she had been as Shaw's more intellectually stimulating Maid. But Malcolm got the job. However MRT also recognized me as a director that season, as well as a new and fascinating leading lady. The play was S.N. Behrman's witty drawing-room comedy about a lady portraitist, *Biography*, and the dazzling Betty Wilson played the role created by Ina Claire.

Betty, daughter of Morris Wilson, head of the Royal Bank, had studied theatre in New York and even made her debut there, when she was called back to Montreal to work in the war effort. She did this through the Junior League (and rose to be president of that organization twice, in Montreal and New York) but continued acting for MRT. She had a distinctive style, crisply effective, which suited the Ina Claire role in *Biography* perfectly.

I then directed a small production of Eugene O'Neill's *Ah, Wilderness!* at MRT's Guy Street Theatre in January 1948. For this, ingenious as ever, I designed a dining room arch for the Nat Miller living room that could also be used as a proscenium for the tavern and beach scenes. My fine cast included Gerald Rowan, who had reportedly gone on for George M. Cohan, the celebrated song-and-dance man who created the role in the original Broadway production in 1933. Eric Donkin, already settled into the career that was to take him all across Canada, playing everything from Lear in Halifax to Julius Caesar and Koko at Stratford to Sarah Binks on the Prairies, was our young Richard. Susanne Avon was his temptress and Douglass Burns Clarke glowed hilariously as the tippling uncle.

The Montreal Repertory Theatre production of Eugene O'Neill's *Ah, Wilderness!* (January 1948), directed by Whittaker. Appearing were Eric Donkin as Richard, Gerald Rowan as Father, Lillian Niderost as Mother, Douglass Burns Clarke as Uncle and Rita Wheatley as Aunt.

Perhaps it was my handling of the sentimental *Ah, Wilderness!* that got me the job of director when MRT secured the rights to John Van Druten's 1944 play *I Remember Mama*. The decision was made that such a popular play, with such a large cast, deserved larger audiences than were possible in the two-hundred-seat theatre on Guy Street. Consequently I was back at Moyse Hall in May 1948 as both director and designer. Elizabeth Leese – Scandinavian dancer and teacher, married to Ken Johnstone, a newspaper colleague – was an obvious choice for the role which Mady Christians had created on

Broadway and which Irene Dunne and Peggy Wood took over for films and television.

I recall attempting to advance my directorial methods by giving the solid cast of MRT players the right to move and react as they felt their characters dictated; I would incorporate those movements into my stage action and business, I promised. But not a soul contributed any movement, which confirmed my growing conviction that Canadian actors are a particularly docile lot, giving their directors greater control than either American or British directors enjoyed. It also suggests that method acting had not yet reached the Montreal Repertory Theatre by the late 1940s.

My feeble attempt to introduce a more inwardly determined approach to acting suggests, however, that some word of Konstantin Stanislavsky's system of examining theatrical performance had seeped through to Montreal. The revered head of the Moscow Art Theatre drew on Pushkin's belief: "truth of passions, authenticity of feelings in the presupposed circumstances – this is what our mind demands of the dramatic author." What was good for the dramatist must be good for his actors, Stanislavsky decided. He cautioned however that "one must be able to summon up subconscious creativity with conscious technique." To a theatre town newly embracing Sigmund Freud, this latter principle appealed less. New York adopted the method as it applied to its current demands and interests. Montreal, I may say, was slow to follow. Our highly individual French-language actors never did.

Elizabeth Leese proved to be a most convincing, if young, Mama. Likewise, an old friend from the YM-YWHA, Charles Lewis, adapted his own formidable accent to Papa's, while a leading member of the Sixteen-Thirty Club, Tom McBride, got the rich role of Uncle Chris and did well with it. The cast of twenty-two included Maud Whitmore playing a visiting celebrity. Griffith Brewer painted the panorama of San Francisco that I had designed for MRT –

this time for a full-scale stage. I also remember Doreen Lewis as producer and her assistant, Jean de Savoye, Lee Prime, MRT stage manager, and Virginia Watt in charge of wardrobe (this time with both Malabar's and Ponton as costumiers).

I honestly don't recall how well *I Remember Mama* went,[4] but, as producing director for MRT, Doreen Lewis must have been sufficiently satisfied with my direction because she handed me another prize assignment after May 1948. I was to direct Tennessee Williams' third play, *The Glass Menagerie*. To have secured the rights to *The Glass Menagerie* only three years after its 1945 New York premiere was more of a coup than it might seem now. Williams' memory play was ideally suited to the small Guy Street studio since it had four characters and called for direct communication with the audience. Casting, however, was a problem since the role of Amanda was by then so closely identified with Laurette Taylor's truly remarkable creation of the part on Broadway.

I was lucky in having Amelia Hall available in Montreal during that period. The Ottawa actress and director offered me the right combination of naïveté and drive that makes Williams' portrait of his Southern mother so pathetic. Amelia was too young, but her vocal quality helped compensate for that. She proved an ideal Amanda, even for those with the memory of the original still fresh in their minds. I also did well to cast Silvio Narizzano, an actor whose later success as a film director depended on a real understanding of what acting is,[5] and Betty Taylor (by now Fenwick), a perfect Laura. In George Powell I had a less experienced player for the fourth role of the Gentleman Caller, but he had just the right kind of breezy normality to contrast with those neurotic principals.

As usual, the MRT stage presented spatial problems. Williams' play calls for a living room–cum–bedroom plus a dining area with a convincing surround of St Louis slum viewable from a practical fire escape. With Hans Berends' help I surrounded the MRT proscenium with dingy brick walls, thrusting the fire escape

Amelia Hall and Silvio Narizzano in the final moments of Tennessee Williams' *The Glass Menagerie* at the Montreal Repertory Theatre (March 1949), directed by Whittaker (with Roberta Beatty).

into the auditorium and making Tom enter from out front. To balance that projection I placed an old upright piano on the opposite side of the brick proscenium, with a pianist to tinkle at the music Williams requests – in the manner of old silent films rather than ghostly offstage recordings. As at the movies, the accompanist could thus comment unobtrusively. It worked wonderfully well.

Projecting the door to this backwater flat at right angles to the stage allowed for a splendid ending. As Tom slammed out of the house, he paused on the other side of the door. At this moment his mother hurled herself in vituperation against her side of the door. Their stubborn positions represented the finality separating them. Silvio spoke the play's final words of farewell directly to the audience, moving out, down, and away from the image of his mother turning to console her fragile daughter.

Years later, at a wedding in Toronto, Hugh MacLennan finally got around to saying what he had always intended. "Herbie," he drawled, "I've always meant to tell you, your *Glass Menagerie* at MRT was better than the original one that I saw in New York." I don't know how well my old friend remembered either production, but his praise was welcome. He may not have been as good a theatre critic as he was a novelist, but it was still nice to hear.

In those years in Montreal, I was ecstatically happy in my double – or rather triple – life as designer, director, and critic, with a heavy side order of theatre committees when it came to drama festival time. So when I received a telephone call from a Mr George Erskine Jones, who identified himself as an uninvolved spokesman for some other party, I was not much interested. He asked if I would entertain an offer from an out-of-town newspaper. From him, I was soon to learn that Robert Farquharson, the managing editor of the *Globe and Mail* in Toronto, thought theatre sufficiently important to his paper to fly down to Montreal in person to persuade me that my future lay in Toronto with his paper.

Later I discovered that Ernest Rawley, manager of Toronto's Royal Alexandra Theatre, had been consulted about a replacement for the *Globe's* recently deceased drama and film critic Roly Young and had recommended me. Gratefully, I learned that John Gielgud had also put in a good word for me. Young had been as heavily active in local theatre productions in Toronto through the Civic Theatre as I had been in Montreal through the MRT. Later, someone told me that his death was brought on by the shock of a long overdue but unexpected raise. The two contenders for his post as drama and film critic, I also heard, were Frank Morris of the *Winnipeg Free Press* and myself.

Bob Farquharson was most persuasive. He assured me that I could continue my work in theatre outside the paper – only adding the rider that I was not to become involved financially in production. As I wavered, I turned for advice to the most professional theatre person I knew – Bobbie Beatty. She and her husband, the much-loved Julius Cohen, spoke practically. Conditions in Montreal's professional theatre, they pointed out, were not likely to improve.

Since Martha Allan's death, the rising French-language theatre was not being challenged by English-language theatre. As a working theatre critic without sufficient command of French, I was much better off employed in a predominantly English city, one which had not been deserted by the touring theatre. To top all of this, Bobbie offered to steer my production of *The Glass Menagerie* through its dress rehearsals if this Mr Farquharson was being so insistent. I was grateful for this offer because I knew she would add that extra pacing which was still my weakness as a director. Doreen Lewis approved and, rather more nervously, so did my actors.

I confess I bid a rather pompous farewell to my *Gazette* readers before *The Glass Menagerie* opened in March 1949. "With this issue, and this article, the writer ends a 12-year association with the *Gazette's* theatre page and an even longer one with the Montreal theatre. He is departing for fields that look, from this distance, a little greener … Perhaps some explanation for the move may be in order … The reason for the change is best answered by a question: How long can one go on being a drama critic with no professional theatre to criticize? Toronto has that necessity for drama critics. Montreal has not … And Montreal will not until some competition stirs its movie-owned legitimate house to action."[6] (So much for Consolidated Theatres and its owner, Mr Hirsch.)

I loftily admonished my fellow Montrealers for not getting behind the proposed Civic Auditorium, and I advised them to insist that it contain a theatre as well as a concert hall. "For until such a building does arise, Montreal will continue to lag behind the other major cities on the continent … When there is a chance to play host to next year's Ballet Festival, the 1951 Drama Festival, the visiting Old Vic or even the massed choirs of Sherbrooke, Montreal should be ashamed to say – "'Of course we're the cultural centre of Canada, but we just haven't a theatre for you.'" Still, I had to admit that Montreal had fuelled my passion for theatre. "May it continue to flourish" was my closing wish.

Chapter Six

OUR FAIR-WEATHER THEATRE

Do the seasons affect our theatre as they did that of the Greeks? Of course they do. We still speak of Broadway and West-End seasons. Canada, a land of violent weather contrasts, plainly favours the summer theatre, sowing the seeds of talent when the sun encourages their flowering. Our summers have been crowned by events such as les Festivals de Montréal, the Stratford Festival and the Shaw Festival at Niagara-on-the-Lake, the all-Canadian Festival Lennoxville, and later the Atlantic Theatre Festival at Wolfville in Nova Scotia. Although we no longer add the caution "weather permitting," our theatre culture has long seemed a fair-weather matter.

In 1940 a few of us decided that what Montreal lacked was a summer theatre. We weren't being particularly original since this was the height of straw-hat activity in the United States, when summer theatres seemed to spring up out of the New England ground like warriors from dragons' teeth. Broadway stars such as Tallulah Bankhead and Ingrid Bergman, film personalities from Harpo Marx to C. Aubrey Smith, made triumphant tours of quaint rustic playhouses, sometimes trailing only a secretary and a leading man or lady.

Stage Magazine depicted glamorous scenes of high-society audiences outside colonial barns, and we in Montreal studied them with envy. When somebody discovered the Lachine Boating Club on the Lakeshore, we saw immediately that we could convert it into a smart playhouse. It had real possibilities, being not too far from town, right on the water with a lighthouse adjoining and with an upper hall big enough to serve as an auditorium. Of course the stage space was limited, but we were used to that where we came from.

The Lakeshore Summer Theatre (summer 1940). Seen are Adelaide Smith, Whittaker, and, in the foreground, Charles Rittenhouse (standing), Chester Lemaistre, Gillian Hessey-White, and Doreen Lewis.

Who were "we" and where did we get our capital? Mostly we were Montreal Repertory Theatre addicts. We were Charles Rittenhouse, myself, and Doreen Lewis. We were Pegs Hessey-White and her daughter Gillian. Pegs, I remember, advanced the generous sum of $1,000 to help launch the project. From the Lakeshore, Ivy Ashworth – who had courageously staged *Julius Caesar* (1937), *Henry VIII* (1938), and the Sanskrit drama *Sakuntala* (1939) as open-air productions at Lachine – was our honorary president, with Robert Dufresne as president and Percy Innes as treasurer. Douglass Burns Clarke, dean of Sir George Williams College (later Concordia University), became our production manager, while I bore the proud title of scenic director. I was also a member of the board along with Douglass, Charles, Bobbie Beatty, Mada

Gage Bolton, Hubert Desaulniers, and Janet McPhee, who lived at Dixie on the Lakeshore.

In retrospect the 1940 and 1941 seasons at the Lakeshore Summer Theatre run together in my mind. But before our venture was terminated by the introduction of wartime gas rationing we came close to emulating that New England straw-hat establishment. I have memories of a favourite Philip Barry comedy *Holiday*, also *Heroes Don't Care* by Margot Neville, George Oppenheimer's *Here Today*, the Edward Chodorov melodrama *Kind Lady*, Emlyn Williams' *Night Must Fall*, *The Distaff Side* and another John Van Druten play, *There's Always Juliet*, during our first summer. Two of Montreal's more charming young actresses, Gillian and Adelaide Smith, were both in that last production.

Another mainstay of the Lakeshore venture, and surely one of the most versatile of local actors, Chester Lemaistre is remembered for a moment on the stage of the Lachine Rowing Club when Pegs Hessey-White lost her lines while putting together a jigsaw puzzle. Getting no help from the prompter she just continued, "And this goes here and this one here …" leaving the other actors stranded. It was Chester who reached over and whipped the puzzle away from her. So shocked was she that her lines came back. One needed to be quick-witted in summer stock and Chester was certainly that. And debonair as well.

In Eleanor Stuart we had a star for *Night Must Fall*. Bobbie Beatty, admiring Eleanor Stuart's special talent, invited her the following summer to play Birdie in Hellman's *The Little Foxes* – a role of importance which must be played strongly to illuminate the evil of the devouring sister-in-law, Regina, and her rapacious brothers. Eleanor accepted but seemed to have something on her mind when Bobbie was driving her home from the first rehearsal. "Bobbie, I'd love to play Regina." "But darling," Bobbie warned, "it's such an unpleasant part." To which Eleanor replied firmly, "I'm sick of playing nuns!" Esther Solloway, who had been cast as Regina, stepped into Birdie's role.

Eleanor Stuart (née Nichol), backstage at the Lakeshore Summer Theatre (1940).

As I said earlier, Eleanor Stuart was a pale beauty, her dark hair worn in classic style, her eyelashes beaded in the old way of applying mascara. But in the Broadway production Tallulah Bankhead had established a tradition by having Regina wear a high red pompadour. Eleanor, however, refused to conform to this tradition: she tossed the rented red wig across the dressing room and dressed her dark hair in her own austere style for the part of Regina. Perhaps Ponton's wig was enough to put her off.

Esther Solloway had her opportunity to shine when Bobbie staged *Kind Lady*, a play based on a story by Hugh Walpole about a gentlewoman whose house is taken over by a sinister body of servants. I designed a mural wall that turned threatening when the coloured gelatins on the lights were changed. Charles gloried in the role of arch villain until Bobbie explained to him that he was betraying the whole plot by telegraphing his evil intentions. Thomas

Archer came out to Lachine to review *Kind Lady*, largely as a tribute to Bobbie whom he admired enormously. He sat with her in the audience while she watched Charles revert in misguided fashion to his sinister characterization. Bobbie blazed with anger at such rank amateurism!

The most poignant of our Lakeshore productions was Mildred Mitchell Wray's *Our Town*, which gained from its rustic setting in a white-painted boat-house perched above the water, with a lighthouse nearby. It is a play that rarely failed then, the novelty of its non-setting balancing the homeliness of its slight story. Its cast included a young actress named Madeleine Thornton, later Sherwood. She had the little girl's lines about addressing a letter care of "the Universe and the mind of God" and delivered them with real wonderment. A decade or more later I witnessed this same Madeleine Sherwood take over the role of the wicked Abigail on the tryout tour of Arthur Miller's *The Crucible*, taking her place with its strong Broadway casts. Madeleine deserved her success.

Moving from designer to director at the Lakeshore, I undertook its one classic offering, Shaw's *Candida*. Snapshots still recapture for me the sunshine of that period, showing me conducting a lawn rehearsal with Fraser Macorquodale as Burgess and Adelaide Smith, a superlative Miss Prossy. Griffith Brewer was my Marchbanks and Douglass Clark a perfect Lexy. The photographs also show my American friends from Dixie, Douglas and Janet McPhee, hovering appreciatively.

The wartime rationing of gas signalled the end of our summer theatre. Even the Montreal Repertory Theatre ceased operations, save for the completely respectable war effort of mounting and touring the MRT Tin Hats, a show for the troops training in Canada.

Fashionable, fleeting, even superficial as was the Lakeshore Summer Theatre, there was another Canadian summer operation that achieved a greater degree of stability. This was the Brae Manor Playhouse, conceived in 1936 and located much farther from Montreal, 68 miles to the east in fact.[1] It survived the period

The dining room at the Brae Manor School of the Theatre, Knowlton. Students seen are Estelle Mendelssohn, Sheila Boland, Dick Easton, Joan Blackman, and David Haber.

of gas rationing because it had roots in the community of Knowlton, Quebec, where its two founders, Filmore and Madge Sadler, were local citizens as well as being important members of the Montreal theatre scene through their work at MRT. Their school was to become a favoured outlet for leading Montreal performers, from Robert Goodier to John Colicos, with Martha Allan herself among them.

In 1977 a Knowlton resident, Constance Chambers, recalled Brae Manor: "We had at least one of the oldest summer theatres offering courses on dramatics for youth. It was run by a highly talented and popular couple. The theatre was intimate. It was a big event for older people – meeting their friends, strolling on the firefly-lit lawn, hearing croaking frogs from the marsh, eating ices or taking cold drinks. A most attractive shop was there, too, and across the yard a lovely old-fashioned white-painted house housed and fed students and visitors. We all delighted in lending all sorts of furniture, etcetera, for the plays."

The Sadlers had tried to establish this same house as a country hotel in Knowlton – their original purpose for the lovely white house. But they had far greater success as teachers in theatre, first at the MRT in 1933 in its Union Street days and later in their own school. In 1936, when their first child David was born, they decided to turn their Knowlton property into a theatre school. A fundraising evening of three one-act plays – Herbert Swears' *The Young Idea*, James Barrie's *The Twelve-Pound Look*, and *Suppressed Desires* by Susan Glaspell – was presented at the Lakeview Hotel. The support of the Knowlton summer colony (primarily English-speaking Montrealers) was enough to justify a full-length play that August – Clare Kummer's *Her Master's Voice*, with Robert Goodier as guest star and my old Everyman friend Margaret Sutherland in the cast. The profit for that first "season" came to $50 at 50 cents a seat. Such financial success augured well for the Sadlers and for Knowlton.

For the next year, 1937, two school terms of two weeks were announced, with the MRT logo lending substance to the venture. After that the local citizens advanced a loan to build a playhouse for the Sadlers. In 1940 Martha Allan came to star in the opening production – Noel Coward's *Hay Fever*. There was a floodlight on the lawn, flower-filled window boxes, a cowbell to summon the audience, and a notice in the *Gazette* proclaiming Brae Manor as "a real Canadian summer theatre." Martha Allan improved the occasion by losing her slip on stage, but she stepped gracefully behind a chair and let it fall without interrupting the comic action. The *Gazette* critic, one Herbert Whittaker, proclaimed *Hay Fever* as "one of the best plays the British playwright has ever written."[2] It still holds up well today – a bit of a classic indeed.

Brae Manor soon achieved its own logo, Cecil West's woodcut of the very simple building in which the theatre was now housed. Later, the adjoining shop was added, then a stage house in 1949.[3] Set back from the road beside that old white house, Brae Manor sported a circular driveway and an air of completely belonging to this Eastern Township setting. As Constance Chambers recalls, it was situated "in beautiful rolling country, green pastures, a gem of a lake five miles long, a hurrying stream through the centre where the old mill stood." Mrs Chambers also recalls that Knowlton got its name from a United Empire Loyalist who had hacked his way from New England through the forests towards beautiful Lake Brome, which was to gain its own fame as source of the prized Brome Lake ducklings.

There was another Brae Manor with a theatre connection in the same township. It was in North Hatley at the Brae Manor Hotel, but its life was brief, lasting only two seasons. Joy Thompson's Canadian Art Theatre also set up shop in the Eastern Townships, in the delightful Haskell Opera House which, most conveniently avoiding customs, straddled the USA/Canada border at Rock Island, Quebec, and Derby Line, Vermont. However, Brae Manor in Knowlton outlasted them both.

Through his position at MRT Filmore Sadler, a cheery outgoing personality, won support from other Montrealers who, like Bob Goodier and Martha Allan, appeared as leading performers in Knowlton. Mildred Mitchell came to play Benn Levy's *Mrs Moonlight* in 1939. The compelling Betty Wilson also appeared. Alex Thompson and Maud Whitmore followed, and later Amelia Hall, who was to have the longest career of them all. Some specially gifted students appeared – talented young people like Anna Cameron and Ann Murray from Toronto, and Montreal's Richard Gilbert, Richard Easton, Bruce Raymond, and John Colicos.

My recollections of Brae Manor are highly personal and warmly affection-ate. I used to take my summer holidays at Knowlton, enjoying the beautiful countryside between the heavy schedule of weekly play production. Checking the Brae Manor papers at the National Archives in Ottawa in April 1978, with Madge Sadler at my side, I traced my involvement from Shaw's *Candida* (1946) through Brandon Thomas's *Charley's Aunt* and Hellman's *The Little Foxes* (1947) to Kaufman and Ferber's *The Royal Family* (1948), then to the double bill of

Terence Rattigan's *Harlequinade* and *The Browning Version*, followed by Garson Kanin's *Born Yesterday* (1950) in the new stage house and, finally, after Filmore's death, Christopher Fry's *The Lady's Not for Burning* in 1954. Brae Manor was the most ideal theatre I was ever to encounter – free from doubt, antagonism, restrictive rules about rehearsal times, and, in its simplicity, free from financial pressures.

The Brae Manor working day started off with a communal breakfast and boisterous exchanges in the sunlit dining room. I remember Joan Blackman, the prettiest of the student actresses, making her entrance late with an elaborate towel turban around her dark locks. The Sadlers' supervisory concerns never relaxed because Brae Manor, even at the height of weekly production, always remained a school. This was its principal source of income and the Sadlers were always conscientious about their charges.

I was a favoured guest, contributing my services in return for lodging, board, and friendship. The Brae Manor theatrical fare rose in quality from the usual straw-hat attractions to works of considerable value. I helped that trend, I suppose, when I arrived to stage Shaw's *Candida*, which I had already done at the Lakeshore Summer Theatre – an interesting link between these two very different warm-weather operations. This production was highly artistic, with Betty Wilson's Candida vivid in a copper-coloured dress against a deep blue setting but with Filmore Sadler a more realistic, rather than romantic, Reverend Mavor. I couldn't have my Lakeshore Adelaide Smith or Fraser Macorquodale again, but Jessie Pitkethly and George Gorman were most satisfactory replacements. My brightest idea was to have Pierre Dagenais, the vivid actor/director of Montreal's l'Équipe, invited as Marchbanks, his heavy accent casually explained away by changing a Shaw line to read: "His father is a real French marquis." Less a poet was Pierre, but an intense artist deeply in love.

Sometime after 1936 the Sadlers established a connection with the wealthy and exclusive Seigneury Club at Murray Bay, like Knowlton another vacation

August 22, 23, 24, 1946

Brae Manor Players

Filmore Sadler, Director

PRESENTS

"CANDIDA"

By George Bernard Shaw

Directed by Herbert Whittaker

CAST (In order of appearance)

PROSERPINE GARNETT .... Jessie Pitkethly
REV. JAMES MORELL .... Filmore Sadler
REV. ALEXANDER "LEXY" MILL .... Leo Ciceri
MR. BURGESS .... George Gorman
CANDIDA MORELL .... Betty Wilson
EUGENE MARCHBANKS .... Pierre Dagenais

———

SCENES

ACT I - Morning.
ACT II - That Afternoon.
ACT III - Evening of the same day.

The action of the play takes place in St. Dominic's Parsonage, London in 1894.

———

Business Manager .... Jean Howe
Production Manager .... Marjorie Sadler
Stage Manager .... Lynne Minter
Assistant Stage Manager .... Dagmar Johnson

———

The Sadlers wish to express their gratitude to all who have played with them, worked backstage, ushered, and loaned furniture, thus contributing to the success of their eleventh season. We have tried to give you a balanced season of plays, and would be glad of any suggestions you might have for next season.

———

THE SHOP will continue to be open during the Fall months.
There are new things arriving daily
DO YOUR CHRISTMAS SHOPPING EARLY!!!

———

Starting Wednesday, August 28th, there will be a special Exhibition and Sale of oil paintings and water colors by Canadian Artists, in the Playhouse.

———

Next Thursday, August 29th, at 8.30 p.m., the Brome Lake Boating Club will give a musical program in the Playhouse. Margaret Messenger, Soprano; Hazel Barrett, Contralto; Marian Gardner, Pianist; and Amy McKeown, Accompanist, will be the artists. Proceeds are for the benefit of the new Club House.

A program for the summer theatre, Brae Manor (1936–56), designed by Cecil West.

outpost of the anglo elite of Montreal and Quebec City, which supplied enter-tainment for the members on New Year's Eve. Because of this, the Seigneury Club was persuaded that year to accept more classical fare. As a result my Brae Manor production of *Candida* was taken there. For most of us, though not for Betty Wilson, this was an excursion into a new world of luxury which we enjoyed without being envious. We knew that the Seigneury Club was a "restricted" establishment. Perhaps out of respect for one member of our com-pany, we decided to insert some obviously Jewish names into the guest list. I can't remember whether we actually did so, but I do remember that the audi-ence at the Seigneury Club proved rather indifferent to Shaw's humour.

In the summer of 1947 I designed and directed two productions, *Charley's Aunt* and *The Little Foxes.* The week previous I worked with Malcolm Morley, a distinguished guest director, designing the scenery for his play *The Beacon Light.* Malcolm's play was a premiere and was dubbed "almost Dickensian" by me in my role as critic. Amelia Hall was found "to come down a little hard" on her role, while Robert Russel was somewhat young as the Nazi menace, although he did "suggest the man of lost cause."[4] Photographs of Malcolm's play show an intense Betty Wilson, a very young Leo Ciceri, handsome in uniform, and a painted overmantel that must have looked very fake indeed, even from the front.

Betty was fast becoming another favourite actress to work with. She stayed on that summer for *Charley's Aunt*, playing the title role with John Colicos as her mature admirer, Bruce Raymond as the famous masquerader, Silvio Nariz-zano as the lawyer, and Gordon Diver the manservant. My setting was black and white, very chic.

I learned something while directing that play. As a rising director I had spurned printed stage directions, having developed some knack for making up my own. Halfway through the week of rehearsal, I realized that much of the success of this famous farce by Brandon Thomas lay in its traditional stage business. So I told the cast that we would now have to apply ourselves to a completely different set of actions while retaining the ones I had given them. Unflinching, they took to their books. The result was undoubtedly the busiest production of *Charley's Aunt* ever contrived.

On opening night Filmore and I stood in the window that led from the rear of the auditorium into the shop. I suddenly realized that the famous tea party gags had driven not only the audience but also the actors themselves out of control with laughter. Without a word to Filmore I dashed around the building, up the stairs to the stage, and started to yell at the actors to get hold of themselves. As I did so, I was aware of a figure in the wings on the other side of the stage doing the same thing. It was Filmore. I remember blasting Bruce Raymond hardest as he left the stage because he was a special guest, a supposed professional.

For *The Little Foxes* in the following week, I designed the Giddens' living room at an angle with the stairs for that final scene ascending to the wings, stage right, thus favouring Betty as Regina. This triangular setting had a hilarious spinoff at the beginning. It forced the offstage dining room area into a small space upstage, so that the cast had to stand stomach-to-stomach to recite their offstage breakfast lines.

They also had to stand there for the opening of the play as Maud Whitmore, a gifted contralto, sang a Negro spiritual off stage to establish our deepsouth setting. My talented cast included Amelia Hall, a perfect Birdie, John Colicos and Filmore as the brothers, Leo Ciceri excellent as the ailing husband, and Silvio Narizzano as Leo. Betty was quite brilliant as Regina – dynamic, flashing, elegant – so much so that her mother went about at intermission assuring her friends that Betty wasn't at all like Regina off stage.

Other talented newcomers strengthened the cast lists when names such as Anna Cameron, Ann Murray, and Richard Easton emerged from student status towards professionalism. Anna Cameron was an excellent example, having come

The Little Foxes at the summer theatre at Brae Manor, Knowlton (August 1947)
in Whittaker's triangular setting (staircase going up into the stage-left wings).
The impressive cast included Filmore Sadler, Betty Wilson, John Colicos,
and Silvio Narizzano, seen above, left to right.

from Toronto where she worked with Robert Gill in the post-war student years
of Hart House. She carried off with ease leading roles as different as Julie
Cavendish in *The Royal Family* and Billie Dawn in *Born Yesterday*.

Although it was to the financial advantage of the Sadlers to cast their paying
pupils, I was never aware of having inadequate talent thrust upon me in my
productions. I hoped that Richard Easton, one of the most promising of the
young Montreal actors, could play the newspaperman's role opposite Anna in
Born Yesterday; but even with a fake moustache it was apparent that Richard still
looked very much like a student. So Harry Threapleton got the part. Anna's

Billie Dawn was well matched by Robert Goodier playing Harry Brock. He was not only Brae Manor's first guest actor, a veteran of many MRT productions, star of the *Meet The Navy* show but also, within five years, a leading figure of the first company at the Stratford Festival. Anna made a superb dizzy blonde and the gin game between her and Robert was quite delicious.

Anna was something of a student of "the method," as were many New York-oriented actors of the day. Goodier, whose quick ear had been honed in *Meet The Navy*, was exasperated only when he tried to teach Anna to sing Cole Porter's title tune from *Anything Goes* – which starts "In olden days a glimpse of stocking …" At that point Anna would always lose the tune. We waited for it nightly.

That was in 1950, the year after the new stage house was built at Brae Manor. It was also the year I directed both Sadlers in *Harlequinade*, which was coupled with *The Browning Version*. Having the Sadlers recreate their acting school roles of Romeo and Juliet as an aging acting couple was great fun. Perhaps *The Browning Version* was the better of these two Rattigan playlets because of a gentle yet superbly true performance from Alfred Gallagher as the frustrated schoolmaster and from the talented young Easton as the schoolboy who gives him the gift.

These two performers certainly stand as representative of the times having changed. Alf Gallagher's talent was well recognized in the amateur field of the day. A businessman, he became a professional actor only upon retirement and wound up his performance career playing in the Stratford Festival company in the seventies. Dick Easton, on the other hand, trained in Montreal by Dorothy Davis and Violet Waters and later by the Sadlers, almost immediately found professional work in radio and theatre, scoring in theatre, film, and television in Canada, England, and the United States. His career was as meteoric as fellow Montrealers, Colicos, Plummer and Ciceri. By age twenty-two he was playing Edgar in *Lear*, Claudio in *Much Ado about Nothing*, opposite John Gielgud and Peggy Ashcroft – and in Vienna, no less!

The joys of being a guest director at Brae Manor started when the play was first read – on the terrace under the trees where Sunday suppers were served. Sometimes these early sessions were in the nature of auditions for the youngsters whom Filmore thought might meet my demands. Usually I worked the actors from that first meeting since, with only a week between plays, there was little time for sitting around.

If I was a slave driver, Brae Manor's resident stage manager was certainly a workhorse. This was David Haber, who was later to become highly conspicuous in Canadian theatre. An orphan from Quebec City who had studied dancing, David found a true home, his first, with the Sadlers. They cared for him as much as they did for their own children. Perhaps fearing all this love would be snatched away from him, David drove himself incessantly. Now and then he would walk on, as he did for me in *The Royal Family*. But his talents obviously lay backstage.

I have a treasured memory from that production of working in the basement with Haber. We were painting paper tape gold to use on white flats to suggest elegant wallpaper for the Cavendish duplex apartment. I had just finished a portrait of John Colicos as Aubrey Cavendish, the father of Tony, the role he was playing. Colicos was waiting for us upstairs in the auditorium, studying his lines for a role that meant a great deal to him because of his affinity for John Barrymore, its prototype, while across the yard, in the old white house, Anna Cameron sat with Richard Gilbert, trying to recapture her impeccable timing of that first line as Julie Cavendish: "A table for one, not too near the music."

I remember, later, Maud Whitmore, as the grande dame of *The Royal Family*, most movingly toasting the Cavendish portrait before her death scene. I remember too, some three decades later, being left unmoved by the celebrated Eva Le Gallienne making the same toast on Broadway to a portrait of Otis Skinner, an actor whose tradition was entirely opposite to her own. The glamour of the Barrymores still redolent, we were all thrilled when Bobbie Beatty

Rehearsing the *The Royal Family* at the summer theatre at Brae Manor, Knowlton (August 1948). Actors are John Colicos as Tony Cavendish, the John Barrymore role, and Anna Cameron (seated) in the Ethel Barrymore role. Madge Sadler, Brae Manor producer, and Whittaker, guest director, are also visible.

came to see our production, complimenting all except Colicos. Her only remark on his dashing study of Barrymore was "Have fun, John?" – a put-down that really hurt.

The following week the Brae Manor production of Sheridan's *The Rivals* was uneasy in its casting of a promising young French-Canadian student as Faulkland. He had trouble with the language of Sheridan and perhaps was intimidated by a solid company that included Filmore as Sir Anthony, Maud Whitmore as Mrs Malaprop, Richard Gilbert as Captain Absolute, John Colicos

as Sir Lucius O'Trigger, and Dick Easton as Bob Acres. By the weekend
Malcolm Morley, the director, had decided that the Faulkland must be replaced.
A car was sent to Montreal to collect Christopher Plummer, reputed to be
quick of study. He learned his lines in the car and was remarkably well in
command of them on opening night. When he dried up on one occasion, he
merely turned to the prompt girl and asked, "What's the line, dear?" (As this
is one of my favourite stories about Brae Manor, I repeat it here again with
much affection.) The prompt girl, as my story goes, fainted.

We all knew Malcolm Morley was looking for talent for his new Canadian
Repertory Theatre and fully expected him to take Colicos back to Ottawa with
him. But Malcolm was so impressed by Plummer's gifts and personality that he
took him instead. Later, when Malcolm bemoaned his decision because Chris
was so undisciplined, I remember saying, "But Malcolm, the boy's only
nineteen."

My last memory of Brae Manor is a warm one because some of my
favourite Brae Manor players were again involved in the 1954 production of
The Lady's Not for Burning. Betty Wilson, back from New York where she had
been in Judith Anderson's *Medea*, and Colicos, back from Britain where he'd
been the Old Vic's Lear, played Jennet Jourdemayne and Thomas Mendip.
Pierre Dagenais, David Gardner, Christina Dreever, Ted Wilson, John Gibbon,
and Ian Fellowes provided their strong support.

For the Brae Manor production I devised a more practical, if less lovely,
setting than the one Harold Town had designed for the Toronto Jupiter Theatre's production – a dazzling design that hardly needed such capable players as
Chris Plummer, Katharine Blake, or Donald Harron in front of it. We borrowed
Town's handsome costumes but put them into a setting that made the mayor's
office a real sanctuary for Jennet Jourdemayne, with a shutter to protect her
from the angry townsfolk. I have the happiest memories of standing backstage,
agitating a positive electric wire in a jar of saline solution to make realistic

firelight for the scene between Betty and Colicos, both of them at their best. This production of the Christopher Fry play was our tribute to Madge Sadler and came when she was trying to keep Brae Manor alive after Filmore's death.

Alas, the beloved Brae Manor did not long survive his death in 1954. After that saddened season, Madge ran the summer theatre for two more years, then closed it down and left Knowlton for the west coast. I went there often to visit her and recall past joys. Of all these summer ventures, Brae Manor has left the most lasting memory for me: an ideal theatre compound of youth, discipline, and dedication – and a strong bond with its audience. By the time of its passing in 1956, it had lasted twenty years.

Twenty years later, in the early 1970s, I went back to Quebec's Eastern Townships for another summer theatre adventure, the new Festival Lennoxville. One day I took a side trip with Charles Rittenhouse over to Knowlton to see if it was as charming as I remembered it. Indeed it was, except for the old house named Brae Manor, once a handsome white-painted building. It was still there but now somehow less glowing. Around it were the graceful trees that had dappled the playing ground of those happy actors rehearsing their plays. But completely missing, now demolished, was that brave little theatre with its stage house and shop. Something so full of life, of such worth, of such good will should have been preserved for the contribution it had made to a growing Canadian theatre, I thought. Canadian theatre resolutely continues to lose track of its past.

Chapter Seven

RIDING OFF IN ALL DIRECTIONS

My heavy work schedule at the *Gazette* did not seem to reduce my activity as a designer and budding director around town. I gloss over productions of Shaw's *Dark Lady of the Sonnets,* a favourite of mine, although one actually had Eleanor Stuart as my Queen Elizabeth. Also the Westmount Women's Club, which engaged me to direct the Ferber-Kaufman comedy *Stage Door* in 1942, where, unfortunately, I encountered my first anti-semitism in casting sessions. An invitation by Charles Rittenhouse in 1948 to direct for the Commercial High School led me to discover John Colicos' extraordinary power as the old Obey hero, Noah, standing out as vividly as I had found Christopher Plummer doing in Montreal High's adaptation of Austen's *Pride and Prejudice* in May 1946.

Also memorable was the Canadian Art Theatre production of *Ghosts* in December 1945. The driving genius behind this creative but short-lived company was Joy Thompson, who had first made her reputation with children's plays. She plunged into the Ibsen drama in her own highly individual way – she sent Griffith Brewer, her Oswald, on a tour of social disease wards. This upset him so much that her Pastor Manders and Mrs Alving, respectively Filmore Sadler and Betty Wilson, persuaded Joy to invite me in as a replacement director, another first for me. After some amicable adjustment, the Victoria Hall audience saw the Canadian Art Theatre presentation of Ibsen as advertised.

Joy continued to cut a swath through Montreal theatre in her distinctive fashion. She launched such eager young thespians as Silvio Narizzano, Bruce Raymond, John Colicos, Arthur Voronka, and many others into their careers.

As mentioned before she briefly ran a summer theatre in the Eastern Townships and, more lastingly, turned the Mount Royal Toboggan Club into the summer-time Mountain Playhouse, bringing the likes of Jack Creeley and Jane Mallett to Montreal audiences. This proved her most successful innovation and was carried on in the 1950s by Norma Springford when Joy moved off into the international high life.[1]

Of all these "sideline" commissions, however, the most lasting was the work I did as a part of the revitalization of the Little Theatre of the YM-YWHA on Mount Royal Avenue, originally founded by Rupert Caplan before he went off to New York. I must have been introduced there by Mada Gage Bolton, for whom I'd managed eleven impressionistic settings for her capsule History of Drama for the MRT School. Mada had been invited by the group to stage Shaw's *Arms and the Man* at the "Y" and told them I was to do the settings. Which I did, bright cardboard cut-outs against the blacks. She and her husband, John, were an American couple who became part of the theatre crowd I hung around with Saturday nights. She was one of many dynamic and versatile women the MRT attracted over the years.

The Y theatre also had its own dynamic director and actress in Ada Span, and it was she who had invited me to do the settings for the Kaufman-Hart Hollywood satire *Once in a Lifetime* in March 1936. I had also directed one of those Shaw *Dark Lady of the Sonnets* with Ada in the title role the previous month. However, it wasn't until March 1944 that I heard from the YM-YWHA again. The offering was exciting: to direct and design Robert Sherwood's 1940 Pulitzer Prize play *There Shall Be No Night*. And a chance, at last, to work on a full-sized stage. We hit it off, the Y little theatre and myself, and I was invited back three more times. And I had my choice of plays. After Sherwood's play, we did Chekhov's *The Cherry Orchard* (January 1945), Thornton Wilder's *The Skin of Our Teeth* (January 1946) – another Pulitzer Prize winner – and, finally, the Jewish classic *The Dybbuk* by S. Ansky (November 1948).

The Cherry Orchard with Isabel Weinrauch as Anya and Adolph Mueller as Trigorin, directed and designed by Whittaker for the YM-YWHA Players (January 1945).

Sherwood's *There Shall Be No Night*, which had started in 1940 as his protest against the Russian invasion of Finland, had to be reset in Athens because of our changed relations with Russia during the war. Starring for the YM-YWHA were Charles Lewis and Fran Malis, who played the roles in which Alfred Lunt and Lynn Fontanne had scored so successfully in New York and later during the blitz in London. While Charles lacked the essential eloquence of the Professor, there was no doubt that the emotional demands of the role were well within his reach, and Fran certainly had the style and graciousness needed for the wife's role.

Art theatre rather than commercial efforts suited a director who was still largely a designer. For example, by emphasizing perspective when using a series of telegraph poles for the second scene of *The Cherry Orchard*, I achieved an easy but impressive optical illusion of space. Griffith Brewer, Marjorie's brother, and his wife, Marie, painted the settings that he had built for me and also lit them very well. I remember vividly that the sky in the second scene was yellow as was the sky backing *The Dybbuk*. What was this obsession with yellow skies?

The rest of my settings were made from the flats on hand at Mount Royal and the costumes were assembled piecemeal, but the effect was not unpleasing. In casting I was indeed lucky. Fran Malis was the Y's great prize, a sensitive and handsome actress with a quite gorgeous voice. Her Madame Ranevskaya was throbbing and compassionate, able to coo without loss of sincerity. For our Lopakhin we had Charles Lewis, another mainspring of the group. Charles had retained his Middle-European accent and his voice was harsh, but he had emotional depths. To him, theatre was a way of matching the climb of the younger brother whom he had helped educate and who was already making a reputation as a political speaker. That younger brother, David Lewis, later became head of the New Democratic Party of Canada, his son Stephen heading the party in Ontario. But Charles' thick harsh speech was a handicap, even in a theatre group like the YM-YWHA that somewhat subscribed to method acting as derived from Stanislavsky. He died without gaining in the theatre the success that his brother found in politics.

In the middle of the 1940s, however, Charles was the vigorous leader of the Y Little Theatre and was backed by such reliable talent as Henry Gamer, Pauline Trehub, Will Allister, Clara Horn, and Adolph Meuller, whose voice was resonant as Charles' was harsh, yet even more incomprehensible. He was our Trofimov, our eternal student. As I remember it, the YM-YWHA audience responded favourably to the production of Chekhov we presented, so I was invited back to direct a third year.

Having established ground with these two productions, we ventured into something more startling for the Y audience: we offered Thornton Wilder's *The*

Skin of Our Teeth in 1946. This comic-book history of the world is surely one of the highest achievements of the Broadway stage. Wilder was equipped to tackle such a theme because he had explored the theatre of other countries. His style can be linked to Japan's Noh Theatre and to Italy's Futurism. Some of his more complex scenic demands had to be rejected for one reason or another on the stage of the Mount Royal YM-YWHA. But his broad sketch of mankind from the Ice Age through the Flood to Armageddon received a good production, I believe, despite our amateurism.[2]

Fran Malis was a charming Sabina, Will Allister a good Mr Antrobus, with Dorothy Boyaner, another experienced Y member, bringing force and determination to the role of Mrs Antrobus. Charles worked hard as producer as well as playing a combined doctor and professor and the role of Mr Tremayne who speaks for Genesis. By the time we got the rights for a Montreal production, *The Skin of Our Teeth* was still pretty advanced in its mixing of pathos and humour and in the manner in which it manipulated time sequences.

For my fourth YM-YWHA production – which proved to be my last – I persuaded my Y actors to attempt the one widely recognized classic of Jewish theatre, Ansky's folk-drama *The Dybbuk*. Many of the Y actors were working in theatre to improve their speech and would have much preferred to tackle Noel Coward comedies. But I won my case with the support of Charles Lewis.

Because Fran Malis had gone to try her luck in New York – actually becoming a pupil of that notable teacher of method acting Stella Adler – I chose as female lead Sarah Kositsky. The rehearsals were illuminated by recollections of the famous Habimah production of the play, conveyed to the actors playing in the Y version by grandparents who had seen it abroad. I welcomed such help in instructing the modern Y actors in the background of their own classic. That Hasidic scholars must never lower their hands below their waists intrigued them. The rhythmic chanting came more easily, being familiar to them from synagogue.

Always with an eye to costs, I cut out cardboard segments of stone walls and hung them against black curtains, trusting spectators to see these as the only areas to catch the light. (This worked only when the actors didn't brush past the blacks, agitating them. Then the effect could be somewhat unnerving.) My city square paid homage to the original Habimah production, but the tomb of its two lost lovers was my own invention – a roughcast stone that held the shape of two figures in close embrace.

Sarah Kositsky won praise from the reviewers as she alternated between the confused Leah and the tortured Dybbuk. Charles Lewis, as the old Rabbi, was the most impressive member of the cast according to the *Gazette* reviewer, Harold Whitehead. Stanley Mann played the Dybbuk "with remarkable and commendable restraint," while others highly praised included Adolph Meuller, Henry Gamer, Ruth Sorel – my first choreographer, who was responsible for the traditional wedding dances – and myself as director/designer.[3]

Later that season *The Dybbuk* was entered in the 1949 regional drama festival. Another production of mine, Trinity Players' *The Linden Tree*, J.B. Priestley's very British family drama, was also entered, a precedent for directors. I remember less about the Trinity show – only that Richard Gilbert as Rex Linden failed to catch my aim at decadent symbolism since he was a much better mimic than an actor.

But it was *The Dybbuk* which found favour with the notable British adjudicator Robert Speaight in the Western Quebec Regional Festival at the Sun Life Auditorium, although he conceded that "*The Linden Tree* was, on the whole, extremely well done." However he thought that none of the actors had the drive and pace to overcome the problems of the auditorium, which he characterized as "the most difficult in Canada."[4] That was a familiar complaint from adjudicators. The actors they saw were used to smaller spaces, but the places in which they played at festival time were rarely helpful.

The Dybbuk did better, coming in second. Speaight recognized that its feeling of authenticity was "easily invoked to introduce us to the heart of a great national and religious tradition" and singled out Sarah Kositsky for commendation. Later, in his final summing up, he surprisingly found her "not the actress for that particular part."[5] The Little Theatre of the Y had to console itself with being runner-up to a vivid recreation of Eugene O'Neill's *The Emperor Jones* by the Negro Theatre Guild, although Mr Speaight did give me a special adjudicator's award as director and designer. This proved a satisfying exit for me from Montreal's festival scene, which had given me such a rare variety of opportunities.

Years earlier I had worked as a designer with the triumphant Negro Theatre Guild when the exuberant Don Haldane led them into Victoria Hall in March 1942, then into His Majesty's Theatre in May to stage Marc Connelly's *The Green Pastures.* I knew that the black community in Montreal was disadvantaged by the low compensation for railway porters, a job held by many men in the community, and that the community's chance at cultural expression on the stage meant a great deal indeed. (I was to recognize a similar cultural achievement when young French-Canadian actors won top honours at the Dominion Drama Festival with Marcel Dubé's *Zone* in Victoria in 1953.) What I didn't know, or even suspect, was that the railway porters worked for tips alone, a shocking example of exploitation. Low salaries I did know about, having suffered cuts at the *Gazette*, where we worked a six-day week – with Saturday afternoons off.

With a cast of one hundred, the Guild had dared the heights to produce *The Green Pastures* at His Majesty's, aided by the Kinsmen Club of Montreal as a benefit for the Milk for Britain Fund. I had no choice but to review it in the *Gazette*, even though I had designed the settings – my most ambitious to date. The Guild got from me the response it deserved, although I couldn't pass over my own contribution entirely.

In my review I see that I mentioned "the greater staging facilities added greatly to the pictorial values of the production" and I even mentioned that "the scenic conception used has the golden steps of Heaven framed by an arch suggestive of a simple Negro church … One of the most effective moments was that of the swift transition from the garishness of the cabaret scene to the serenity of God's Heaven above." I never mentioned my own name in this, though, preferring to credit Hans Berends who painted the settings. But I could give full credit to Horace Phillips as De Lawd, "a tremendous part in physical and emotional demands as well as religious implication … He played with consistent sincerity and perfect simplicity."[6]

I remember a very late dress rehearsal for this Connelly play, with its cast members sprawling about and sleeping in that venerable auditorium, uncomplaining although most of them had very early morning jobs to get to. They recognized the importance of the Guild's venture into the hallowed ground of His Majesty's.

When the Guild launched into Eugene O'Neill's *The Emperor Jones* six years later, I was able to give more extravagant praise, having no connection with its production. "In Percy Rodriguez, the Guild is fortunate enough to have found an actor to measure up to the magnificent title role. On his first appearance, you recognized the physical force for it … an acting jolt of genuine emotional force."[7] One of the real satisfactions of the critic's profession, I had learned by then, is "the discovery" of distinct talent on its way up.

Under the joint direction of two other good friends of mine, Joan Dunbar and Beatrice MacLeod, the Negro Theatre Guild well deserved the Martha Allan Trophy for best production in English or French in 1949. Percy Rodriguez, its Jones, was accorded the best actor's Festival Plaque, that for best actress going to Madeleine Sicotte for her intense performance as Phèdre, staged by le Conservatoire LaSalle (to which also went the new award for the runner-up in the alternative language from the Notre Dame de Grâce Women's Club). Impressed that the Montreal festival presented works dealing with French, French-Canadian, Jewish, and Negro themes in either French or English, Robert Speaight happily concluded that "Bilingualism was the most exciting aspect of Canada." He compared Percy Rodriguez's Emperor Jones with Paul Robeson's and spoke of his extraordinary dignity, his consistent beauty of voice and movement, and declared that it was also "a technically armour-proof performance."[8]

The Negro Theatre Guild had trouble raising the money to pay its entry fee into the final festival in Toronto, so Bobbie Beatty and I paid it between us. Rodriguez won again in Toronto and was offered a scholarship at the Lorne Greene Academy of Radio Arts. Being a family man whose income was augmented by serving as doorman at a Montreal nightclub, he had to decline; but eventually his well-recognized presence and talent took him on to Broadway and Hollywood.

After those two near misses in the Western Quebec Regional Drama Festival, I was soon busy, as I have written before, directing and designing another major production for the Montreal Repertory Theatre: Tennessee Williams' *The Glass Menagerie*. I recall walking one night on my way home from work at the *Gazette* in a state of exaltation – past Sun Life's wedding cake of a building on Dominion Square, the formidable fortress of Canadian Pacific's Windsor Station, the Anglican buttresses of St George's Church, the Archbishop's Palace behind St James' Basilica, and the seedy dignity of the Windsor Hotel – and exclaiming "Montreal belongs to me!" Incautious exclamation indeed!

Chapter Eight

THE CRITIC, RETROSPECTIVE

In the thirties and forties Montreal was a fascinating, by now highly expressive, bicultural city for a young, theatrically minded adventurer. For one thing, it was visually attractive. From the old St Lawrence harbourfront it progressed through the then-deserted old French town, past the high commerce of St James Street, on to the lower public commerce of St Catherine Street. Then it rose again to the dignity of Sherbrooke and on, up sharp mansioned slopes to Mount Royal, a crown of green still topped by Jacques Cartier's cross. In the wings, stage right and left, were balanced many poor French dwellings, sloping off to St Henri, and a few wealthy ones; a smaller body of poor English houses edged out into the middle-class areas towards Montreal West.

I could walk my way down from a poor-to-middling English section of the well-off northern French area of Outremont, down over Fletcher's Field towards the old town, when I approached the *Gazette* at 100 St Antoine Street. Past Sherbrooke Street, where the Church of the Messiah had welcomed me into its artistic congregation, past the first home of the MRT, the Coffee House – both on Union Street – and, at the bottom, Windsor Station. There was the *Gazette*, with some old stone shops still surviving across the street to remind me of printer Fleury de Mesplet, whose journal was its early predecessor. Eventually my mother and I moved downtown into a smaller apartment on Lincoln Avenue, near His Majesty's Theatre and the second home of the MRT on Guy Street. Our apartment was also within walking distance of the *Gazette*, which was fortunate when I returned late at night.

My decade at the *Gazette* reflected wartime changes in Canadian theatre, but some Broadway productions still came to Montreal at His Majesty's. I didn't review them at first, of course, for that was still the responsibility of my colleague Tom Archer. Yet I saw most of them, for by then I was included on the free list. As second-string critic I was sometimes allowed to interview important figures of the stage. With some of them, I even became friends. I even dared to take Irina Baronova, one of the celebrated three Baby Ballerinas, to our Samovar, Montreal's remarkable Russian nightclub, to celebrate her birthday. I came to know her and others, including Leon Danielan, when she was touring with Colonel W. de Basil's Ballet Russe de Monte Carlo.[1]

On that particular night at the Samovar I discovered two things that I'll never forget: one, that ballerinas are not easy to partner on the dance floor; the other, that in wartime even champagne goblets become practical. When the delightful Irina, responding to the birthday toast, had to smash her glass on the table after draining it, dangerous chunks of common pressed glass flew all about.

But it was Tatiana Riabouchinskaya of the three Baby Ballerinas who most enchanted me professionally, even after seeing her backstage in the grip of a common cold. Snivelling, with a shawl over her shoulders, she astonished me by instantly turning pure swan before my eyes as she heard her cue, sailing out into the great lighted area of the stage where it seemed as if no germ could ever reach her.

I had to wait until Saturday night – my night off most weeks – to see the various actors and actresses after Tom had reviewed their performances. For instance I had Saturday tickets for *No Time for Comedy*, the S.N. Behrman comedy which Katharine Cornell brought to Montreal in 1940 – her first appearance in that city. After reading Tom's notice on Tuesday, I couldn't wait until Saturday and so sneaked into the Wednesday matinee. It was worth it, although *No Time for Comedy* was perhaps not the kind of play or the kind of playing for which this magnificent star became famous. The handsome Czech

A drawing by *The Gazette's* Grant Macdonald
of prima ballerina Tatiana Riabouchinskaya.

actor Francis Lederer had replaced Laurence Olivier as her leading man. Cornell
was so enchanting that I didn't miss Olivier. I also enjoyed the advertisement
taken out by Consolidated Theatres that claimed the play to be "the most
pretentious theatrical event of the season."

Two actresses of international repute, France's Gaby Morlay and America's
Helen Hayes, brought Laurence Housman's episodic *Victoria Regina* to Montreal
within weeks of each other back in 1939. Miss Hayes and her sumptuous
Broadway production won the greater attention. Designed by the English stage
artist Rex Whistler, the production won him a great many admirers before he
died in the war, at age 39, in 1944. Miss Hayes won her greatest fame in this
role of the dominant little British queen and her full-scale tour of the American

A publicity photo of Helen Hayes as Queen Victoria in the touring production of *Victoria Regina*, seen in Montreal at His Majesty's in January 1939.

continent was an unqualified success and earned its producer, Gilbert Miller, a return of more than $1.3-million. In Canada in 1939, with our close connection to royalty, we were properly thrilled by the time Miss Hayes was wheeled out for her Jubilee. Her tour must have had, I think, some political impact on the isolationist stance then held by the United States.

In 1939 we still had some visiting theatre from Britain. The faithful Colborne and Jones Company brought both Maurice Colborne's *Charles the King*, written for Barry Jones to play Charles I, and the latest work by the legendary George Bernard Shaw, *Geneva*. There was also Charles Morgan's impressive intellectual drama *The Flashing Stream*, with the stunning Margaret Rawlings opposite Godfrey Tearle, also pretty impressive and resembling Franklin D.

Roosevelt in a remarkable way. (This is to say that we all remarked on it.) Broadway also sent us one scintillating English star, Gertrude Lawrence, in Rachel Crother's *Susan and God*. That was a respectable lot considering wartime restrictions and all of them virtuoso material, particularly Miss Lawrence's Susan, a dazzler on a serious theme, and the young and very talented Jessica Tandy as Queen Henrietta Maria.

The play of greatest interest to me today is Shaw's *Geneva*, which marked the great playwright's withdrawal from public life during the war years. We had grown up with Shaw second-hand, finally accepting his great originality after having first seen him as merely an Irish upstart and a bit of a comedian. Now we Canadians were seeing his latest work presented by a company on which he was definitely keeping his eye. Our first-hand connection was sharpened by the fact that Shaw's faithful Theatre Guild of New York had decided against producing *Geneva* because it presented Hitler as a Wagnerian warrior factitiously named Battler – anathema to a subscription audience that contained a considerable Jewish component.[2]

Geneva, Shaw's examination of the need for an international body of peacemakers like the League of Nations, was acted for us by solid players – Colborne and Jones were backed by Jessica Tandy, Lawrence Hanray, Norah Howard, and, most important to Canada, Earle Grey. The management, we knew, received several telegrams from Shaw himself making changes and additions to the script to bring his play in line with the turbulent times as Europe tottered towards chaos. Shaw's attempt to laugh chaos out of court satisfied few, including the great Irish dramatist. Originally a success in London (it had a run of 237 performances) it continued to be adjusted to face the gathering storm. There were no less than eight different versions, according to Michael Holroyd, that most conclusive of biographers. The Colbourne and Jones company were kept up-to-date as *Geneva* crossed Canada. How I wish we could find those telegrams today; they would make a very distinguished exhibit for the Theatre Museum.

A publicity photo of Flora Robson and Isobel Elsom appearing in *Ladies in Retirement* at His Majesty's (March 1940), Robson's stage debut on the Atlantic side.

Plays from England almost ceased after war broke out. We got along with expatriate British players in American productions or with English fare played by Americans, as well as with some rather pale American ventures. But we did get one considerable prize in 1940. This was Reginald Denham and Edward Percy's able thriller *Ladies in Retirement*, with Estelle Winwood and Isobel Elsom in support of the distinguished Flora Robson. Much less impressive but still welcome was Noel Coward's mixed bag of playlets, *Tonight at 8:30*, with a largely American cast. I later discovered with delight that *Hands Across the Sea*, my favourite of these Coward playlets, was based on the home life of the Louis Mountbattans and that Lord Louis had not been amused by it.

Having seen the original West End production of Emlyn Williams' *Night Must Fall* in 1935, I was rather snooty about Florence Reed, Violet Heming, and Douglass Montgomery playing the roles created by Dame May Whitty, Angela Baddeley, and the author. But I could have no complaints about the replacement for Monty Woolley in *The Man Who Came to Dinner*, even if he wasn't properly an actor at all. This was Alexander Woollcott, the New York critic and columnist who was the actual role model for this comedy by Kaufman and Hart. Woollcott was very much himself and was well served by a strong supporting cast. After this benefit tour for the Red Cross, we got more humdrum fare: Elliott Nugent's comedy *The Male Animal*, with Conrad Nagel; the Chodorov and Fields' *My Sister Eileen* with Betty Furness; and Ruth Chatterton and her husband, Ralph Forbes, in Coward's *Private Lives*. About this time we also managed to see the Scottish charmer Sophie Stewart in a revival of James M. Barrie's *Mary Rose*. Again the cast included Earle Grey, who was to settle in Canada and make many varied contributions – as actor, broadcaster, Shakespearean producer, and committeeman – to his newly adopted country.[3]

As the war broadened violently to include the United States, theatre in Canada went into a slump except for two troop shows that awoke memories of a wartime ancestor from World War I, *The Dumbells*.[4] *The Army Show* revealed the comedy gifts of Johnny Wayne and Frank Shuster, who were to keep Canadians laughing for so long after, while *Meet the Navy* forwarded the careers of John Pratt, Robert Goodier, Cameron Grant, and Lionel Murton, the dance team of Alan and Blanche Lund, and conductors Eric Wild and Victor Feldbrill.

Meet the Navy and, in particular John Pratt, became the more familiar to me. In outsize overalls that emphasized his height and thinness, supported only by a mop, Pratt's rendition of "You'll Get Used to It," sung with the utmost lugubriousness, delighted audiences everywhere. The young navy artist Grant Macdonald, who drew for the *Gazette* on occasion, has captured that memorable

Princesses Elizabeth and Margaret, Hon. Vincent Massey,
King George VI, and Queen Elizabeth greet Robert Goodier,
Barbara Whitley, and John Pratt of *Meet the Navy* in London.

image for future generations. Pratt – politician and MRT performer – was as
surely a Canadian star then as Gratien Gélinas, John Drainie, or Lorne Greene,
although without their staying power. Pratt and *Meet the Navy* won admiration
from royalty as well as from Marlene Dietrich, Noel Coward, and Sir Harry
Lauder when the show played abroad. Its guiding spirit, it must be recorded,
was Capt. J.D. Connolly, NCNVR director of Special Services.[5]

In summer 1944 I was extremely fortunate in getting to meet my long-time
idol, the great designer Robert Edmond Jones. He had won the attention of
Canada's Special Auxiliary Forces with his advocacy of wartime entertainments
by the troops themselves, in the fond tradition of village concerts. He was
invited to Montreal in June and I was able to interview him. My Saturday

Ruth Gordon in a scene from *Over Twenty-One*, Miss Gordon's new comedy hit at His Majesty's (March 1945).

Gazette article, aptly headed " A Visionary in the Camp," was so appreciative it won me an invitation to drop by next time I was in New York. Several such visits followed and I had a chance to absorb the philosophy of this fine artist of the theatre. On one of them, he took me to the Players Club and spoke movingly of John Barrymore's *Hamlet*, for which he had contributed a famous design. "When Gielgud spoke 'Alas poor Yorick,' it was cue for a great soliloquy; when John spoke it, it was grief for an old childhood friend." There is, I began to perceive, a difference between English and American acting.

Near the end of the war I interviewed Ruth Gordon when she visited Montreal in March 1945, performing in another wartime comedy, *Over Twenty-One* – one that she had written for herself in order to play the wife of a military man well beyond recruiting age. I don't remember too much of Miss Gordon's play, but when I knocked at her dressing room door at His Majesty's, it was flung open by a highly irate actress who proceeded to lambaste me about the disgraceful conditions, indeed the filth, of this particular dressing room. I shouldn't have been so taken aback at the lady's outburst, but I had got used to Consolidated Theatres disregard of His Majesty's, putting paint and polish only where the public would see it. "I'm wearing $500 Molyneux dresses in this show! Do you expect me to hang them in this dump?" I was terrified. "I know it's nothing to do with you," she added casually and proceeded to be as nice as possible to a still-frightened interviewer.

Then on vj Day, 2 September 1945, I found myself caught up in the general excitement, accompanying the *Gazette's* star photographer Buster Arless into Chinatown. There we came upon a street roped off to accommodate a stage where a Peking Opera was in progress. Fearless, and with the photojournalist's conviction that he himself is invisible, Buster moved onto the stage to record the action of these exotic artists. I followed him, as I was assigned to catch the flashbulbs he discarded. When people ask me where I spent vj Day, I can truthfully say that I was appearing in a Peking Opera.[6]

No other theatre matched that exotic scene in Montreal that season, I am convinced – not even the dramatic Yiddish Art Theatre, visiting from New York, which I so enjoyed. That was a company as authentic as the Peking Opera, as proud and positive in its highly theatrical art. I was thrilled by its *Yoshe Kalb* and its *Brothers Ashkenazi* (based on novels by I.J. Singer), and a play I remember as *The Little Holy Tailor*, although I don't find its name among the many plays listed in *The New York Times' Directory of Theatre* – nor among the titles *Jew Suss*, *Shylock and His Daughter*, or other plays which its actor–manager, Maurice Schwartz, himself wrote.

A remarkably imposing personality, Maurice Schwartz dominated this American troupe of actors. I recall that, as that little holy tailor, he wore a shining gabardine and was accompanied by a follow spot as faithful as that of Sonja Henie, the skating star. Why did I embrace wholeheartedly the big acting of the Yiddish Art Theatre on its visits to the Monument-National and His

Majesty's while treating an equally out-of-date company such as that Donald Wolfit brought us in 1947, so scornfully? Because Schwartz and his fellow actors had a fervent religious conviction about their place in the universe. That universe went far beyond New York's 14th Street, where the company had its headquarters, to an older, uncompromising, European strength. The broad exotic productions and the leadership of Schwartz, who was plainly an Old Testament prophet, defied Stanislavsky and his "methodists" to proclaim a powerfully and richly theatrical art form.

One anecdote about Maurice Schwartz, who was as imposing in real life as on the stage. Interviewing him in a hotel dining room, I brought up the announcement in *The New York Times* that Billy Rose planned a production of *King Lear* to star Paul Muni. The news proved explosive, the great Schwartz voice filling the dining room. "Muni Weisenfreund? That little actor!" This was accompanied by an expansive gesture that completely condemned the film star's pretension in invading territory clearly belonging to Schwartz. (He used Paul Muni's original name not to denounce him but to put him firmly in his place when it came to the hierarchy of the Yiddish stage.)

The great German actress Elisabeth Bergner won my utter devotion when she appeared in *The Two Mrs. Carrolls* by Martin Vale in June 1947 and Margaret Kennedy's *Escape Me Never!* in December 1948. I remember that her first arrival prompted me to draw a Hirschfeld-style cartoon for the paper, which it used. I revelled in the heady Europeanness of Bergner and her reputation as a leading ego of the world of the stage, which concealed a very sharp judge of theatrical value. I discovered that she was not to be measured by the somewhat tawdry melodramas in which she was appearing.

During her stay in Montreal with *Escape Me Never!* the great Bergner played "cat and mouse" with me. My adoration – betrayed in my *Gazette* review – she accepted as one used to such worship. But we could meet only without her supporting company knowing, as I had given them and their play a hard time in that review. So we met for drinks after our nightly work – hers on stage at His Majesty's, mine at the *Gazette*. Her winsome charm was unabated, but I discovered her shrewdness in judgment of other performers. She must have been amused that I was so deeply stage-struck – particularly in her presence – but also felt that, as a young critic, my education was worth her attention. After she left Montreal I received a telegram wishing me a happy New Year and giving me her telephone number in New York (Butterfield 8-8966) in case I ever got there. In time I did and learned more about great acting and something of great actresses.

I also have a vivid memory of Tallulah Bankhead from a 1947 interview. It was a group affair with the press gathered around the star in her hotel after her opening in Cocteau's *The Eagle Has Two Heads*. She reclined on a chaise, suffering huskily from the final fall downstairs at the end of the play. The Montreal press suggested the names of some doctors as Bankhead demonstrated how she had bruised herself. But she must have become bored with this, for she perked up when I asked her about the report in the *New York Times* that she planned to appear in a drama based on the life of Sarah Bernhardt. She stunned me by saying that the *New York Times* story was in the nature of a "trial balloon," in case any investors showed interest. Using the sacred *New York Times* like that shocked us, as perhaps the lady intended.

Bankhead told us that when she was beginning her career in London she had once given a very creditable impersonation of the Divine Sarah, although she herself had never witnessed Bernhardt playing. "Show us," I urged her, accounting myself a good judge of Bernhardt. Bankhead's aches and pains vanished immediately. She disappeared into the bedroom. "Hand me my fur coat," she commanded from the next room. "Turn off that light and put on the lamp." All this done, she made her entrance, striking a familiar Bernhardt pose. The likeness was indeed startling until the deep Bankhead voice destroyed the illusion. No *voix d'or* that, although it was mightily hypnotic.

Not all the stage visitors I encountered in Montreal came from Broadway. Although the war had broken the tradition of the British theatrical tours, one man sought to revive them – an actor who yearned for the laurels of the old actor-manager abroad. This was Donald Wolfit, now the head of his own company and glorying in the great Shakespearean roles. He had won that rank and those roles in the face of the enemy – quite literally. In 1940, under Nazi barrage, he played Shakespeare for the British public in a three-month season during the Battle of Britain. Because the theatres were closed at night, he played at lunchtime. His roles included Hamlet, Shylock, Petruchio, Malvolio, Othello, Benedict, Touchstone, Falstaff, Richard III, and Bottom.

When he returned to Canada in early 1947, playing some of these great roles, I reviewed him as Richard III, Touchstone, Shylock, Hamlet, and, in his most admired performance, Lear, as well as Volpone, a role for which I personally believed he was best suited. Regarding his 1948 tour *Time* quipped cruelly: "Oh to be in England now that Wolfit's here." Of his famous curtain calls, which had him visibly fighting fatigue to pay his humble tribute to "the master dramatist, William Shakespeare," I wrote that they were among the best acting he did, especially that after *The Merchant of Venice* when he'd had the whole of the Belmont scene to recover from his exertions as Shylock. He took umbrage to the tone of my reviewing since I found his style overly theatrical and his company, save for a rare exception such as David Dodimead, less than supportive. "I am too exhausted by my Shylock and, besides, the lights hurt my eyes," he wrote me testily.

I blush to recall one occasion when I was dispatched early one January to interview Wolfit as he was passing through Montreal by train. "What do you think of the Queen's New Year's Honour List, Mr Wolfit?" I asked. I realized too late that he had hoped for himself in that direction but that Ralph Richardson instead had been named a knight designate. "Any honour to the theatre … is an honour to the theatre," was all he could muster. I slunk away ashamed.

The touring stage star Donald Wolfit –
surprised by a flashbulb when arriving
New Year's Night in Montreal (1947).

I was genuinely pleased when Her Majesty's New Year's Honour List for 1957 finally announced a knighthood for Donald Wolfit.

There was much about Wolfit's theatrical dream to which I could have been more receptive, for it was an extension of the grand old tradition crowned by Sir Henry Irving and Sir John Martin-Harvey. But Wolfit's egotism and a continuing strain of coarseness detracted from his art. His Hamlet was marred by this for me, but his bold Touchstone, his totally avaricious Volpone, and particularly his Richard III were enhanced by it. His Richard, plainly allied with Mr Punch, maintained an interpretation that had dominated the scene before John Barrymore's super-subtle Plantagenet of 1922. Wolfit's Lear, beset by poor stage-management and weak acting support, was an outdated remnant of the old school by the time we saw it in Montreal.

A party at the Montreal Repertory Theatre's Guy Street playhouse after the opening of the touring production of *The Importance of Being Earnest* (January 1947). Revellers are John Gielgud, Roberta Beatty, and Jean Adair.

In contrast to the old-style fare of Wolfit, *The Importance of Being Earnest*, with John Gielgud, splendidly crowned the season of 1946–47 and also my Montreal theatre reviewing. Along with Gielgud, under John C. Wilson's banner came the delightful Pamela Brown, Jane Baxter, Robert Flemyng, Margaret Rutherford, and Jean Adair to offer something as near to perfection as I could imagine – with its equilibrium delicately maintained between high comedy and farce, between realism and exquisite style. After my ecstatic review in the *Gazette* Gielgud spoke of me to several people as "the best critic in America," I later learned, and had an important influence on my career as critic.

"Mr Gielgud's uncanny sense of style in presenting a period comedy of this calibre should not be mistaken for anything like an accurate reproduction of the original production. He goes beyond anything so dull as studious research, although doubtless that is part of his approach, and soars into the creative planes. This is a sublimation of the Wilde comedy, treated consciously as a masterpiece must be, and adds to the joys of the original the comment of deep appreciation. This production pictures for us a world of ideal Victorianism. Each characterization is a refinement of that age, each setting and dress a loving tribute to its foibles, grace and charm."[7] That was just part of my published tribute.

It was a happy accident for me that I was reading at lunch in the restaurant Dinty Moore's when Gielgud and some of his company came in. Recognizing me from the press conference, Gielgud stopped at my table. By another happy accident I was reading Granville-Barker's *Prefaces to Shakespeare*, which he knew well. And he knew Barker himself well. That coincidence prompted an invitation to bring my coffee over to his table. Which I did, launching a long and rewarding theatre friendship.

The possibility of Gielgud's bringing his other touring production, Congreve's *Love for Love*, inaugurated an exchange of telegrams between us, culminating in his invitation to me to see it in Ottawa when Consolidated Theatres said "no" to performances in Montreal. Which I did, giving another ecstatic commentary in the *Gazette*. My theatre-going was to be most gloriously enriched by the high art of John Gielgud, immensely extended by his off-stage commentary on all things theatrical. On that day back in Dinty Moore's, I couldn't have dreamed of such a happy outcome.

Montreal's multicultural character attracted a variety of performers who would not, for instance, have found their audiences elsewhere in Canada then. In particular modern dancers felt at ease. I have fond memories of Kurt Jooss's company staging its great satire *The Green Table*, and the slow ravishing *Pavanne d'une infante morte*. I hugely enjoyed Trudi Schoop's comic expressionism and Serge Lifar's company with *La chatte*, Colette Marchand glittering among black oilcloth settings. There were Spanish and Argentinean companies with the great Escudero and José Greco. And there was Harold Kreutzberg, billed as "the world's greatest dancer."

I had discovered the wonderful world of ballet during my London trip of 1935 after racing up stone steps, having queued for a place on the backless benches of the Covent Garden Opera. Tatiana Riaboushinskaya was "the Firebird" in Fokine's *L'oiseau de feu*, set to Stravinsky's music – dazzling against the Byzantine backdrops designed by Natalia Gontcharova. Back in Montreal my enthusiasm for ballet was rekindled by a new friend, Kay Walker, who had turned balletomane while training as a physiotherapist at London's St Thomas Hospital.

Together we shared the best of the touring companies – the Ballet Russe de Monte Carlo, Colonel W. de Basil's Ballet Russe, and, later, American Ballet Theatre. My first Giselle was danced by Lucia Chase in a company headed by Mikhail Mordkin, who had danced with Anna Pavlova – a link with the Imperial Ballet of Russia. We had a direct line to that hallowed institution, we felt, through the local impresario, Nicolas Koudriavtzeff. Through him I managed to get invited to some of the ballet parties, some of them at the St Matthew Street home of the photographer Basil Zarov, of which I have happy memories. That very White Russian, Koudriavtzeff, ran the Canadian Concerts and Artists series, which brought all the leading musical attractions to a scene happily well-developed musically. They added to the air of cultural metropolis that Montreal proudly sported in those halcyon days.[8]

Within a few seasons, in the early forties, we were enthralled by works such as "Aurora's Wedding," which is all a travelling company could bring us of *The Sleeping Beauty*; Fokine's *Schéhérazade*, with the sumptuous Bakst decor matching Rimsky-Korsakoff's music; those Polovtsian dances from Borodin's *Prince Igor*; and Fokine's exquisite *Les Sylphides*, set to Chopin. This was to us the essence of classical ballet, and we approved Benois' use of a Corot background. But I took a lasting dislike to the effete design for the male dancer, which Benois could perhaps get away with when Nijinsky wore it but not when Paul Petroff and Romain Jasinsky did.

In all this discovery, my scenic sense was inflamed by the giant canvases of famous designers. The Gontcharova epic *L'oiseau de feu* was not seen again, as I remember, but there were Benois' productions of *Giselle*, *Nutcracker*, *Raymonda*, and *Graduation Ball*, the latter recreated by Mstislav Doubjinsky who had designed *Ballet Imperiale* for Balanchine. In addition to Benois, there was Bakst, represented by *Carnaval*, *L'après-midi d'un faune*, and *Le spectre de la rose* but most significantly by *Schéhérazade*. These Montreal seasons were full of glamour and excitement, and not only for ballet alone but also for other disciplines of dance. Yet it was classical ballet that made the great difference to me.

However as early as summer 1947 I was becoming aware that as far as legitimate drama was concerned, my beloved Montreal was no longer getting its full share of the best available. I blamed Consolidated Theatres, which preferred its attractions in cans, pre-sold. Toronto put us in the shade. A party of MRT enthusiasts planned an excursion to that city to see John Gielgud's *Hamlet*, with the added excitements of Lillian Gish and Judith Anderson in his company. Then came the word that Montreal would be getting this prize attraction. We cancelled our excursion, only to learn later that Montreal was not included in this tour of *Hamlet*. Although Forbes-Robertson had played Hamlet when he was more than seventy, Gielgud would not play it past forty and had qualms about doing it even at that age. It had been our last chance to see this century's greatest Hamlet.

I looked to New York in order to keep in touch with the larger stage of the day. On my holiday trips to New York I was to recognize a major musical genre in 1943 when I saw how the American musical could be developed, as it had never been before, in Rodgers and Hammerstein's *Oklahoma!* Within a comparatively few years I saw their *Carousel* and *Allegro*, and Lerner and Loewe's *Brigadoon*, Loesser's *Where's Charley*, Berlin's *Annie Get Your Gun*, and *Kiss Me Kate* by Cole Porter. New York shows were a "must" for theatre-minded Montrealers then. We were establishing a bond that was later to puzzle the rest of Canada. Why, it asked, was Quebec so afraid of the influence of "les Anglais" on provincial culture and never that of the more pernicious one from its Southern neighbour? The excuse for French Montreal was that its language would protect it. For English Montrealers, there seemed to be none. Few of them made the trip to Toronto to see theatre, even when aware that it was flourishing better there.

In 1946 I went again to New York and saw the delicate *Lute Song*, adapted by Sidney Howard and Will Irwin from a Chinese play called *Pi-Pa-Ki* to Raymond Scott's music, which caught my heart. I have a special affection for *Lute Song*. This was partly because of Robert Edmond Jones' exquisite Chinese designs, partly because of the beguiling Dolly Haas (succeeding Mary Martin) as its Chinese heroine, and partly because of the company it kept. There was also Orson Welles' audacious musical *Around the World*, a spectacle very much to my liking. But the most striking treat was a British import.

That year in Montreal a small group of us had just finished staging *King Lear* at Moyse Hall. Shakespeareans all after that experience, we were determined to see the Old Vic when it visited New York. The stage-struck travellers included our director Pierre Dagenais, our designer (myself), our Cordelia and Edgar, Adelaide Smith and Leo Ciceri, and Don Haldane.

We were to see England's Old Vic at a particularly brilliant period of theatre history. We had heard all about the Old Vic and of its recent rise to new power under two familiars, Laurence Olivier and Ralph Richardson, with John Burrell as third partner. For its visit to New York in spring 1946 the Old Vic's programme was drawn from its past two seasons and included the two *Henry IV*s, Chekhov's *Uncle Vanya*, Sophocles' *Oedipus Rex* and Sheridan's *The Critic*, to be played at the Century Theatre.

We were able to appreciate both Henries, with Harry Andrews a most imposing Owen Glendower, Margaret Leighton the loveliest possible Lady Percy, George Ralph the Earl of Worcester, all lending magnificent support to Richardson's superb Falstaff and Olivier's Hotspur under Burrell's sound direction. We hugged ourselves over the brilliance of Olivier's choosing to stumble on his "Ws" for a Hotspur who must die trying to utter "worms." Further-

Photo from the program of the Old Vic production of *Henry IV Part I* with Ralph Richardson as Falstaff and Laurence Olivier as Hotspur.

more, Burrell had contrived a stunning final image for *Part One* with Richardson holding Olivier by the heels – an image that could be taken for a reversible comedy/tragedy, a substitute for the usual masks. In *Part Two* there was a marvellous scene between Miles Malleson as Justice Silence and Olivier, now Justice Shallow, both sitting in the fading sunshine of their days. "Dead?" "Dead!" Silence. The pair of them conjured the seventh age of man perfectly and memorably.

The next day, in a record heat wave, we shared the Chekhov, staged by Burrell and designed beautifully by Tanya Moiseiwitsch. After seeing Olivier impersonate a young stuttering rebel and a dying old judge perfectly, it was truly astonishing to see how Russian he could become as Dr Astrov in a

Photo from the program of the Old Vic production of Sophocles' *Oedipus Rex*
(May 1946 – New York).

splendidly controlled performance opposite Richardson's lost Vanya. Then, as if
more demonstration were necessary, came the actor's Oedipus, followed immediately by his Mr Puff. No wonder we were intoxicated. We were shattered by
the two famous cries he emitted as Oedipus when he could no longer deny his
guilt in John Piper's darkening Thebes. How hysterical we became when he
swung down on the curtain to put an ending to Sheridan's wonderful theatre
piece (and nearly so for his audacious dandy, Mr Puff). Miles Malleson had the
wonderful role of Sir Fretful, surely one of the wittiest parodies in literature;
but it was Richardson's silent Burleigh which caught my fancy second, with
Joyce Redman's starkly mad in white linen Confidante third.

Finally, when the double sensation of *Oedipus* and *The Critic* hit us, with
Olivier dazzling in both leading roles, we headed home, singing and dancing

as we walked around Central Park, to an apartment on 72nd Street belonging to our absent friends the Ravens. For me, that still remains the richest single programme in a lifetime of rewarding theatre-going. How I wished the Old Vic could have come to Montreal, but I was proud that my *Gazette* readers were made aware of such magnificence.

Such New York theatre-going helped compensate for the fact that the owners of His Majesty's, Consolidated Theatres, were plainly interested only in their film palaces and that Montreal would never regain its pre-war status as a touring stop. And there was so much theatre in New York, so much visual art, so much music – so many surprises. One evening I went to a nightclub where another legend, Edith Piaf, was singing, and I remember now how that forlorn gamin broke everybody's heart with her songs. Yes, New York was indeed the place to be! Even the most involved of the theatre-struck Canadians agreed to that – if they could afford the excursions.

The rise of professional French-language theatre was both result and consolation; but the decline of the city as a once-great touring stop was depressing. Our premonitions were right: Montreal's day as a major city for English-language theatre was over ("Ils s'en fouent"). That it would never return was symbolized by the demolition of Her Majesty's Theatre in 1964 to make way for a parking lot.[9] That wonderful old house had known greatness and I had been lucky to share in some of it. By spring 1949 I had had to find my theatre elsewhere.

Chapter Nine

LE RIDEAU SE LÈVE

As previously discussed, during the war years I had spent my summer holidays learning how to handle larger groups of actors in a wider range of plays and, at the same time, had been moving from the modest status of a greenhorn second-string reviewer at the *Gazette* to that of established theatre critic at a most exciting period of Montreal life. The town was bursting with wartime activity. Most significantly, the French-language theatre and drama were now beginning to attain greater importance and independence. It had been building slowly through the years, of course – as my colleague Jacques Laroche recorded in *La Presse* under his nom de plume "Jean Béraud."[1] Now it began to explode!

Quebec's French-language stage was to achieve the first truly independent dramatic expression in Canadian life, although the Montreal Community Players had declared in 1920 that their purpose was "to facilitate the production of plays dealing with Canadian life or written by Canadian authors. Up to the present time, such plays have had practically no chance for production in the Dominion." That proclamation was issued over the signatures of Sir Andrew MacPhail, B.K. Sandwell, Ramsay Traquair, and C.W. Simpson, R.C.A., Anglos all! The Community Players' edict was to be restated a decade later when Martha Allan revived those aims under the banner of her Montreal Repertory Theatre.

But their high ideals were always touched with modesty – a true colonial well-bred modesty that recognized the undeniable superiority of the English theatre, its performers, its audiences, and above all its playwrights. Canadians only wanted to emulate these high national expressions: even if we could manage to develop a Broadway of our own, we'd be respectful of the British supremacy.

It was very different with our fellow Canadians, the Québécois. They had no great respect for the theatre of France, save in an academic way, and that I believe was somewhat resentful. New France, being settled by worthy servants of *le Roi*, withdrew in revulsion when the bourgeoisie rose against His Majesty and cut off his head in the most bloodthirsty fashion. It took the settlers a century to forgive France's revolution. And the British embargo on French ships blocked any news of that revolution's aims and successes from the lonely folk in New France. It was not impressed with revolutionaries and told Benjamin Franklin so when he came wooing with an army of the New Congress at his heels, expecting to persuade the French-speaking neighbours to join with the American revolutionaries. "*Merci, mais non*" was their reply to Monsieur Franklin, no matter how persuasive his good French was. But Franklin's visit left a tangible symbol of Quebec independence. He had brought with him, for propaganda purposes, a printing press and its operator, Fleury de Mesplet. When the new Americans retreated, the new Congress refused to pay for the return of this press, so de Mesplet stayed behind, starting a journal that was to evolve into the *Gazette*, for which I am eternally grateful.

So, as I have chronicled above, it came about in my time that the theatrical folk of Montreal were united in their dream of a living theatre of their own — even though it wasn't the same dream. *Les Anglais* never learned the difference.

English Montrealers could well envy their French counterparts the language barrier, which made it easier for them to cast aside colonial handicaps. The linguistic isolation of French Canada was to prove even more effective than the isolation of distance for the rest of the country. Winnipeg, for instance, exploited its geographic isolation boldly, creating its own Royal Winnipeg Ballet, the Winnipeg Symphony, and the Manitoba Theatre Centre to supply its needs when the foreign tours petered out. But Quebec created an entirely indigenous theatrical culture. It had, of course, endured its years of profound colonialism too. France sent its theatre to this outpost of French culture to dazzle the impressionable natives, to take home worthwhile profits, and to leave the local artists overshadowed. Those great names of the 1880s – Bernhardt, Coquelin, Monet-Sully, and Réjane – were followed by others from Paris, including the Comédie-Française itself, Gaby Morlay, Sacha Guitry, and Yvonne Printemps – powerful rivals to the native Quebec artists who were trying to establish themselves.

It took time for native and local names to achieve any kind of recognition and respect. The true pioneers were the actors, as ever exploited because of their need to act, to keep alive in their profession. Led by the beloved veteran Fred Barry, their heroic ranks include names such as Albert Duquesne, Jeanne Demons, Jeanne Maubourg, Bella and Rose Ouellette (la Poune), Olivier Guimond *père et fils*, Pierre Durand, Henry Deyglun, and so many more.[2] In those days, when working actors got a radio or, later, a television call, a fellow player would go on-stage for them. It was a practice accepted by l'Union des artistes, which was founded in 1937. But dropping out from even one performance would never be condoned by the US-affiliated Canadian Actors Equity.

I became aware of these vedettes slowly, even after I became a newspaperman, for the *Gazette*, with its English-reading circulation, did not cover the French-language stage. I had heard of theatres such as the Stella, the Arcade, the big Saint-Denis, the Salle du Gesù, and the Monument-National but rarely visited them, my curiosity unable to overcome my language deficiency. Handicapped or not, I think I first became aware of the French majority through its theatre – not in Outremont, the French-language equivalent of Westmount where I lived, but when I ventured downtown to Union Avenue into the Montreal Repertory Theatre, Martha Allan's world.

The MRT had first allowed me to serve as stage crew in 1933 at the Salle du Gesù on Bleury Street, just south of St Catherine Street, for the production of

Obey's *Noé*. I remember meeting Gratien Gélinas who I think was in the cast. He certainly played Dr Caius in Edwyn Wayte's production of *The Merry Wives of Windsor* for MRT. That performance, which I marked "excellent" on my programme, was undoubtedly what later led me to cover Gratien's popular revues, his *Fridolinades*, which were winning a very special audience for him and helped launch him into an astonishing stage career. It established this tiny woebegone genius as one of the country's most important stars, one able to transcend the language barrier through his art.

Gratien Gélinas' excursion into the language of Shakespeare at MRT was in 1935. After graduating earlier from Collège de Montréal, he tried selling insurance for a living, but he carried on with the theatricals he had become involved with there, acting with les Anciens du Collège de Montréal. It was inevitably radio that, like many of his generation, took the young graduate into the professional world. He became attached to poet Robert Choquette's popular and endless serial *Le curé de village* on CKAC.[3]

Jean Béraud and Louis Francœur co-authored Gélinas' first professional revue, *Télévise-moi-ça!* Its scale can be established by the theatre it played in, since the Saint-Denis was the French-language equivalent to His Majesty's. Gélinas' success in that and on radio combined to lead to his creation of the first *Fridolinades* in 1938 – bright satirical sketches centering on the sharp-talking, apple-eating, impudent little gamin Fridolin that he had first played on a radio programme called *Le carrousel de la gaieté*. By 1939 Gratien Gélinas was hailed as "comedian of the year" by the magazine *Radiomonde*.

Gélinas found a new spirit and a new identity as Fridolin as he swept the town, causing waves of laughter even up the slopes of Westmount. He didn't spare *les Anglais*, even though they weren't widely represented in his audience. They were fair game, especially, I recall, when the little gamin, straddling his chair downstage centre, his cloth cap pulled over his ear, got around to the baby bonus, punctuating his wry comments on life with bites he took of his apple:

Miriam Hopkins and Gratien Gélinas in the touring production of *St Lazare's Pharmacy* which was performed at His Majesty's in December 1945.

"It wasn't going to help *les Anglais* much, for they were known to have a preference for dogs rather than babies." The Quebec audiences, renowned for large families, roared with laughter, enjoying his comments on their own foibles just as hugely. If there were priests in the house – and there nearly always were – the area around them would become quiet when Gélinas became too out-spoken about the Church. Much of his humour was too "in" and too "joual" for my untrained ear, but his personality as Fridolin needed no interpreter.

The attention he attracted eventually spread across Quebec and beyond the boundaries of Canada. Eddie Dowling – the American who had just directed and starred in Tennessee Williams' first great success, *The Glass Menagerie* – heard of the bright French-Canadian comedian when he adapted Miklos Laszlo's drama *St. Lazare's Pharmacy* to a Quebec setting for Broadway and film star Miriam Hopkins. With Gélinas in the cast, the Laszlo drama played in Montreal in December 1945, then in Chicago, but did not become a Broadway

A photo of the milestone
production of Gratien Gélinas'
Tit-Coq (May 1948), with the
author–actor himself, Fred Barry,
and Huguette Oligny.

hit. When Dowling went on to direct O'Neill's *The Iceman Cometh*, Gélinas
returned to Montreal to produce another Fridolin revue, which then became a
profitable touring production throughout the province. This taste of more legitimate drama encouraged Gélinas to write *Tit-Coq* in 1948, which was to be a
milestone in Canadian theatrical history.

Gratien achieved what few Canadian actors have, a long run in a star role,
with time to polish that role to perfection. I recorded his success as Tit-Coq,
and in the subsequent (and delicately anglicized) Ti-Coq. I said, in part, "As
an actor of unusual personality and talent, as a producer of taste and imagination, and as the author of as strong and earthy a play as *Ti-Coq*, Gratien Gélinas
stands at the top of the Canadian theatre today."[4]

If Gratien Gélinas was my first link with Quebec's new theatre, père Émile
Legault provided an even stronger one. His productions for les Compagnons de

Saint-Laurent were easier for me to review, especially when one could first read the play in translation. Père Legault had been detailed by his order, the Congregation of the Holy Cross, to carry on the work in religious drama for youth that Henri Ghéon had spearheaded in France. In 1937 père Legault formed les Compagnons de Saint-Laurent for that purpose – a company that under his vigorous leadership became a small acting troupe of great style rather than a body dedicated to mass religiosity.[5]

After a provincial scholarship took him to France, père Legault emerged as a most imaginative director. Les Compagnons were established at the Collège du Saint-Laurent, from which they took their name. By 1940 they had moved to Montreal, finding a studio there the next year on Côte des Neiges. They played at l'Ermitage and at the Salle du Gesù where Montrealers (even those in the English-language press) had a chance to discover them. When, in 1947, les Compagnons de Saint-Laurent entered Molière's *Le médecin malgré lui* in the Dominion Drama Festival and were awarded the Bessborough Trophy by Emrys Jones, the first Canadian adjudicator, French and English theatre groups united in their approval.

Père Legault's troupe advanced the quality of Montreal's theatre – as Gélinas had done by the sheer exuberance of his comedy and as Pierre Dagenais did by the fierceness of his intellectualism. Les Compagnons were earthy, extroverted, and popular. Their playing made a sharp contrast to traditional British restraint and to the American emphasis on psychology, both reflected in Canada's English-language theatre. Jean Gascon, Jean-Louis Roux, Thérèse Cadorette, Guy Hoffman, and Jean Coutu were all members of the company, equally distinctive and characteristic in their art. Famous visitors such as Jacques Copeau and Louis Jouvet applauded the young Canadian company's achievement.

I believe I first saw Jean Gascon in the company of the illustrious Ludmilla Pitoëff, wife of Georges Pitoëff – a pair born in Tiflis, Russia. They had both made major contributions to France's intellectual theatre: she had been a notable Saint Joan in Paris before she brought her family to Canada as war refugees.

She gave some remarkable performances in Montreal, one of them as Racine's *Phèdre* at the Université de Montréal in March 1946. I saw the youthful Gascon in support as Thesée, with Jean-Louis Roux as Hippolyte. Gascon was later to pay great tribute to her influence on his own performing style.

Visitors of special renown from abroad enrich any theatre scene. Ludmilla Pitoëff was certainly one of these as were Fyodor Komisarjevsky, Adeline Genée, Tyrone Guthrie, and Michel Saint-Denis. I recall the fascination of Pitoëff's *Maison des poupées*, staged at l'Ermitage with special effects achieved by using child-sized chairs against a strong red curtain. With red light trained on this curtain, the effect was almost unbearable. She had a marked impact on les Compagnons de Saint-Laurent, with whom she also appeared in Claudel's *L'échange*.

The year after the company's first success in the DDF with Molière's *Le médecin malgré lui*, les Compagnons entered Anouilh's *Antigone* with Thérèse Cadorette in the title role. In deference to the Church, père Legault made a few textual adjustments. The bilingual adjudicator Robert Speaight noticed them immediately and gave the Bessborough Trophy to the London Little Theatre for its *Saint Joan* with Olga Landiak as Joan. Yet when Speaight later returned to Canada to recreate his great role as Becket, it was in Legault's production of Eliot's *Murder in the Cathedral*. In 1951 les Compagnons won the Bessborough a second time with a fantastic comedy, the Martens/Obey *Les gueux au paradis*.

In 1978, père Legault wrote to thank me for my appreciation of his company: "Je vous remercie from the bottom of my heart. C'est vrai que j'ai toujours eu pour vous une particulaire amité et j'ai deploré votre départ de *La Gazette*. Vos critiques dramatiques étaient toujours intéressantes et sympathétiques; jamais démolissantes." I have had no more appreciative tribute. We met at the finals of the DDF, sometimes as competitors, until 1952 when he was withdrawn from theatre by the Church. By that time many of père Legault's

outstanding players had moved to the professional stage – to the notable enrich-
ment of theatrical history in modern Quebec – Gascon and Roux, for example,
launched le Théâtre du Nouveau Monde in 1951.

Gascon remained a friend and colleague for the rest of his highly productive
life in theatre, for his concerns were close to mine. Les Compagnons, le Théâtre
du Nouveau Monde, the Stratford Festival, and the National Arts Centre bound
us over the years and I am very proud to have known such a major contributor
to Canada's theatre in its two founding languages. He was always highly expressive – as actor and director. Our loss, Canada's loss, by his death in 1988 has
not yet been fully recognized, I believe.

His talented colleague, designer Robert Prévost, I knew less well but
admired equally. He began his career as a designer in his native Montreal but
was self-taught and never went to l'École des beaux-arts. In fact, he started out
as an actor with les Compagnons de Saint-Laurent when he was a student at
the college. Very soon, though, he became principal designer for les Compagnons, working with them from 1946 to 1952. Yet his talents were not limited
to backstage: he turned journalist for a while, working in Val D'Or.

The vividness of his imagination, however, expressed in exciting illustrations
and designs, soon brought him back into the fold. He designed his first opera,
Puccini's *Tosca*, for the impossible area of Molson Stadium in 1949. Opera
remained his major employer over the years, interspersed with theatre work,
much of it for le Théâtre du Nouveau Monde. And he continued to work with
Gascon at Stratford. I have elsewhere expressed my deep admiration for his *Le
tartuffe* produced there in 1968. He loved Italy and spent time there but also
remained in touch with Canada's theatre – a great ornament to it himself –
until his death in 1982.

When Jean Gascon crossed over into Stratford's management, Jean-Louis
Roux upheld le Nouveau Monde's status as the leading theatre company of
French Canada. Roux had progressed theatrically as a star on stage and screen.

He was also recognized widely as the rebel "Ovide" in CBC-TV's folkloric *La famille Plouffe*, scripted by Roger Lemelin. Later, he became an administrator of both le Nouveau Monde and the National Theatre School and, still later, president of the Canadian Theatre Centre (UNESCO) and chairman of the Canadian Conference of the Arts. As playwright, author, and translator of Shakespeare, his contributions were equally distinguished and widely recognized by his contemporaries. One thing is certain: the name of Jean-Louis Roux will be remembered as long as theatre flourishes in this country. Being named head of the Canada Council in 1998 restored the dignity lost by an abbreviated stint earlier as Lieutenant-Governor of Quebec.

But the creative figure of French Quebec to whom I became closest was the brilliant Pierre Dagenais – a young actor, director, playwright, and eventually critic – who also made his own company, l'Équipe, into a major contributing element to this new theatre of Quebec. I came to know Pierre Dagenais not as a critic but as a confrere, designer, director, and friend. Pierre was of middle height, slight but with a burning intensity of passion and a depth of voice that commanded attention and helped him function successfully as director and actor.[6]

He soon gathered around him some of the brightest of the young Quebec actors. When I came to know l'Équipe these included both Denise Pelletier, who was to emerge as the greatest of the Quebec actresses of her day, and her brother Gilles; Janine Sutto (the first Mme Dagenais), Roger Garceau, Yvette Brind'Amour (who was to found le Théâtre du Rideau Vert), Guy Maufette, Robert Rivard, and Nini Durand (the second Mme Dagenais).

Pierre fought for l'Équipe valiantly, even going to jail – proudly and defiantly – for an unpaid amusement tax of $800. And he maintained l'Équipe from late 1942 to early 1948, staging thirteen productions that had a great impact on Quebec theatre. It was his personal debt and the poor reception of his play *Le temps de vivre* at le Monument-National that eventually brought l'Équipe down.

Dagenais produced a variety of avant-garde plays for an often-shocked Catholic community, as well as exploring diverse worlds such as Marcel Pagnol's Marseilles (in *Marius*) and Shakespeare's Athens. His outdoor presentation of *Songe d'une nuit d'été* (*A Midsummer Night's Dream*) in 1945 was at its most French in its handling of the quartet of lovers. It was an outdoors production, played in the gardens of l'Ermitage on Côte des Neiges. As played by young Robert Rivard, its Puck was a truly amoral animal spirit.

In complete contrast to that frantic Attic romance, I was honoured to be present in the ballroom of the old Windsor Hotel the next year when Pierre's l'Équipe repeated its North American premiere of Jean-Paul Sartre's *Huis clos*. Yvette Brind'Amour, Roger Garceau, and Muriel Guilbault were the splendid players in a performance arranged for Sartre himself, then in Quebec on a lecture tour. Sartre demanded that they repeat it immediately, so pleased was he!

In recognition of his brilliance, Montreal's English theatre community invited Pierre to stage the Shakespeare Society's 1946 *King Lear* and François Mauriac's *Asmodée*, called *The Intruder*, the latter for the MRT. As discussed elsewhere, I myself directed Pierre in Brae Manor's *Candida* (August 1946). In return Pierre asked me to direct *Le héros et le soldat* (Shaw's *Arms and the Man* in the Hamon translation) for l'Équipe in December 1946. Hoping that this would improve my French, I did so. But in the end I had to admit that, while the French-speaking players all learned more English, the only French word I got out of it was *bibliothèque*. The dazzling cast consisted of Denise Pelletier as Mme Petkoff opposite Roland d'Amour, her brother Gilles as the first-act soldier, Albert Cloutier as Bluntschli, and dashing Guy Maufette as Sergius. Nini Durand was the fascinating Raina, Yvette Brind'Amour as the smouldering Louka, while Pierre played Nicola superbly.

I designed a war-cracked pink castle against the silhouette of a black scarred landscape, beautifully painted by Griffith and Marie Brewer. All of the characters wore pure operetta costumes except Cloutier, who drove home our point that war is a matter of survival, not a path to glory, by sporting Canadian battledress. Those two future Quebec vedettes, Denise and Yvette, displayed the qualities which were to make them pre-eminent later. Yvette was determined to be good; Denise was distressed when she was not perfect. Once, when she asked me how to play a certain scene, I answered by asking what she herself thought about it. She responded by bursting into tears. Having Denise and Yvette in my cast was a measure of Pierre's generosity to a guest director. He gave me two actresses who were to become the most respected in Quebec theatre.

They were strongly contrasted, in contribution as in personality. Denise Pelletier, a pupil of Sita Riddez, joined les Compagnons de Saint-Laurent while still in her teens and was not much older when Pierre invited her to play a character role in the Shaw play. Tall, aquiline, and fair, she was recognized early on as *une vraie vedette*. She won a television public as Cecile in the popular serial *La famille Plouffe* and was in Gélinas' English-language *Ti-Coq* when it went on tour. Star roles came her way. She played Mary Tyrone in O'Neill's *Long voyage vers la nuit*, Brecht's *Mère Courage*, and that half-buried monologist in *Oh les beaux jours* by Samuel Beckett. For les Festivals de Montréal, she did another Shaw play, *Saint Joan*, in 1954 under the direction of Charles Rittenhouse. She had yet to demonstrate her great range and power in our Shaw comedy, but the maturity and temperament were there. Denise's early death in 1976 robbed a country that always seems short on stars. But she is not forgotten, nor will she be. A theatre in Montreal bears her name.

Even back then Yvette Brind'Amour offered strong competition. Shorter, dark, and more intense than Denise, she was to contribute equally as an actress-manager. I had known her first as a youngster (she was older than Denise) at

A photo of l'Équipe's production of *Le héros et le soldat,* the Hamon translation of Shaw's *Arms and the Man*, designed and directed by Whittaker (December 1946). Seen are Denise Pelletier as Madame Petkoff, Roland d'Amour as Mr Petkoff, Nini Durand as Raina, and Guy Maufette as Sergius.

MRT. Six years later she was part of the production of Sartre's *Huis clos* that had so pleased its author at Windsor Hotel one sunny afternoon. Perhaps his encouragement sent her off to Paris to study with Charles Dullin. But she was back soon to launch, with Mercedes Palomino, le Théâtre du Rideau Vert in 1948, which profited mightily for many years from her vivid style and personality in starring roles such as Jean Giraudoux's *Ondine* and *La reine morte* by Henri de Montherlant.

Nini Durand, who played the leading role of the capricious Raina in *Le héros et le soldat*, held her own vivaciously against such formidable competition, while Albert Cloutier made Shaw's point as the chocolate soldier. Guy Maufette, our Sergius, who like Denise was to become a popular Radio-Canada favourite, was always searching for a talisman that would provide a key to his role. He found it for *le héros* in a pair of elaborate tasselled boots at Ponton. Pierre himself brought to the small subservient role of Nicola much brooding and sinister social significance to counter Yvette's burning ambition as Louka. It was a splendid cast, and I know that Pierre gave his actors the kind of expert textual assistance that Charles Rittenhouse had given his actors in his Shakespearean productions.

My own regret was that I could not understand what members of l'Équipe's audience were saying when they came to congratulate me after the opening at the Salle du Gesù. Years later Pierre told me that his French-Canadian confreres never forgave him for associating with *les Anglais.* I tended to think that Pierre was exaggerating but it was true that he did not achieve the career as a director that his special gift warranted. When Jean Gascon returned to Montreal from his decade at Stratford, he told of meeting the same kind of mistrust.

Did the Anglos never notice incipient separatism in those early years of the century? I suppose everybody had some little incident that they could bring forth on occasion – but never fearfully, only humourously. Like my boyhood recollection of shouting "mougy peasoup" to French-speaking students on my block and then running as fast as possible, in those carefree days in Outremont. But I was unaware of any animosity when I went to evening classes at l'École des beaux-arts later on. Nor did I take seriously Gratien Gélinas' saucy sneers at *les Anglais* in his *Fridolinades* revues. Surely we Anglos were blind because it suited us to see nothing.

Years later I took tea with the owner of Toronto's burlesque house, the Casino. We spoke nostalgically of burlesque, Canada's first underground theatre. When I contributed the name of Montreal's most beloved stripper, Lili St Cyr, along with "artistes" such as Gypsy Rose Lee and Sally Rand, I drew a blank.

She never played the Casino, I was told. She belonged to Quebec and wouldn't give Toronto the advantage of her art. All we knew in Montreal was that burlesque comics, and also those promoted into vaudeville, could always get a laugh by announcing, "I spent a month in Toronto last week." We joined in the laugh at Toronto's reputation as "Toronto the good and the dull." It was just another example of the healthy rivalry between Canada's two major cities, not any unhealthy rivalry between Canada's two founding nations. What was Hugh MacLennan going on about? Was the dance music of the Titanic band distracting us from watching out for icebergs?

But the Ottawa office of the Dominion Drama Festival was well aware of conflicts and divisions. It was stalwart in maintaining its original mandate to uphold union in Canada's theatre, as set down by His Excellency the Earl of Bessborough, Governor General of Canada, with very useful guidance by a Canadian amateur actor of talent, the Honorable Vincent Massey, in 1933. After the war the patriotic restraints that had been placed voluntarily on Canada's English-language stage, save for troop shows, were lifted and the Dominion Drama Festival started once again to organize its national competitions. To my satisfaction I was teamed with Jacques Laroche in reorganizing the Festival in 1947. We were joint vice-chairmen of the Western Quebec Regional Festival under the chairmanship of Jean de Savoye. I suspect that Mrs de Savoye's impeccably French name was a factor in her choice; she had, however, done Trojan work for the Montreal Repertory Theatre and was later to be its producing director at the end of its career. Though she was "a verra frank-talking Scot" her name had its value on paper as head of a committee which was carefully chosen to keep both French- and English-speaking contingents working together for the DDF's greater glory. And survival.

As mentioned above, Laroche was a much-respected critic, contributor to, and chronicler of, Montreal's growing Québécois theatre. My own connection was that of a critic and also a stage director who was already involved in the workings of the DDF. I had made my bow before the DDF Executive Committee as far back as 1938. I had gone to Winnipeg when the DDF made its first move out of the sacred precincts of Ottawa as director of one of the winning regional entries, Irena Groten's translation for us of Pushkin's *Festival in Time of Plague.* I was made aware of the difficulties between the two language groups. Naturally, the dissatisfaction felt by the French Canadians over the management of the DDF by the English Canadians was centred in Montreal. The Montreal French believed that there was no solution other than the division of the DDF into two separate operations – one French, one English. When I went to Winnipeg, it was not only as the director-designer of the production by the Sixteen-Thirty Club but also as bearer of this demand from the Montreal committee. Though no action was taken in that direction by the DDF Executive, their committment to the Festival's founding principles of bilingualism and national unity meant that much discussion of the "French fact," or lack thereof, in the DDF was engendered.

Re-establishing the DDF in 1947, with the determination that both cultures would work together and accept whatever the finals handed out to them without complaints was a stern challenge. The next festival's adjudicator was to be a Canadian drama professor, Emrys Jones, of the University of Saskatchewan. It was definitely a step forward to have a Canadian adjudicator. Perhaps inspired by the sense of nationalism that the war had generated, English dramatic groups were back in full swing. Meanwhile the French groups were stronger by the addition of les Compagnons, bursting with talent under père Émile Legault. However, what was to be the major confrontation of that May 1947 DDF Final in London's Grand Theatre had begun much earlier in our bicultural committee meetings.

The new element in the post-war DDF was professionalism and it was not entirely welcome. The young actors of les Compagnons represented it in its pure state. After all what did they do for a living but act, although you couldn't say that they acted for profit! But this contribution was matched by real professionalism from the Montreal Repertory Theatre. Under Bobbie Beatty's direction MRT mounted very strong competition to les Compagnons' production of Molière's *Le médecin malgré lui* with *Amphitryon 38*, S.N. Behrman's adaptation of Jean Giraudoux's play which the Lunts, Alfred and Lynn Fontanne, had made such a Broadway hit.

To oppose the lively Compagnons under père Legault's direction, Bobbie Beatty had mustered Cicely Howland, a young English actress moved into Canadian journalism, and John Dando, a lecturer at McGill University. The imported English regional adjudicator, Virginia Vernon, was perfectly bilingual – she had translated the plays of Noel Coward for the Paris stage with her husband, Frank. She was a good judge of professional theatre, both English and French. She chose the MRT's *Amphytrion 38* as winner of the Western Quebec Regional Drama Festival at the Sun Life Auditorium. Bobbie Beatty received the top festival award onstage from the hands of A.B. Woods, President of Sun Life. Les Compagnons, a very good second, were also invited to the finals in London. That decision might have upset the French applecart entirely but the French entries respected Mrs Vernon. Of course, there was still a good chance that les Compagnons would come out the better contestants in the finals with another adjudicator. And so they did.

In the 1947 DDF finals Emrys Jones chose les Compagnons' *Le médecin malgré lui* as winner of the Bessborough Trophy, naming the MRT's *Amphitryon 38* as the best presentation in English. The best presentation in French, exclusive of the Bessborough winner, was judged to be that of Le Caveau, the long-established little theatre group from Ottawa – Paul Gury's dramatization of *Maria Chapdelaine*, which also took the Sir Barry Jackson Trophy for the best presentation of an original play. Montreal also came out well in the acting awards: Cicely Howland was second to Vancouver's Aileen Cocleugh (later Aileen Seaton), who was named for her Mrs Massingham in *Angel Street* while

John Dando and les Compagnons' Henry Groulx were named runners-up to Bill Walker in Regina's production of *Ways and Means*. Both Vancouver and Regina winners went on to long careers in Toronto's CBC studios. A practically perfect balance had been struck, but still the cry for separate festivals was heard from Quebec.

The efforts of the DDF executive to keep that balance between both language groups doubled. The executive, primarily British in thinking, gave dogged deference to its French-speaking representatives. I cheered the committee on, a voyeur in this battle of the languages, as Ottawa's dominant executive wooed Quebec's burgeoning creativity. I gradually came to participate more and more in DDF deliberations over the next quarter of a century, and the bilingual cause became my cause. Jacques Laroche was replaced as my opposite number in committee by Guy Beaulne, another professional man of the theatre with strong convictions who, I felt, shared my hopes for equal honours.

There were others in Quebec who also believed in the DDF's linguistic equality. In my last year on the Western Quebec Regional DDF committee, Gratien Gélinas was named chairman, with radio's Ferdi Biondi, Henri Trudel, and Mme Paul Goyette also serving. In 1959 Col. Yves Bourassa, a leading Montreal advertising man married to the attractive French star Nicole Germain, brought his strong personality to the position of chairman of the DDF. This balance thus prevailed as long as the festival lasted, allowing the noble aims of Lord Bessborough to be upheld until the very end of the DDF itself.

Renamed Theatre Canada in May 1970, the united DDF continued until 1978 when its Ottawa office closed because of lack of money and interest. It had been superseded by more powerful forces in the Canadian theatre – indeed, by the dual professionalism it had worked towards. Canada was moving forward and in this the Dominion Drama Festival played a leading role. It is still on record as the closest our country has come to a truly national theatre and lives on in spirit through the myriad theatre festivals now across Canada.

I certainly had no such historic premonitions about its role when I left Montreal for Toronto in 1949, although I found the DDF's Central Ontario Drama league in even better shape than the bilingual one I had left behind. My reputation as both successful competitor and active executive member had preceded me and gave me some recognition within DDF circles, beyond my rank as new drama critic of the *Globe and Mail* – which was considerable, if I may say. A step up all round, one could say.

But I could not tear away from my hometown so easily. For one thing my family was there, my mother having moved to Pointe Claire to be near brother George and his family: his wife Lillias and their two bright children, Jeffrey and Leslie. And then there were the long-time friends, including the Macorquodales, and Bobbie Beatty and Julie Cohen, at whose home I also shared Christmases. Whenever I could justify a return visit for reviewing purposes, I did. I flew down for Rosanna Seaborn Todd's newsworthy Mount Royal production of *Cymbeline*, directed in modern dress by the celebrated Russian Fydor Komisarjevsky, and for Louis Jouvet's splendid staging of Moliere's *L'école des femmes* at Her Majesty's. As it was sold-out, I was allowed an extra chair up close, to revel in the bedazzlement of these Parisien actors and their exquisite production, designed by Christian Berard. In its height, wit, and ingenuity that setting matched, but did not obscure, the sheer brilliance of Jouvet's comic technique and the irresistible charm of his ingenue, Dominique Blanchard. I lingered after the performance to go backstage and discover how a single stagehand had made Berard's setting open up so entrancingly when needed.

This, in March 1951, was my last visit to my beloved Her Majesty's, and the performance was worthy of comparison with the Gielgud *Earnest* and that long-ago Martin-Harvey *Hamlet*. Two years later I was invited back by les Festivals de Montréal to design a mammoth setting atop Mount Royal for a revival of the Shakespeare Society's *King Lear*, a truly spectacular farewell to the Montreal stage for me.

I SPEAK THE EPILOGUE

No partnership in my Montreal days was livelier and more rewarding for me than the one I had with Charles Rittenhouse. Starting with high-school productions at West Hill, it survived his absence while he attended the Yale Drama School and ended actively only when I left for Toronto. Charles' quickness of mind was particularly appreciated by me as a stage designer, where my imagination was matched by his practicality. Our years of collaboration climaxed with our last hurrah together, the production of *King Lear* at les Festivals de Montréal in 1953.

It was, in general, a happy hectic reunion of the team that had created the successful *King Lear* at Moyse Hall in 1946: once again Pierre Dagenais was to direct with Charles Rittenhouse to oversee his creativity as producer and I as the designer – the trio that had brought the Shakespeare Society to its finest hour within the protective confines of the Arts Building of McGill University.

In August 1953, however, we were out in the open with a vengeance – on top of Mount Royal. Our team was on the same great personal terms that had produced the earlier success, and we were all delighted that our Lear this time was to be John Colicos. This gave our reunion added excitement because we were welcoming John home after his truly spectacular breakthrough to glory as an overnight Lear at the Old Vic. His astonishing performance when the Old Vic's touring star Stephen Murray was unable to go on in Helsinki made world-theatre news. It certainly made news in Toronto when this twenty-three-year-old actor from Montreal "went on" to achieve overnight fame: to my surprise, his picture as Lear appeared on the front page of the *Globe and Mail*. Who inspired this happy choice I don't to this day know, but the committee of les Festivals de Montréal leapt at it.

Still, there was a catch here – our new production of *King Lear* was scheduled for only one night. We were to recreate, stage, and blow up our original

1946 production of the great tragedy to festival proportions, mounting it on an eighty-two-foot wide stage outdoors on top of Mount Royal – and all for one night only! Staging a single performance of a play as complex as Shakespeare's *King Lear* is like leaping over a mountain and landing on the head of a predestined pin.

This time, everything would obviously have to be bigger, bolder, more noticeable. The characters, I realized, would have to be more easily identifiable. Thus Cordelia's green dress and cape became blue – blue to link her with the King of France for the benefit of audiences not knowing the play as well as those in Moyse Hall. The properties as well as the setting had to be enlarged. There were many more drawings to be made of them, all bold and easily identifiable. Gone my Shakespearean scheme for the permanent or static setting, in its place a sprawling panorama of Stonehenge arch and monolith, walls and stairs, flanked by huge poles bearing shields and weapons to serve as proscenium frames and to conceal great floodlights.

Almost all of it permanent – mind you, for only one night permanent – except that I contrived one wall to swing out to provide the shelter on the heath. I was proud that, in the swinging out, there came a rope with a noose, anticipating Lear's "And my poor fool is hang'd" in the last scene. We closed that shelter scene, our Fool alone on stage, making his last appearance of the play, singing "With a heigh-ho, the wind and the rain."

Ivor Francis was again a brilliant Fool and Adelaide Smith again a Cordelia of character. Colicos was a Lear to the life, full of great grandeur and deep pathos. This was most apparent in the one dress rehearsal, for bad weather threatened the actual performance, as the storm must always threaten its Lear. Recruited happily from the 1946 production were Fran Malis as Goneril, Ken Culley as staunch Kent, Myron Galloway as Oswald, Robert Goodier, again Albany, and Alfred Gallagher, a most fragile Gloucester. The rest were recruited, some from the French acting colony, to play roles such as the King of France and Burgundy, with local militia to fill out the wide stage in the battle scenes, which were somewhat chaotic.

Subtleties of the text were blown away in the high wind that tossed our players about during that memorable night. I left Pierre to handle his own lighting cues because I couldn't trust my inferior French to give the stage crew of les Festivals the right instructions. Pierre shared producing responsibilities with Charles this time, communicating with the production departments – scenic, properties, and costuming. It was very much a les Festivals production for the visiting Shakespeare Society. We were part of a larger picture – a one-performance part – with Pierre Dagenais as our most recognizable name, along with the other star attractions of Wilfrid Pelletier and le Théâtre du Nouveau Monde.

Having been away for almost four years, I understood that Montreal was a very different city from what I had thought it to be while growing up there. The floodlights provided by les Festivals de Montréal showed a great old British tragedy against the night sky, in vivid illumination with its bright characters moving larger than life. But below that Mount Royal lookout thus transformed lay a city very different indeed from Toronto. It was a French city, and we were up there as its proud guests. For one night only.

AFTERWORD: A CONTEXTUAL COMMENTARY

Jonathan Rittenhouse

PROLOGUE: A STAGE SET

On 12 August 1953, at the Chalet Terrace on the top of Montreal's Mount Royal, William Shakespeare's *King Lear* was performed for one night only. The production was an extravaganza, sponsored by the summer festival organization les Festivals de Montréal.[1] Our author, Herbert Whittaker, had returned from Toronto to be part of this *Lear.* He held the position of theatre critic for the *Globe and Mail*, a post he had taken up when he left Montreal and a similar job at the *Gazette* in March 1949. Whittaker, who for twenty years had designed and/or directed close to eighty productions, designed the mammoth set and colorful costumes for *King Lear*. He worked alongside two of his closest Montreal friends – Pierre Dagenais and Charles Rittenhouse – with whom he had collaborated on theatrical productions throughout the 1930s and 1940s. Dagenais directed and Rittenhouse, my father, was both producer and the evil Duke of Cornwall in the play. Playing King Lear was a young Montreal actor, John Colicos, whom Whittaker had directed in a 1948 high school production of André Obey's *Noah*, and who had just returned to Montreal having successfully played the same role in London at the Old Vic.

Such a moment and event deserves preserving and, as you have read, in this book's Epilogue Whittaker recounts his eyewitness sense of the extraordinary production. There he notes the ambition and scale of the undertaking and the very personal nature of the production. For Whittaker it was a homecoming with his closest Montreal colleagues, as well as, he suggests, a symbolic last hurrah for English-language theatre in Montreal, whose cultural presence in this increasingly French-speaking metropolis had become less and less influential. Whittaker's recollection of the event reveals a fascinating historical imprint in Montreal's evolving culture.

The production represented local English-speaking culture at les Festivals de Montréal and, in the year of the experimental opening of the Shakespeare Festival at Stratford, Ontario, it was not surprising that Shakespeare was chosen as the torchbearer of English culture. In both instances the canonically unchallengeable Shakespeare provided credibility for local theatrical producers. That the production was a hybrid of professional and amateur efforts (a paid technical crew, full-time entertainment professionals like Dagenais and Colicos collaborating with local amateurs or occasional professionals like Whittaker and my father) was also not unusual as mid-century Canada's indigenous culture evolved from amateur or isolated professional activities to pervasive and institutionally supported professional activities.[2] The 1953 *King Lear* is interesting evidence of an intermediate, pupae-like, cultural production – not entirely caterpillar or butterfly, not entirely British or Canadian and/or Québécois, not entirely amateur or professional.

Perhaps even more important to the narrative of *Setting the Stage*, which provides such a detailed picture of the cultural importance that English-language theatre once had in Montreal, is that of the four primary figures of this *King Lear*, only Pierre Dagenais continued to flourish professionally in Montreal, primarily through his work as producer, director, writer, and performer for the French-language Radio-Canada. John Colicos' subsequent professional career kept him in Toronto, London, New York, and Hollywood, and Whittaker was never again involved in Montreal theatrical production. My father effectively "retired" from such visible theatrical/cultural activities and, while he stayed in Montreal, devoted his skills to the somewhat less complicated territory of English-language education and high school drama.

The ephemeral nature of this one-night only *King Lear* – a small part of a summer festival whose orientation was towards French-speaking Montrealers and an indiction of the isolated or simple lack of cultural opportunities for Montreal's English-speaking artists in that most social of the arts, the theatre – has great significance for me personally. Though less than a year old on the night and so without any personal recollections of this theatrical moment (or any other detail mentioned in Whittaker's book), I have, to some degree, been shaped by the socio-cultural forces that "produced" that play on Mount Royal. I am an ex-Montrealer, though my anglo-exodus has been to another region of Quebec, the Eastern Townships. I became a theatre historian of events Shakespearean and/or Canadian, and I was able to continue to function professionally, as my father did, as an English-speaking educator in a French-speaking province. To function culturally in Quebec, as an artist *en anglais*, has in my lifetime (the post *King Lear* era, if you will) been a confusing, contradictory, and problematic experience. This reality reflects the difficulties encountered when cultural paradigms shift. On the other hand, during this same period and in the exact same geographic space, French-speaking or French-influenced cultural forms have freed themselves from many socio-cultural restraints and Quebec artists have affirmed themselves in diverse ways, to Quebec's and Canada's increased cultural well-being.

In a complicated and contradictory fashion, then, there is for me (and perhaps for other readers of this book) a nostalgic way to read about an era either never directly experienced or no longer with us. On such readings one Herbert Whittaker could be unselfconsciously "at home" in English and in Quebec, in a cosmopolitan city where being an active artist was what one did. We no longer live at *that* time or in *that* city and a one-night-only production of *King Lear* on Mount Royal to celebrate the new millennium would, no doubt, mean very little to Montreal and its present-day inhabitants. However, the extraordinarily simple and evocative closing words of that great tragedy of western culture, "Speak what we feel, not what we ought to say," provide a compelling accompaniment to Whittaker's story of so many artists – known and unknown, amateur and professional, local, transplanted, passing through and passing on – who "spoke" by involving themselves on the stage and giving voice to those thoughts and emotions that often remain unsaid.

CHARACTER DEVELOPMENT: HERBERT WILLIAM WHITTAKER

Herbert Whittaker has been, and still is, an avid promoter, critic, and practitioner of theatre. His writings about, involvement in, and promotion of things theatrical and cultural in this country have led to many honorary awards (including an Order of Canada), distinctions, and memberships in this country's prestigious cultural institutions. For his long-standing tenure as theatre critic of the *Globe and Mail* (1949–75) and in particular his championing of our home-grown theatrical cultures, he is respected and fondly referred to as "Herbie." In the Preface to *Whittaker's Theatre*, a collection of theatre reviews and essays culled from his long career at the *Gazette* and the *Globe and Mail*, Ron Bryden captured Whittaker's stylistic reluctance to write a simple theatre review – good/bad, thumbs up/thumbs down.[3] Bryden argued, as I have done elsewhere,[4] that Whittaker's lifelong involvement in the theatre as director and designer prevented him from reductively panning or praising the work he saw, leading him instead to offer "appraisal by description." Of course, such an analysis of Whittaker's theatrical career doesn't mean that he avoided judgments or that he did not have any opinions about what he liked or didn't. Herbie has had very firm opinions about everything he ever saw (during his eighty plus years and counting), yet his writing was not opinionated in the sense that his critical opinions pushed description of the work into the background.

More recently, in their essay on Whittaker for *Establishing Our Boundaries: English-Canadian Theatre Criticism*, Jennifer Harvie and Ric Knowles fine-tuned and reconsidered the positive description of Whittaker the critic. There they interestingly suggest that Whittaker's skills at description were shaped by his critical coming of age during the war years and that his critical style, much like a war reporter or sportscaster, mixed "the apparent objectivity of the news reporter with advocacy." Through rhetorical analysis of his writings they point out many metaphors and images of martial and missionary zeal in which Whittaker, like many of his generation, linked the "true" creation of a nation to the constant battle to develop a national culture and theatre. They also compellingly argue that such cultural discourse and perspective on Canadian nationalism were thoroughly inflected with the non-objective tones of imperialism, whose values were seen as neutral, objective, and universal.[5]

I agree with Harvie and Knowles that Whittaker was, and is, guilty of the exclusionary rhetoric of cultural nationalism, a rhetoric that borrows heavily from the verbal storehouse of imperialism. However, such rhetoric and advocacy of "what's good for us" was, I would argue, a necessary and inevitable prolegomena to the 1949–51 Massey-Lévesque Report of the Royal Commission on National Development in the Arts, Letters and Sciences, the primary document of Canadian cultural nationalism.[6] This text, like Whittaker's critical prose, was *both* a conservative and liberal blueprint for the deliberate creation of state-encouraged and supported culture that is in fundamental opposition to the free trade, free-market philosophy of American culture, where control of distribution and exhibition always determines what gets produced. However problematic his language or agenda, Whittaker spoke clearly for cosmopolitan values and boundary-breaking ideals in a hoped-for future of Canadian theatre and culture. And, particularly given his coming of age in Montreal during the roaring, depressed, and wartorn years, his words should not be defined only as *parti pris* boosterism for "what's good for us" but seen as necessary and useful clarions for a saner, less prejudiced, and more open cultural environment – like the world he discusses at length in this book.

Whittaker's book takes us back to the beginnings of his voluminous curriculum vitae, back to his formative years in his hometown of Montreal where he learned to appreciate, create, and write about theatre. He was a first generation Canadian of English parents whose family came to Canada's then largest metropolis – Montreal – before the First World War. From there he developed his passion for theatre around the globe; from there he began his lifetime of writing about the theatre and designing and directing productions. His vision of theatre was and still is remarkably heterogeneous, open to both European and American innovations and developments as well as nurturing of Canada's cultural formation. In this memoir of Montreal theatre Whittaker traces his own theatrical journey – his own evolution – through the contemporaneous development of Montreal's theatre cultures: its imported product, its indigenous amateur fare, and its tentative steps towards professionalism.

In an era when the print media meant everything for popular entertainment and knowledge, when film and theatre were still the most pervasive products of our culture, Whittaker thoroughly immersed himself in those worlds as he grew up in Montreal. Though his immersion took place in a city whose language in the street, in the home, and in the church was primarily French and whose culture off-island was overwhelmingly Catholic, French-speaking, and rural, Whittaker's world was English-speaking, urban, and spiritually and culturally eclectic. Influenced both by the high ideals of European art theatre and the popular products of the American and British entertainment industry, Whittaker, like many of his generation, struggled to define and attain some sort of Canadian identity. His book speaks of the cosmopolitan possibilities for his Montreal, of respect for the creative development of French-language culture in his home province and its successful pursuit of national identity. It also laments the loss of the vibrant cultural activity that was English-language theatre in Montreal and hints at the difficulties it has had in redefining or reanimating its creative voice.

Setting the Stage speaks of a world no longer with us and refers to local names and institutions few people remember.[7] Taken as a whole, however, Whittaker's fond and specific memories of evanescent moments help us more fully sense Canada and Quebec's mid-century years of transition and crisis. Few of his generation exposed themselves so thoroughly to all media and cultures – newspapers, radio, theatre, live entertainment, film, ballet, and opera. Few of his generation were so willing to support the full breadth of cultural activity while also recognizing the importance and significance of evolving local professionalism. Few of his generation took as much advantage of *all* that Montreal had to offer. In some respects then, Whittaker's book, while providing a wealth of specific anecdotes and personal moments is, in the most positive sense, a larger testament to one of his home territory's most famous mottos, "*Je me souviens.*"

MONTREAL AND ITS CULTURES (1920–1950)[8]

Simple or popular versions of Quebec's social history evoke a static, rural, Catholic, and conservative world that was merely marking time until the Quiet Revolution of the 1960s. In reality, outside pressures from the Americanization of global capital and culture in the 1920s; the pervasive Depression of the 1930s; and the Second World War, immigration, and massive reconstruction of the 1940s irreversibly affected Quebec's and, particularly, Montreal's economic and social evolution. Such forces and pressures also speeded up Quebec's cultural development. While comprehensive state intervention came into being in Canada only during the Second World War and significant state attention to the arts only became operational only in the late 1950s and 1960s, the early markers for such fundamental changes can clearly be seen in the alterations in Montreal's socio-cultural landscape between and within the war years.

THE TWENTIES: PROTESTANTS, PARTIES, AND POPULAR THEATRE

In the 1920s Montreal was still the financial capital of Canada. It was economically dominated by local English-speaking business leaders – Canadian-born, recent expatriates from Great Britain or branch-plant Americans. The Montreal Stock Exchange was the second most important on the continent, and the Canadian head offices of financial, industrial, insurance, energy, and transportation sector companies were still in Montreal. Only a select few had positions on the Exchange and most of the same people served on the boards of these companies.[9] Making money with money was, increasingly, the major occupation of the very powerful, wealthy, and primarily anglo-Protestant elite of Montreal, whether it was the "old" money of the Allans, Drummonds, and Ogilvies or the newer money of Sir Herbert Holt, J.W. McConnell, I.W. Killam, and the Websters.[10] The largest cheques in the country were still cashed on St James Street, Canada's Wall Street of the era, and the Sun Life Assurance Company, its Montreal head office the largest office building in the British Empire, had assets of $400 million by the end of the decade.[11] The downtown core was completely dominated by the homes, businesses, schools, hospitals, and clubs that this small but powerful group built, financed, and patronized. This same group also partied hard in the twenties, though unlike the sin-city activities in lavish or seedy public places that Montreal positively encouraged in the forties and fifties, the extraordinary round of 1920s balls, parties, sporting trips, and innumerable club events took place in the private spaces of people's homes, clubs, or estates. For such people Montreal was a playground of privilege.[12]

While during this decade the movers and shakers of the Canadian economy were local players who also created a local culture of leisure, the purveyors and suppliers of high culture effectively ensured that art, music, and theatre in Montreal primarily came from elsewhere. In the arena of popular culture, as Whittaker notes in this book's opening chapters, the influence of local theatre owners in determining audience taste through programming decisions based only on financial considerations restricted what English-speaking Montrealers saw in their major live entertainment space, His Majesty's Theatre.[13] Opened in November 1898 and built by a local chartered company, the West End Theatre Company, on the east side of Guy Street (the western edge of downtown) just above Montreal's major commercial artery, St Catherine Street, Her Majesty's lasted until the 1960s. The theatre was typical of "opera house" construction at the turn of the century with orchestra, box seats, and two galleries providing close to two thousand seats.[14]

Almost all entertainment construction during the twenties, however, was for the cinemas that offered the increasingly popular silent films from Hollywood. In the 1920s Montreal had almost 100 single-screen venues to choose from. These public pleasure palaces were the immense and ornately decorated downtown cinemas (the Loews, Capitol, and Palace) or the somewhat more functional neighbourhood cinemas.[15] Even these latter were occasionally "atmospheric" in design, as suggested by their names – Rivoli, Granada, Seville – attesting to interior motifs suggestive of Italian gardens or Spanish courtyards. These cinemas eschewed elaborate and expensive ceiling domes and ornamentation for decoration that evoked an outdoor setting in an indoor space. Their trademark effect – a simply painted blue ceiling upon which lighting effects denoted dusk, twilight, and starry night in an auditorium appointed in clever *trompe-l'œil* style – could be found in many cinemas around town.[16]

One of the most famous events in Montreal's history occurred in a neighbourhood cinema, the Laurier, when seventy-eight children under sixteen perished in a horrific fire in January 1927. Officially Quebec public amusement regulations absolutely forbade unaccompanied children in cinemas, yet fire marshal regulations had been easily evaded for years. This unfortunate incident encapsulates the deep contradictions and paradoxes of Quebec society, where conservative and Catholic ideology enunciated a strict moral code, which was routinely and casually ignored in the anonymously urban and secular space of popular entertainment, influenced by the laissez-faire economics of the Canadian political system that imposed few regulatory restraints on American branch-plant industries.

Throughout the 1920s the Liberal government of Louis-Alexandre Taschereau ruled Quebec in this traditional hands-off fashion. New business interests, usually American, were allowed to flourish with few constraints. The government was equally conventional in its wariness of federal legislation or initiatives that threatened provincial autonomy in such areas as health care, social welfare, or education. Any attempts by the Quebec government to take the initiative in such areas, for example the child adoption policy it finally put into place in 1924, inevitably met a wall of conservative opposition.[17] In the area of health care there was painfully slow progress against the scourge of tuberculosis – Montreal's rate of disease was three times higher than Toronto's.[18] Pro-union legislation was non-existent; instead, union development in the province was advanced by the Catholic Church. The Church encouraged Catholic-only unions to "protect" workers from the radical and/or progressive thinking of secular unions that had led to strikes across Canada at the end of the First World War.[19]

In the area of suffrage, the Quebec government again demonstrated its deeply conservative perspective. Though the federal government had granted women the vote during the First World War, the Quebec government never allowed any suffrage bill past first reading in its Legislative Assembly. Such recalcitrance was indefensible but indicative of the fundamental paradoxes in Quebec society, where women comprised more than 20 per cent of the total workforce, greater than any other province in the country.[20]

The greatest proportion of that female workforce was in Montreal. From 1911 to 1931 Montreal's population more than tripled – from 225,000 to 818,000. The great wave of immigration before the First World War, some natural increase, and the depopulation of rural Quebec for Montreal all contributed to this great increase. Home to almost 30 per cent of the total Quebec population in the 1920s, over 60 per cent of the city's population was French-speaking. The Jewish and Italian communities of the province increased in numbers and were almost exclusively located in Montreal. The British/Irish presence in the province also became increasingly localized in the Montreal area.[21]

During this decade of laissez-faire politics, free trade economics, and cosy closed elites, the city was undergoing massive demographic change and alteration. Theatre in Montreal reflected these contradictions in its complicated two-language search to survive in the commercial world of popular entertainment or the amateur and elite appeals to the serious mission of the stage. While at the beginning of the decade French-speaking audiences could still partake of stock companies performing at le Family, le Saint-Denis, le Monument-National, le Chanteclerc, le National, and le Théâtre Canadien-français, Parisian imported fare diminished throughout the 1920s to the point where local, amateur, and indigenous productions eventually became the bulwark against the Americanization and anglicizing of popular culture. Most of what got produced in French was traditional theatre of the nineteenth century – popular and conservative – with almost no reference to the European art theatre of the early twentieth century.

Julien Daoust, founder of le Théâtre National in 1900 and an important pioneer in local French-language theatre production,[22] continued his involvement locally by directing shows (*Le mariage forcé,* November 1922) and writing plays (*Geneviève de Brabant,* March 1925). Henry Deyglun's first play, *Bonne Maman,* is produced at le Théâtre Arcade (April 1925) as he began his life-long career in Quebec theatre. Stock company stars of the decade who would continue to perform through the 1940s (when Whittaker eventually caught up with them as a reviewer) included Bella Ouellette, Jeanne Demons, Fred Barry, and Albert Duquesne. Performances of popular, localized, satirical revues by Olivier

Guimond père, for example his *Tizoune* (May 1925) and *La ruelle tranquille* (April 1926) at le National, established one of the strands of Quebec culture – topical and self-referential entertainment – that continued to evolve successfully through the development of local television in the 1950s.[23] Another popular success of the decade was in the commercial genre of melodrama – the locally written and produced *Aurore, l'enfant martyre* which dramatized the murder of a ten-year old girl by her father. Debuting at le Théâtre Alcazar in January 1921, the play was a continuous theatrical fixture in various Montreal venues for over thirty years.[24]

Influential amateur troupes like les Compagnons de la Petite scène, le Cercle dramatique de l'Université de Montréal, and le Cercle Lafontaine developed by performing French classics or influential local works like Louis Fréchette's nineteenth-century *Papineau* (April 1924) that appealed to nationalist aspirations. Certainly the dominant intellectual figure of the era was l'abbé Lionel Groulx, holder of the chair in Canadian History at l'Université de Montréal from the First World War on. He was instrumental in promoting the gospel of Quebec nationalism through his support for l'Association catholique de la jeunesse canadienne-française (established 1903–4) and the publication of such nationalist organs as *L'Action française* (1917) and *L'Action nationale* (1933). His work helped foster the idea in elite cultural circles that the development of local, catholic, and distinct art was vital given the hegemonic forces of both the British Empire and American capitalism.[25] By the end of the decade the influence of Quebec's Catholic Church on theatrical culture, as Montreal theatres came to rely less and less on imports from France, became more marked. Perhaps the most significant example of this trend was Léopold Houlé's *Le presbytère en fleurs*, a conservative religious play that became famous worldwide after its local debut at le Monument-National in May 1929.[26]

In English-speaking Montreal tentative attempts after the First World War to establish a community- or urban-based theatre that would cut across traditional church-based or highly localized amateur groups led to the formation of the Community Players, who produced such works as John Galsworthy's *The Pigeon* in November 1920. The group never set any significant roots in the community and disappeared by mid-decade, while Montreal's older established amateurs – Trinity Players, YMHA Little Theatre, the Dickens Fellowship – survived through clear community links and direction from the few theatre people with professional experience. Whittaker's book provides some details about William Tremayne and Rupert Caplan, for example, both of whom had experience in American professional theatre and worked with many amateur groups in the city.[27] As Whittaker notes in chapter 2, Tremayne's career in Montreal had its ups and downs. He directed for the Trinity Players, the Weredale Dramatic Group, and the Little Theatre Players and his own plays, *The Black Feather* (April 1924) and *A Romance in Bohemia* (January 1927), were staged by the Trinity Players.

The domination of the major theatre spaces – His Majesty's and the Princess – by the touring stars that Whittaker recalls so vividly in chapter 1 – Sir John Martin-Harvey, George Arliss, Robert Mantell, Walter Hampden, and others – uncontroversially assured a kind of passive acceptance among English-speaking Montrealers that things theatrical and cultural emanated from elsewhere. The 1920s equivalent of *Les Misérables* or *The Phantom of the Opera*, a touring production of the all-but-forgotten *Chu Chin Chow*, a musical tale of the East by Frederic Norton and Oscar Asche, started the decade at His Majesty's with record-breaking engagements (edging out the Bernhardt record at that theatre).[28] Theatrical imports would occupy the live entertainment spaces for the rest of the decade.

Popular stock companies with touring visitors, locals, or visiting artists who stayed were relatively successful at the Orpheum. Such companies provided traditional Fall and Spring repertory of light theatrical fare. As Whittaker notes, one such stock company star, Mildred Mitchell, ended up staying to become a fixture in Montreal's theatre world as actor, director, and producer. She appeared in local stock at the Orpheum as far back as 1927. This playhouse, like most other local entertainment spaces, often altered its programming or linguistic orientation. In September 1923, for example, it hosted a stock company from Paris, then returned to English-language shows. In December 1924 it even brought in such a touring war horse as *Uncle Tom's Cabin*, the perpetually performed adaptation of Harriet Beecher Stowe's pre-Civil War novel about slavery. At the end of the decade it even flirted with showing the faddish new arts phenomenon, the talking picture.

THE THIRTIES: DEPRESSED AND DEVOTED TO THEATRE

The Thirties, as an era of depression and radical political movements, was heralded, of course, by the famous stock market crashes of October 1929. In Montreal it was also a bellwether year for significant movements and alterations in the city's entertainment landscape, changes that marked the entire decade.

The crash affected everyone in Montreal. A number of wealthy Montrealers were wiped out in the stock free fall and a definite chill came over the party-time atmosphere of the anglo-elite. More significantly, perhaps, the powerful Montreal Stock Exchange reformed itself in order to prevent the improper speculation that occurred before the crash. The unfortunate and unlooked-for result was that by 1933, the depth of the Depression, the Toronto Stock Exchange had become the most active market in Canada – a position that it has never relinquished. Further, the branch-plant structure of Canada's economy was thoroughly solidified during the decade. American capital established its Canadian centres in Toronto and Southern Ontario at a more than 5 to 1 ratio in relation to the waning financial centre of Montreal. The slow pace of economic power-shifting in the first three decades of the century was galvanised into fast-forward by the consequences of the crash and Montreal's economic and political significance in the Dominion waned apace.[29]

If Montreal had needed more bad economic news, it got it in 1933 when the United States finally repealed Prohibition. The Quebec Liquor Commission, which had had revenues of $20 million just before the crash, saw its revenues plummet to $5 million.[30] With decreased revenues, risk capital going elsewhere, and fewer dollars circulating in an ever-enlarging metropolis, Montreal suffered severely during the Depression, with some neighborhoods reaching 40 percent unemployment rates. Those who did find work increasingly joined unions, either affiliates of American unions or the rapidly growing Catholic unions, which more than doubled their membership during the decade.[31] Amidst economic turmoil and an increase in radical intellectual and political rhetoric (to both the right and the left) which had been much more muted or close to non-existent in the previous decade, the state moved strongly to its rural, Catholic, and conservative roots. The l'Union nationale party under Maurice Duplessis formed the Quebec government for the first time in 1936. Incorporating much of the rural and xenophobic strands in Lionel Groulx's ideological positioning, made concrete in the pages of the "purist" publications of *L'Action nationale* and *Le Devoir*, one of Duplessis first significant state interventions was the passing of the anti-communist law in 1937 – the so-called Padlock Law. This law provided the state's police force with extraordinary rights of entry and the authority to "padlock" subversive organizations or institutions. (The law was not declared unconstitutional by the Supreme Court of Canada until the 1950s.)[32]

The movement in Quebec society was not, however, swinging completely to the right – even the deeply conservative Catholic Church had given encouragement to unionism in the 1920s and 1930s and to a non-corporatist, social gospel. "Freer" thinkers within the Church, like frère Marie-Victorin, the scientific founder of Montreal's Botanical Gardens, found some freedom to question the hierarchy's infallibility. In many cultural spheres members of the clergy, such as the theatre director père Émile Legault, became influential leaders. The unquestioned control over publication in Quebec by the Church, and its simple invoking of Rome's *Index* to prevent unwanted French-language texts from being published or read, began to unravel in the 1930s with the independent publication of, for example, Claude-Henri Grignon's not-so-pretty picture of rural Quebec, *Un homme et son péché*, in 1933.[33]

Perhaps as a result of there being so little money about – one was not going to get rich doing much of anything in Montreal – the 1930s was a very active era for local artistic talent. This hive of "free" activity with its occasional language and class-crossings makes the previous staid, controlled, and cultural-importing previous decade seem backward-looking indeed. Such activities also provide a glimpse of Montreal's still innocent urban world that stood out in stark contrast to the totalitarian terrors that had gripped so many of the world's other major cities.

A noteworthy event just one month after the famous crash brought together the cultural elite of Montreal, still dominated by anglophones, who gathered at Victoria Hall, Westmount, on the evening of 23 November. The event showed that English-speaking Montreal moving westward from its earlier enclave downtown (often referred to as the Square Mile) to its next residential district of significance, Westmount. *The Gazette* predicted that the evening's meeting would be an "epochal event" and that it would constitute "the first serious effort to establish on a substantial basis a Little Theatre in the city of Montreal."[34]

As Whittaker describes in chapter 4, Sir Barry Jackson, knighted in 1925 for his decade-long efforts to establish and maintain a permanent repertory company outside the commercial West End theatre district of London in the industrial Midlands city of Birmingham, spoke passionately in favour of the little theatre movement. Among the influential locals who listened were the Honorable Athanase and Madame David, General Sir Arthur and Lady Currie, Lord and Lady Atholstan, Sir Montagu and Lady Allan, and Mr Justice E. Fabre Surveyor. Canada's most famous stage actress, Margaret Anglin, who happened to be in town performing in Oscar Wilde's *Lady Windermere's Fan*, also spoke in support of local theatre. Sir Duncan Campbell Scott described the Ottawa Drama League, its little theatre successes and suggested how it could prove a model for Montreal. S. Morgan-Powell, dean of theatre critics for the *Montreal Daily Star*, put forward the resolution to form a little theatre in Montreal, particularly noting "the demoralization of the legitimate stage by moving pictures and particularly by 'talkies.'" Martha Allan, who had co-ordinated the evening's logistics and as a result of the event would herself establish and maintain the Montreal Repertory Theatre (MRT), also spoke.[35] Significantly the purchase of His Majesty's, the city's main stage house, by a motion-picture exhibition chain, Consolidated Theatres, and the transformation of the traditional stock company theatre the Orpheum into the Popular Talkie Playhouse the very week after the November meeting further galvanized Montreal's cultural elite into supporting Martha Allan's initiative.

Unlike its chequered and unsuccessful predecessor, the Community Players, by mid-decade the MRT had established a traditional subscription series of plays, an experimental studio wing, a French section of the MRT, a school for theatre training, an extensive library collection of theatre books and memorabilia, and an organization magazine, *Cue,* that kept subscribers up-to-date with all kinds of theatrical information.[36] The centre of all this activity, Martha Allan, turned the MRT into a reasonably eclectic cultural institution. As a privileged daughter of the fabulously wealthy she did not shy away from using her many connections with Montreal's English and French elite to demonstrate "society" support for the venture. She was, however, even more passionate about demanding the highest artistic standards for all MRT activities and encouraging other local amateur groups to achieve the same levels of artistic consistency. Moreover the MRT was much more open than other significant anglo-controlled institutions of the city that were still firmly closed to French Canadians, Jews, and others.

A case in point was the unfortunate polarisation along linguistic lines in the development of Montreal's symphony orchestra. The Montreal Symphony Orchestra had disbanded as a result of the Crash, which had seriously affected patronage for the arts. Further, the coming of the talking pictures eliminated the need for musical accompaniment to silent movies and left Montreal musicians with few employment opportunities. In 1930 a number of these musicians asked the head of the McGill Faculty of Music, Douglas Clarke, to establish a new orchestra. The resulting Montreal Orchestra survived until the early years of the Second World War but was completely oriented toward the English-speaking community in terms of programming, audiences, and choice of musicians. Major cultural leaders of Montreal, the Hon. Athanase and Mme David, repeatedly asked for a greater place for competent French-speaking soloists and offered government subsidies to the orchestra to encourage such artists. Because this did not occur, in 1934 la Société des concerts symphoniques de Montréal was formed so that Montreal had two orchestras (whose composition was very similar) with two distinct audiences. Wilfrid Pelletier eventually took over la Société in 1936 and held the baton through the 1941 demise of the Montreal Orchestra.[37]

A far more positive force for cultural development, the MRT reinvigorated older performing groups and encouraged an amateur theatrical climate that helped to increase public interest. With strong support from Martha Allan, Governor General Bessborough inaugurated the Dominion Drama Festival in late 1932, for implementation in 1933. This Festival brought together the best local theatre groups in the country and so provided them with encouragement.[38] What the MRT unfortunately failed to achieve in the 1930s, despite attempts by Allan to rally local wealth and political support, was the purchase of an existing theatre or the construction of a new one. As a result the MRT remained an itinerant institution, fully "at home" in Montreal but always homeless. It was, perhaps, a victim of in-fighting amongst the anglo-elite as well as indifference or hostility from church and state to the creation of a Comédie-Française type of institution, given that le Monument-National and His Majesty's already existed and the United States (through Canadian subsidiaries) dominated most of the entertainment spaces in town.[39]

By the beginning of the Depression almost a third of Montreal's homes had radio receivers and numbers steadily increased throughout the decade. The Americans had been transmitting programs northward for many years and, as Montrealers purchased more and more receivers, there was much official concern, from both French and English-speaking communities, that yet another popular medium would exist only in its American form. Unlike the federal government's inaction with respect to the movie industry, where American companies and subsidiaries had, in effect, monopolistic control of production, distribution, and exhibition, the federal government intervened and established a national broadcasting network. A radio commission was set up in 1932 and then the Canadian Broadcasting Corporation was formally created in 1936, thus ensuring that French and English voices, perspectives, and artistic achievements would be heard.[40] Private and local Montreal stations, particularly CKAC (French) and CFCF (English), along with the local affiliates of the national network, provided many opportunities for local artists and their creative activities. By the end of the decade writers, actors, performers, and producers could eke out a living through Montreal radio as daily serials and weekly shows became a staple of Quebec culture.[41]

At the same time that the amateur but well-organized MRT was created in 1930, Fred Barry and Albert Duquesne made one more major attempt to start a traditional and professional repertory troupe by turning the old le Chanteclerc into le Théâtre Stella. They began production with *La lettre,* a French adaptation of a Somerset Maugham play. But surviving professionally in legitimate theatre was still next to impossible in the depressed 1930s. Even though in its last season, 1934–35, innovative attempts were made to save it, including the hiring of local favorite Antoinette Giroux to manage the theatre and the successful mounting of local playwright Yvette Mercier-Gouin's *Cocktail* in April 1935, the theatre closed in 1935.[42]

French-language professional entertainment continued throughout this period. Local comedy-burlesque, revues, and melodrama played on as the Guimonds, now *père et fils*, la Poune (Rose Ouellette), Arthur and Juliette Pétrie, and many others entertained Montreal and the province. La Poune solidified her reputation as entertainer par excellence by taking over le Théâtre National in 1936 and running it successfully for years. In addition the long-lasting *The Mousetrap*-style success of the popular melodrama *Aurore, l'enfant martyre* through to the 1940s, indicated the strength of locally inflected popular fare. Mercier-Gouin wrote a number of plays during the decade, continuing in the tradition of Julien Daoust and Henry Deyglun though her works were more focused on the local morés of upper-class Montreal. Her first work, *Ma-Man Sybille,* was presented by the MRT in May 1933. Such fostering of French-language artists by the MRT was a common occurrence during the decade, a dominant trait of the Allan-led institution.[43]

The major "break-out" artist of Quebec's popular entertainment world, Gratien Gélinas, became a successful star by the end of the 1930s through his skilful transmutation of the traditional Quebec genre of revue into his annual *Fridolinades.* Starting in 1937 on CKAC with *Le carrousel de la gaieté* and the introduction of his character Fridolin, Gélinas transformed his radio show for presentation at le Monument-National in Spring 1938.[44] Also in 1937 the creation of the first performing arts union in Quebec, l'Union des artistes, further proved that the French-language and French-language artists, even in the depressed 1930s with American popular culture dominant everywhere, could and must survive in order for Quebec society, particularly its French-language component in Montreal, to emancipate itself from social, political, or economic barriers.[45]

The Catholic Church had played an influential role between the wars in encouraging Catholic-based unions and an active increase in their membership to extend the Church's visibility in the metropolis. Similarly the Catholic Church also encouraged some of its members to advance the Church's cause in the socio-cultural sphere.[46] There were two celebrated practitioners of this theocentric and nationalist-inflected theatre. Gustave Lamarche, with his spiritually inspired plays and religious pageants, was influenced by the works of Paul Claudel and Henri Ghéon. His first of thirty-five works, *Jonathas,* was performed at le Collège Bourget in May 1933 and *La défaite de l'enfer* (1938), perhaps his most ambitious work, was performed on the mountain in Rigaud before ten thousand spectators. As well, père Émile Legault created his particular brand of classical art theatre and in 1937, following on Henri Ghéon and his Paris-based Compagnons de Notre-Dame – "Pour la foi, par l'art dramatique. Pour l'art dramatique, en esprit de foi" – established his Compagnons de Saint-Laurent. This famous troupe of amateurs and future professionals (Guy Maufette, Thérèse Cadorette, Georges Groulx, Jean-Louis Roux, Jean Gascon, among others), committed to an ensemble and a unified sense of art theatre, set high standards for themselves and their audiences.[47]

In chapter 9 Whittaker touches on much of this French-language activity. The bulk of his story, however, describes the burgeoning little theatre movement in English-speaking Montreal, providing first-hand accounts of its various participants and the local significance of its many efforts. The creation of the Dominion Drama Festival in 1933 was an important spur for locals, especially since touring theatre from elsewhere had declined.

The older Trinity Players, Weredale Dramatic Club, and the Dickens Fellowship eventually found themselves part of a growing list of local groups

committed to theatre production and led by the flagship MRT. The Sun Life
Players, a social-business club of Montreal's major insurance company, the
community-based St Lambert Players, and Westmount Dramatic Club, for
example, produced such lighthearted theatre as the latter's April 1933 version of
the American comedy of a famous stage family, *The Royal Family*. All also did
more experimental works as well. Even the Sun Life Players, for example,
performed Maurice Maeterlinck's mood piece *Interior* in the 1937 DDF Regionals. The old YMHA Little Theatre became revitalised and produced serious plays
by the likes of George Bernard Shaw (a November 1936 *Arms and the Man*)
and, along with the more radical New Theatre Group, were ready to perform
the controversial plays of Clifford Odets. In one of the major theatre venues in
Montreal, Victoria Hall in Westmount, the New Theatre Group put on *Waiting
for Lefty* (May 1936) and *Awake and Sing* (April 1938).[48] More art theatre orientation was provided by annual productions from 1933 to 1940 by the Everyman Players at the Church of the Messiah. This group was led by the influential
Montreal musician George M. Brewer. He and the Players' much-appreciated
work are discussed at length by Whittaker in chapter 2. In that same chapter
Whittaker describes the efforts of the ambitious youth group affiliated with the
Everyman Players, the Sixteen-Thirty Club, led by my father Charles Rittenhouse, and Whittaker himself.

All of these groups performed regularly during the 1930s, borrowing eclec-
tically from the repertoire of modern and contemporary theatre from Europe,
Great Britain, and the United States and occasionally venturing into the performance of the work of local writers. At one time or another all organized
their performance schedule to be able to produce a play for the Regionals of
the DDF in the hope, of course, that some famous theatre professional function-
ing as adjudicator would recognise good work or talent and encourage those
involved to consider (or dream) of a professional career.

THE FORTIES: MOBILIZING THE TROOPS/TROUPES

At the end of the thirties, when the world was on the brink of war, paradoxical and contradictory Montreal reached a zenith of sorts when in May 1939 the King and Queen came to town. As William Weintraub details at length in the opening chapter of his book *City Unique*, hundreds of thousands cheered their arrival by train at Windsor Station. The old bedrock of Montreal wealth and influence and innumerable citizens lined the streets for the monarchs' motorcade through the many neighborhoods of the city. Children assembled to cheer the royal couple in the two largest stadiums in town, Delormier for the French-speaking and Molson for the English-speaking. The King and Queen eventually dined in the halls of the Square Mile sector with the likes of Sir Herbert Holt, almost as wealthy as they were, yet were officially greeted by the populist mayor *par excellence*, Camilien Houde, and honoured by Montreal's famous distilling family, the Bronfmans, with their new Seagram's product, Crown Royal.[50]

The festive, adulatory, and positive atmosphere that ruled during that May visit ironically ended a long and financially debilitating decade for Montreal and, equally ironic, inaugurated the next half dozen years of total war. For the whole of the 1940s Montreal lurched itself out of its economic doldrums "thanks" to the war and the massive relocation of peoples into Quebec after that war. These new immigrants made Montreal even more open and cosmopolitan than before. With this extraordinary influx of new peoples, Montreal would have more than one million inhabitants by the end of the decade.

As a province, Quebec asserted its rights over federal legislation and actions on the issue of conscription and when Mackenzie King's federal government put the issue to a national referendum Quebecers, alone, firmly voted no. Montreal, however, effectively oriented almost its entire economy to war and the war effort (the establishment of aircraft and armament factories, for example) so that the city had the largest number of war-related contracts in the country.[50] As the most important and protected seaport in the country, Montreal also teemed with wartime activity. This occasionally led to skirmishes between conscripts and anti-conscription Montrealers, as in the zoot suit riots of 1944 where the latter wore tailored suits so obviously beyond wartime restrictions that they enraged visiting servicemen.[51]

With money finally flowing more freely in Montreal, labour tensions rose even higher in the 1940s, as even the Catholic unions, relatively quiet and corporatist during the previous twenty-year period, participated in increasingly militant strikes. Some church leaders, such as Mgr Charbonneau, encouraged and/or articulated messages of social reform even greater than those in the 1930s. After the fall of France the Church's *Index* was all but ignored and independent publications flourished. In Montreal, those involved in the publication of *Cité libre* advocated a more independent sense of political thinking and writing, while the Catholic l'Université Laval and l'Université de Montréal established, finally, faculties that were no longer controlled by theologians and oriented their research and students more and more to the social sciences.[52] In the political arena, the radical Bloc populaire garnered well more than 10 percent of the popular vote in both provincial and federal elections.

Most fundamentally, in the early 1940s both levels of government (both Liberal) put into place legislation for government intervention that was both a delayed response to the many social welfare ills revealed during the Depression and a proactive response to national needs in times of war. The federal government implemented the War Measures Act, granting it temporary but significant control over areas that Quebec had always regarded as being within their jurisdiction. Having already established the CBC in 1936, the federal government went into another cultural-communications territory by starting up the National Film Board in 1939, setting up its headquarters in bilingual Montreal. They eventually put into place the underpinnings of the federal welfare state in

1944 by passing the family allowance plan, preparing for a comprehensive unemployment insurance plan, old-age pensions, and massive funding for the country's universities.[53]

With Duplessis and his party briefly out of power, the provincial Liberals implemented equally interventionist policies on issues of fundamental importance. These included the long-delayed granting of the vote to Quebec women in 1940, a series of legislative actions granting workers greater opportunities to form or join unions, a compulsory education act for all children aged 6–14 in 1943, and the nationalization of hydro-electric power in 1944 with the creation of Hydro-Québec.[54] This action radically diminished private influence in a utility sector long-controlled by Montreal's English-speaking elite. The seemingly inevitable shift of financial action to Toronto was accelerated when another traditional arena of English-speaking domination in Montreal, the insurance industry, moved over twenty of its head offices to Toronto, including the massive Prudential of America.[55]

Although Maurice Duplessis returned to provincial power in 1944 and stayed in control until the Quiet Revolution election of Jean Lesage's Liberals in 1960, the post-war years in Montreal were not solely redolent of stultifying conservatism either from the Catholic or nationalist right or the Board of Directors' cronyism of the English-speaking elite. In fact, Montreal became a wide-open city attracting all kinds of gangsters and depending on the sin-industries for much of its economic activity. It also was internationally influenced as a result of the war effort and the vast wave of immigration, making post-war Montreal a creative city with many and various energies.

While Montreal could not boast a popular culture industry like the extraordinarily successful Hollywood movies of the 1940s, the National Film Board began its innovative work in documentaries, short films, and experimental techniques in Montreal. The city was, perhaps, the only one in the world with a vibrant radio culture in two languages, each offering its practicing artists opportunities for professional work. Montreal was also the site for the most significant experiment in professional sport in the decade and probably this century. In 1946 the city's minor league baseball team, the Royals, had as its starting second baseman Jackie Robinson, the first African-American integrated from the Negro baseball leagues into the previously all-white world of major league baseball. And the other long-established professional team sport, ice hockey, saw a Montreal Canadien, Maurice "Rocket" Richard, establish one of the great milestone marks of his sport in the 1944–45 season – fifty goals in fifty games.

While a listing of events has the whiff of civic boosterism, such popular and exciting activities reflected a city which had gained a reputation for public fun and mayhem for out-of-towners "on the town" and Montrealers became much better paid than ever before. Their activities were being recorded by journalists such as Herbert Whittaker as print and radio journalists in both languages competed with each other in providing colorful copy for their daily, weekly, or magazine-style papers or broadcasts.

Popular and "street" culture boomed. Illegal gambling sites proliferated throughout Montreal, either locally or as "branch plants" controlled from outside. Brothels, always present, were now more blatantly integrated into Montreal's social system than ever before. And after-hours blind pigs (bars providing illegal liquor) were a definite staple of Montreal's desire to out-New York New York. The downtown territory, the area along St Lawrence Boulevard often called "the Main," and the black Montreal area by St Antoine Street offered varying kinds of entertainment. Huge dancehalls like the Bellevue Casino and Chez Maurice's Danceland flourished. More than a dozen New York-style nightclubs like the El Morocco, Chez Paree, and Faisan Doré booked all types of comic and singing acts. Louis Metcalf's International Band played at Café St Michel on St Antoine Street. Innumerable lounges opened and closed.[56]

Paralleling the Rocket's fiery career for *nos glorieux* was the most famous stripper of the era, Lili St Cyr, a semi-permanent fixture in Montreal, plying her trade at the Gayety and glamorizing the many late-night spots in town with her presence. Her significance in Montreal grew so large that it led to condemnation in the pages of *Le Devoir,* a subsequent trial on morality charges, acquittal, and the permanent exit of the stripper in 1951.[57]

The 1940s also saw the significant representation of Montreal's local social landscapes in serious literature, whose impact went far beyond the bookshops of Montreal to reach a critically appreciative and North American audience. Gabrielle Roy's *Bonheur d'occasion* portrayed lower-class life in Saint-Henri and lower Westmount. Hugh MacLennan's *Two Solitudes* depicted English-speaking and French-speaking Montreal in their conflicts and possible reconciliation. Both novels fictionalized the real circumstances of life in Montreal but exposed the reality that Montreal's public high life and private wealth masked the city's continuing and systemic poverty. Montreal's paradoxes – the city's increasingly cosmopolitan and open spirit that co-existed with the continuing wariness, distrust, and occasional ententes of its traditional linguistic communities, were given fictive "truth."

While the theatrical staple of Montreal theatre – imported shows– obviously diminished during the war years and only returned in the second half of the decade, there was some American fare. Most striking, however, was the successful evolution of high-level amateur activity into early experiments with locally produced professional ventures. That a formalized state-supported granting system for the professionalization of arts was necessary in Canada was not officially affirmed until the Massey-Lévesque Report of the Royal Commission on National Development in the Arts, Letters and Sciences in the following decade. The Commission was established, however, in April 1949, in the charged atmosphere of high hopes and dreams with limited means and opportunities. The forces behind its establishment can certainly be seen and felt in 1940s Montreal.

In English-speaking Montreal the impact of the war on the amateur theatre was significant. The Dominion Drama Festival ceased operation from 1940 to 1946 and smaller amateur groups ceased to function. A new initiative like the Lakeshore Summer Theatre (1940–41), which Whittaker discusses in chapter 6, showed that theatre-minded people of that era leaned towards more commercial, for-profit ventures. Much like ordinary citizens becoming soldiers for awhile during wartime, so such theatre people and activities experienced a certain level of professionalism.

In groups that continued the scale of production, much like Montreal's, Quebec's, and Canada's wartime economy, became bigger. Full-length plays regularly replaced the one-act plays that had been the staples of the little theatre movement for the past two decades. Larger casts were "mobilized" for greater effect. Some details about three productions from the first half of 1942, all of which Whittaker was involved in, help make this point.

In February 1942 Victoria Hall saw the Westmount Women's Club production of the Kaufman and Ferber *Stage Door*. This was an amateur activity but the chosen vehicle was a popular full-length Broadway comedy and the cast involved at least twenty-five local amateurs performing for two nights (not just one) in one of the major theatre venues in town. In March 1942 the amateur Negro Theatre Guild produced another full-length large-cast play at Victoria Hall. Marc Connelly's *The Green Pastures* was very successful in its three-day run and, as a wartime benefit for the Milk for Britain Fund, the show transferred to the most important professional theatre venue in town, His Majesty's, for another three-day stint. Moreover Daisy Pickham, a professional costumer from New York, was brought in to design for the show and worked with Whittaker. Finally in April 1942 an original full-length play by local playwright Janet McPhee (co-written with Whittaker) was also staged at Victoria Hall. McPhee had written one-act plays for the now-defunct Sixteen-Thirty Club (*Divinity in Montreal,* 1939, and *Bus to Nowhere,* 1940). The new play, *Jupiter in Retreat,* was produced by the mainstream MRT and was a popular melodrama.

Coincidentally, this last production was delayed by what may have been the most important event for Montreal's English-speaking theatre community: age forty-seven Martha Allan died and left a void in leadership at the MRT and in Montreal's cultural communities. But the MRT did not collapse. Instead it managed to find, finally, a permanent home on Guy Street and solidify a more middle-class subscription base. It provided opportunities for up-and-coming artists to apprentice as pre-professionals before moving on to more fertile professional pastures as well as offering older theatre people, who were working in the new media or in complementary professions with challenging and creative work. Both aims were achieved in efforts such as MRT's collaboration with the Shakespeare Society of Montreal on an ambitious project of major full-scale productions of Shakespeare at McGill's Moyse Hall from 1945–47. Whittaker discusses these shows in chapter 5.

One aspect of MRT's evolution to a middle-class supporter base was that it began to orient itself more exclusively to its English-speaking clientele. By the time of Allan's death the MRT no longer officially supported French-language productions, though it still provided artistic opportunities for French-speaking artists (Pierre Dagenais, for example) who wished to function *en anglais* at the MRT as actors or directors.

As Whittaker discusses in chapter 8, touring shows and stars made some important stops in Montreal during the 1940s. Paul Robeson performed his famous *Othello* (September 1944), Maurice Schwartz' Yiddish Art Theatre from New York appeared (May 1945), Donald Wolfit toured his Shakespearean repertory in January 1947, the same month John Gielgud brought the Wilde classic *The Importance of Being Earnest* to His Majesty's. However, the lack of a modern and available theatre building in Montreal for just such entertainment made legitimate stage programming a haphazard affair. For Whittaker, now the first-string theatre critic for the English-language daily *The Gazette*, such an obstacle for the further development of professional theatre in Montreal (at least in English) was frustrating, indeed. So much so that when an offer came in March 1949 from the Toronto *Globe and Mail*, he felt obliged to accept.

On the French side of the ledger, however, local theatrical culture, of many stripes and kinds, flourished during the decade, laying even firmer foundations for the indigenous professional theatre to follow. Les Compagnons de Saint-Laurent under père Legault went from success to success in serious dramatic fare. In March 1942 they collaborated with the touring star from Paris, Ludmilla Pitöeff, in one of her favorites, Paul Claudel's *L'échange*. Later that year, in October, they used medieval scholar Gustave Cohen's expertise in their production of *Le jeu d'Adam et Eve* and *Le jeu de Robin et Marion*. They performed the classics: Racine (April 1940), Beaumarchais (April 1944), and Molière (November 1946). In 1948 they secured a more permanent home and inaugurated it with a French-language adaptation of Tennessee Williams's *The Glass Menagerie*. The company eventually metamorphosed into professional status at the end of the decade and in 1951 the still dominant Montreal institution le Théâtre du Nouveau Monde was created by les Compagnons stars Jean-Louis Roux and Jean Gascon.

Gratien Gélinas' *Fridolinades* revues were increasingly professional through the war years. He then went off to work with a major American star in a strictly for-profit production, an adaptation of a Miklos Laszlo story into a Quebec setting by Broadway actor and director Eddie Dowling. In *St. Lazare's Pharmacy* Gélinas starred opposite Miriam Hopkins (Hollywood and Broadway actress) in a less than successful show. He concluded the decade, however, with the incredible triumph of his own play *Tit-Coq* and its English-language version *Ti-Coq*. The play debuted at le Monument-National in May 1948, ran more than two hundred performances at la Salle de Gesù, was published in French by

Beauchemin in 1950, translated into English and performed in Montreal the same year. It eventually went to Toronto to great acclaim and onto Broadway where it had its least successful run.[58] While the play was a somewhat melo-dramatic tragedy of *le p'tit gars*, the bastard who loses his girl in the end, the play and production acted as a cathartic triumph for French-speaking Quebec. "[Dans *Tit-Coq*] le public voit son pareil, son frère, son ami, dans une halluci-nante transcription; et comme ce petit gars de chez nous, né dans l'absurde, cherche de toutes ses forces d'âme à dompter le destin, et qu'il accède au grand tragique sans cesser d'être marqué fortement de tous les signes de sa race, on comprend pourquoi l'auditeur est pris aux entrailles."[59] The play and produc-tion then were yet another powerful sign for French-speaking Quebec that it could create works of art and passion that led to better understanding of itself.

Also continuing their successful careers were la Poune with her comedy-burlesques at le National and Henry Deyglun with his annual revues, almost a match for Gélinas at le Monument-National. Mercier-Gouin continued to write her social plays about Montreal for le Théâtre Arcade (*Le plus bel amour,* April 1941, and *Sous le masque,* April 1944). Other popular-oriented theatre companies like la Comédie de Montréal (1941–43) and le Jeune Colombier (1941–44) flourished briefly with the aid of exiles from France. Another strand of theatrical activity, the Orson Welles-like intensity, genius, and radical secu-larism of Pierre Dagenais and his work for his theatre company l'Équipe, pro-vided one more example of theatre style and variable professional opportunities for Quebec artists. Although his venture, conceived in 1942, foundered on financial insolvency in 1948, it demonstrated both that the arts community was still not providing support systems for its artists and, a more positive indicator, that local artists were aiming high and dreaming big. Dagenais produced a full-scale production of Pagnol's *Marius* for le Monument-National in May 1944 and an open-air *Songe d'une nuit d'été* in the gardens of l'Ermitage in August 1945. His own *Le temps de vivre,* produced at le Monument-National in February 1948 just a few months before the opening there of *Tit-Coq*, was unsuccessful and led to his disbanding l'Équipe. That Dagenais himself would, in the end, survive by the professional opportunities then readily available in radio (as actor, writer, or producer) and later television demonstrated the strides that indigenous Quebec culture had made through the crises of the Depression and the war.

However, many local English-speaking artists around town concluded by the end of the decade that while Montreal might provide a fertile territory for apprenticeship, they could best flourish elsewhere – among them Oscar Peterson, Christopher Plummer, Mavis Gallant, and Herbert Whittaker. Radical artists like Paul-Émile Borduas ended the decade with the manifesto *Refus global*, decrying the many stultifying and institutional constraints imbedded in Quebec's conservative and Church-dominated society. That Quebec culture, in its various French-speaking or French-influenced forms, was able to break through so many of those limits in the next fifty years confirms the aptness of Whittaker's final chapter heading "*Le rideau se lève.*" Perhaps a memoir like Whittaker's, that so resoundingly speaks of a generous and cosmopolitan sense of identity in a world long past, can provide food for thought for the cultural *future* for his "*terre de nos aïeux.*"

CHRONOLOGY OF MONTREAL THEATRE
1920–1949

The chronology that follows includes highlights of Montreal's theatrical activity as well as entries providing useful references to individuals or acting troupes that made a long-term or important contribution to Montreal's theatre life from 1920–49. Entries referred to in *Setting the Stage* are followed by an asterisk (★) and a page reference. The entries in this chronology have been culled from a much more extensive chronology of theatre events prepared by Rebecca Harries, aided by a student research assistant, Lisa Gaskell.

1920
JANUARY–FEBRUARY
- The touring show, Frederic Norton and Oscar Asche's *Chu Chin Chow,* at His Majesty's for a two-week engagement, grosses $58,000 and bests Sarah Bernhardt's box office record.

APRIL
- Pierre Barbier's *Le martyre d'une femme* opens at the stock company house le Family. Its star, Mme Jeanne Demons, will become a long-time Montreal-based actress.
- The stock company Orpheum Players, which plays for fifty consecutive weeks under the management of Harold Hevis, present their typical weekly fare. During April it includes Louis Anspacher's comedy *Our Children*, the anonymous *Mam'zelle* with "vaudeville and souvenirs," and Hal Reid's *The Confession* (aka *To Serve the Cross*).
- *Seventeen* by Booth Tarkington, based on his extraordinarily successful novel, is presented by the touring New York Company at His Majesty's.

OCTOBER
- Jeanne Demons' troupe, constituted from local talent, debuts, again at le Family.

NOVEMBER

- H. V. Esmond and Eva Moore, with their touring English company, present Esmond's *The Law Divine* at His Majesty's.
- Le Théâtre Canadien-français shows a staple of its regular fare, *Tu n'dis pas*, a revue by Pierre Christ.
- The amateur little theatre group The Community Players present *The Pigeon* by John Galsworthy at the New Empire Theatre.
- La Troupe Castel shows two one-acts (a Sunday matinee tradition) at le National – *Le baiser* by T. de Banville and *Le cart-circuit* by B. Rabier and F. Jouillet.
- *Adele*, the third operetta of the season, opens at the Orpheum.
- Eugène Brieux's *Maternité* opens at le Théâtre Canadien-français – for adults only.
- La Troupe Bella Ouellette, led by another long-time performer in Montreal, shows Meilhac and Halevy's *Frou-Frou* at le Family.
- The endlessly touring World War I entertainment group the Canadian Dumbells makes one of their many visits to Montreal during the 1920s. This time they bring the second edition of *Biff! Bing!! Bang!!!*

DECEMBER

- The Community Players offer an unusual bill of fare: George Calderon's *The Little Stone House*, J.G. Hoare's *Squirrels,* and Lord Dunsany's *The Glittering Gate.* (Hoare would later be involved as producing director for the Montreal Repertory Theatre.)
- Olivier Guimond *père* opens one of his first locally oriented francophone revues.

1921

JANUARY

- Sir John Martin Harvey presents *David Garrick* by Tom Robertson (adapted by Charles Wyndham) and *The Burgomaster of Stilemonde* by Maurice Maeterlinck.
- *Aurore, l'enfant martyre* debuts at Montreal's le Théâtre Alcazar, presented by the Petitjean-Rollin-Nohcor troupe. This melodrama was based on the murder of a

ten-year-old girl by her father. An outstanding success on stage for thirty years, film and novel versions followed.

APRIL

- Sir John Martin Harvey and Company present John Rutherford's *The Breed of the Treshams* and Wills and Langbridge's *The Only Way*, an adaptation of Dickens's *A Tale of Two Cities*.
- The Community Players conclude their initial season with Stanley Houghton's *Hindle Wakes* and *It's a Farce* by Merton S. Threlfall.

NOVEMBER

- La Troupe Jeanne Demons stages Sardou's *La Tosca* at le Chanteclerc.
- La Troupe Bella Ouellette offers *La vièrge des bouges* at le Family.
- Fred Barry and Albert Duquesne are featured in Bella Ouellette's troupe's production of *Les trois mousquetaires.* These two actors will become major figures in Montreal's acting community.
- A gala performance of *Le mirage* at le Théâtre Canadien-français with the honourable Athanase David in attendance. He and his wife were prominent members of Montreal's French-speaking elite and were present at and supportive of almost all culturally significant events during this period.
- The Petitjean-Rollin-Nochor company take their smash hit *Aurore, l'enfant martyre* to le Laurier.

1922

MARCH

- The New Empire Theatre hosts an experiment with the modern. Led by Henri Letondal and Antoinette Giroux, two mainstays of Montreal theatre in the coming decades, a company styling itself le Petit Théâtre produces Charles Vidrac's *Le paquebot Tenacity.*

- Robert Mantell and Genevieve Hamper bring their touring company to His Majesty's. They perform such Shakespearean classics as *Julius Caesar, Hamlet, Macbeth*, and *The Merchant of Venice.*
- Another perennially touring company, led by E.A. Sothern and Julia Marlowe, present more Shakespeare: *Twelfth Night, The Taming of the Shrew, Hamlet*, and *The Merchant of Venice.*

APRIL

- The Orpheum's traditional spring repertory of stock company fare includes Rinehart and Hopwood's *Seven Days,* George Broadhurst's *Bought and Paid For,* Anne Flexner's *Mrs. Wiggs of the Cabbage Patch*, and *White Sister* by Crawford and Hackett.
- Anna Pavlova and the Ballet Russe arrive at le Saint-Denis.
- Somerset Maugham's *The Circle* opens at His Majesty's with John Drew and Mrs Leslie Carter.
- The Community Players present three one acts at the New Empire Theatre: Lady Gregory's *Spreading the News*, Duncan Campbell Scott's *Pierre* (a French-Canadian play), Emma Gendron's *Na Maunah* (an Indian play).

SEPTEMBER

- Le National is reopened by Louis Bourdon with the new name of le Théâtre des Nouveautés and a house troupe of French actors: they are a great success although their lead actor, Gaston Séverin, returns to Paris in December.

OCTOBER

- J.-Albert Gauvin brings Maurice de Feraudy's troupe to le Saint-Denis. Performances include Molière's *L'avare* and *Le médecin malgré lui*, and *Les affaires sont les affaires* by Octave Mirabeau.
- The perenially touring San Carlo Opera Company brings traditional opera to His Majesty's. They will continue to make an appearance in Montreal through the 1930s.

NOVEMBER

· Stars of la Comédie-Française, including Mlle Cécile Sorel and M. Albert Lambert, bring a wide range of plays to le Saint-Denis. Repertoire includes *Le demi-monde* by Dumas fils, Molière's *Le misanthrope* and *Le tartuffe*, Shakespeare's *The Taming of the Shrew*, and a mixed grill called *Victor Hugo Night*.

· D'Ennery and Edmond's *Le mariage forcé* opens at le Théâtre Alcazar; Julien Daoust, the original founder of le Théâtre National in 1900, directs.

· A Benefit for W.A. Tremayne (following a serious automobile accident) is organized at Stanley Hall: Calderon's *The Little Stone House* and Alice Gerstenberg's *The Potboiler* are produced by members of the Community Players, Trinity Players, St Lambert Players, and the Weredale Dramatic Group. Tremayne had been a professional writer for the Broadway stage and directed on a freelance basis for amateur groups in Montreal, principally for the Trinity Players.

· J.E. Robichaud engages a French troupe for le Théâtre Parisien. Their well-received debut is *Amour, quand tu nous tiens*.

DECEMBER

· Famous touring star Walter Hampden and company are at His Majesty's. Their repertoire includes Shakespeare – *Othello* and *Macbeth*, *The Servant in the House* by Charles Rann Kennedy, and Philip Massinger's *A New Way to Pay Old Debts*.

1923

JANUARY

· Le Théâtre Parisien and le Théâtre des Nouveautés both announce their closing.

· William Archer's *The Green Goddess* with George Arliss opens. (*16)

FEBRUARY

· Le Théâtre des Nouveautés closes its doors but reopens as le National.

· The Quebec government gives its first grant for the study of professional acting to Antoinette Giroux, who goes to Paris for that purpose.

APRIL

- The Community Players present A.A. Milne's *The Truth about Blayds* and Shaw's *Androcles and the Lion*.
- La Troupe Bella Ouellette presents *La dame aux camélias* by Dumas fils at le Family; Jeanne Demons is a part of that troupe.

MAY

- The Trinity Players show Arnold Bennet and Edward Knoblock's *Mike Stares* at Victoria Hall in Westmount, directed by W.A. Tremayne.

AUGUST

- La Troupe Bella Ouellette has a season at le Chanteclerc.
- L'Association Saint-Jean-Baptiste encourages the production of local theatre at le Monument-National under the traditional banner of les Soirées de Famille. Small groups like les Compagnons de la Petite scène, le Théâtre Intime, le Cercle Michel Scott, and le Cercle académique Lafontaine perform over seventy-five times during the 1923–24 season.

SEPTEMBER

- A Parisian troupe led by André Calmettes appears at the Orpheum. Their debut performance is *Terre inhumaine* by François Curel. Other plays include *La huitième femme de Barbe-bleue* by Alfred Savoir and Paul Armont's *L'école de cocottes*.

OCTOBER

- Les Compagnons de la Petite scène produce Charles Vidrac's *Michel Auclair*.

NOVEMBER

- The New York Theatre Guild Co under the direction of Joseph Gates, with Basil Sydney, presents *He Who Gets Slapped* by Andreyev, Shaw's *The Devil's Disciple*, and Ibsen's *Peer Gynt* at His Majesty's.

DECEMBER

· Louis-Napoléon Sénécal's short playlet *La messe de minuit* is produced as part of the extraordinarily successful les Veillées du Bon Vieux Temps at le Monument-National. Producer and performer Conrad Gauthier is responsible for these evenings of variety entertainment which continue to be put on into the 1940s.

1924

JANUARY

· Sir John Martin-Harvey presents *Hamlet* at His Majesty's Theatre. Martin-Harvey's tour also includes Sophocles' *Oedipus Rex*, *A Cigarmaker's Romance*, and Francis Crawford's *Via Crucis*. (★11–13)

APRIL

· Le Cercle académique Lafontaine, an amateur group in the tradition of *les cercles,* presents Louis Fréchette's famous nineteenth century play *Papineau*; Guilbault Lefebvre directs at l'École de Réforme.
· The Henry Duffy Players present *The Cat and the Canary* by John Willard at the Orpheum as the theatre reopens in gala-style as English-language stock theatre.
· The local duo of Barry/Duquesne directs *L'amour pardonne* at le Chanteclerc.
· The Trinity Players present *The Black Feather* by W.A. Tremayne.

JUNE

· The famous Yiddish Lithuanian touring troupe the Vilna play New York and then le Saint-Denis.

SEPTEMBER

· The Yiddish Players establish a long-standing presence at le Monument-National (until 1937) with their seasons of yiddish and modern works. The troupe is led by Hannah and Isidore Hollander and Menasha and Sara Skulnick.

DECEMBER

- An adaptation of Harriet Beecher Stowe's *Uncle Tom's Cabin* appears at the Orpheum; "Tom" stock companies had been performing this play for seventy years.

1925

MARCH

- Julien Daoust's *Geneviève de Brabant* opens at le Chanteclerc.

APRIL

- Friml and Hammerstein's comic opera *Rose-Marie* comes to His Majesty's.
- Henry Deyglun's first play, *Bonne Maman*, is successfully produced at le Théâtre Arcade. Deyglun, like Daoust, was a playwright who had a long career in Montreal theatre.
- Les Compagnons de la Petite scène stage Racine's *Les plaideurs*.
- Le Cercle dramatique de l'Université de Montréal presents Labiche's *Les petits oiseaux* at le Monument-National, the troupe's debut performance.

APRIL–MAY

- The original New York Theatre Guild production of Shaw's *St Joan* comes to His Majesty's.

MAY

- *Tizoune*, with Olivier Guimond in the title role of this new revue, begins at le National with a new troupe of forty persons.
- La Salle du Gesù is used as a theatre for the first time in a long while when les Anciens du Gesù perform Racine's *Athalie*.

NOVEMBER–DECEMBER

- Le Théâtre Canadien-français opens with Victorien Sardou's *Les vieux garçons*.

1926

APRIL

· Julien Daoust and Germain Beaulieu's *La Passion* opens at le Chanteclerc.
· The revue *La ruelle tranquille* with Pizzi-wizzi and Macaroni opens at le National.
· For one night only, the YMHA Players presents Clemence Dane's *A Bill of Divorcement* at His Majesty's.
· Friml and Hammerstein's *Rose-Marie* comes to the Princess. (★17)

MAY

· Sir John Martin-Harvey is back at His Majesty's: *Richard III*, *David Garrick*, Dion Boucicault's *The Corsican Brothers* and *The Only Way*. (★13)
· Winthrop Ames produces John Galsworthy's *Old English* starring George Arliss at the Princess. (★16).

NOVEMBER

· The long-running amateur group the Weredale Dramatic Club stages Roi Cooper Megrue's *It Pays to Advertise* under the direction of W.A. Tremayne.

DECEMBER

· Michael Arlen's *The Green Hat* shows at the Princess, starring Katharine Cornell.

1927

JANUARY

· W.A. Tremayne's *A Romance in Bohemia* is presented at Trinity Hall.

APRIL

· Third week of Lasalle's *La Passion* at le Saint-Denis, M. J.P. Filion stars as Jesus.
· La Société canadienne de comédie presents a program comprised solely of Canadian works, including *Un jeune homme nerveux* by Henri Letondal and other sketches, at le Monument-National. They performed there for three seasons, producing five shows a year.

- The new director at le Chanteclerc, Arthur M. Pétrie, changes the program from melodrama to burlesque. Pétrie and his wife, Juliette, would become fixtures of Montreal's entertainment scene.
- Sigmund Romberg's *The Student Prince* comes to the Princess. (★17)

MAY
- Ibsen's *Ghosts* at His Majesty's starring Mrs. Fiske. (★16).
- The YMHA Players bring their production of S. Ansky's *The Dybbuk* to His Majesty's.

MAY–JUNE
- The best Montreal actors make a Quebec-wide tour, led by Fred Barry.
- The French company of Sacha Guitry and Yvonne Printemps tours Quebec.
- Le Cercle académique Lafontaine presents Guinon and Bouchinet's *Son père*.

NOVEMBER
- Avery Hopwood's *Why Men Leave Home* is at the Orpheum starring stock company regulars Mildred Mitchell and Victor Sutherland. Mitchell stays in Montreal after she eventually leaves the stock company and occasionally performs and directs for the next twenty years. She becomes producing director for the Montreal Repertory Theatre in the 1940s.
- The Little Theatre, a short-lived successor of The Community Players, debuts with Sir Henry Arthur Jones' play *Mrs. Dane's Defense*. W.A. Tremayne directs.

DECEMBER
- The McGill Players stage three one-act plays at Moyse Hall: Stanley Houghton's *The Dear Departed*, *Trifles* by Susan Glaspell, and George Kelly's *Finders Keepers*.
- The YMHA Players again present S. Ansky's *The Dybbuk* at His Majesty's.

1928
JANUARY
- Another New Year opening of Sir John Martin-Harvey at His Majesty's with Rafael Sabatini's *Scaramouche* and Charles Reade's *The Lyons Mail*. (★13)

FEBRUARY
- After four weeks in New York, Sir Harry Lauder brings his popular show to His Majesty's. (★19)

APRIL
- The spring season for the Orpheum stock company includes Fred Jackson's *A Full House*, *Alona of the South Seas* by Hymer and Clemens, and *Murray Hill* by soon-to-be-famous actor Leslie Howard.
- Winthrop Ames presents Shakespeare's *The Merchant of Venice* with George Arliss at The Princess. (★15).

MAY
- Ferenc Molnar's *The Play's the Thing* is presented by Gilbert Miller at the Princess, starring Holbrook Blinn.

OCTOBER
- Shakespeare's *Julius Caesar* and *The Merchant of Venice* are presented by the Memorial Theatre Company with Kenneth Wickstead, Wilfred Walter, and Eric Maxon. (★15)
- La Troupe Barry-Duquesne shows Birabeau's *L'ombre du passé* at le Chanteclerc.

NOVEMBER
- Le Théâtre de la Porte Saint-Martin offers G. Ohnet Georges' *Le maître de forges* and *La marche nuptiale* by Henry Bataille at His Majesty's. This Parisian touring company performs often in Montreal.
- *Paris Bound* by Philip Barry stars Madge Kennedy at the Princess.
- La Société canadienne de comédie shows Scribe and Legouvé's *Bataille de dames* at le Monument-National.
- The new season of the Little Theatre Players begins with Edward Massey's *Plots and Playwrights*, directed by W.A. Tremayne at Victoria Hall. Upcoming season fare announced includes *The Limpet* by Woodhouse and MacClure, Sutton Vane's *Outward Bound*, and George Kelly's *The Show-off*.

- Le Théâtre de la Porte Saint-Martin troupe is at the Princess: Rostand's *Cyrano*, *l'Aiglon*, and *Chanteclerc*, Corneille's *Le Cid*, and Georges' *Le maître de forges*.

1929

JANUARY

- The American Opera Company is at the Princess. Directed by Vladimir Rosing; music direction by Frank St. Leger; *Faust* designed by Robert Edmond Jones. Productions include Puccini's *Madame Butterfly*, Bizet's *Carmen*, Mozart's *The Marriage of Figaro*, *I Pagliacci* by Leoncavallo, and Gounod's *Faust*. (★19–20)
- Impersonator Bransby Williams does his version of Dickens's *Oliver Twist* at His Majesty's.

APRIL

- At McGill, a night of Canadian theatre and music arranged by Martha Allan. By year's end she will become the leading figure in Montreal's English-language theatre.
- Le National shows Guimond's *La belle-mère à Tizoune*.
- Majority control of the Princess Theatre is now in hands of Consolidated Theatres Corporation, a major cinema chain in Montreal and the province. This adds to the company's control of the other theatre houses in town that cater to an English-speaking clientele – His Majesty's, the Orpheum, and the Gayety.
- Bransby Williams and company bring his adaptation of Robert Louis Stevenson's *Treasure Island* to His Majesty's.
- Jacob Ben-Ami brings his Yiddish troupe to le Monument-National. They perform Dostoyevsy's *The Idiot* and Ibsen's *A Doll House*.
- The all-talking, singing film *The Broadway Melody* opens at the major downtown cinema, the Palace. (★49)
- The Little Theatre Players produce George Kelly's *The Show-off* at Victoria Hall. Martha Allan directs.

MAY

· Léopold Houlé's *Le presbytère en fleurs* opens at le Monument-National, its conservative and religious sentiments reflect the influence of the Catholic Church on Quebec culture at this time. The play will become one of the most famous written by a French Canadian.

· *That Year of Grace,* a Noel Coward revue starring Canadian-born Beatrice Lillie, ends its two-year tour at His Majesty's. (★17)

NOVEMBER

· The Barry-Duquesne troupe stage R. deFlers and G.A. de Caillanet's *Primrose* at le Saint-Denis.

· Montreal Repetory Theatre is formally announced, originally as the Montreal Theatre Guild. (★60).

· The Orpheum Players at His Majesty's showcase Margaret Anglin, Canada's most famous theatre actress, in Wilde's *Lady Windermere's Fan.*

· The Orpheum becomes a movie house – "The Popular Talkie Playhouse."

1930

MARCH

· The Montreal Repertory Theatre's first production is A.A. Milne's *The Perfect Alibi* at Moyse Hall. (★60)

APRIL

· Noel Coward's *Bitter Sweet* is presented by the Calvary Players with Florence Ziegfield and Arch Selwyn at His Majesty's.

· The Yiddish dramatic society of the YMHA presents two plays in Yiddish: Samuel Daixel's *Whom the God's Love* and *A Bit Off* by Jane Rose.

MAY

· Molly Picon, star of the Yiddish stage in New York, appears in *The Little Clown* by Kalich and Rumshinsky at le Monument-National.

AUGUST

· Fred Barry and Albert Duquesne, having assumed ownership of le Chantecler earlier in the year and renamed it le Théâtre Stella, present their first production, *La lettre* by Somerset Maugham.

OCTOBER

· *Candida* by George Bernard Shaw is presented by the MRT as the first production of their first full season. Martha Allan directs and stars, a double task she will assume a number of times over the next decade. Co-director is Rupert Caplan, a mainstay of the local YMHA Players, and Cecil West is designer. West will become a fixture at the MRT, in particular overseeing its experimental Studio Theatre. (★60)
· Mary Travers, who became famous as la Bolduc and a singer of popular Quebec songs, debuts at le Monument-National in Conrad Gauthier's Veillées du Bon Vieux Temps.

NOVEMBER

· The McGill Players present A.A. Milne's *Ivory Door*; Cecil West directs.
· The Dickens Fellowship, an experienced amateur troupe, presents an adaptation of *Barnaby Rudge*, directed by Edwyn Wayte. Wayte directed for many troupes in Montreal through the 1940s.

DECEMBER

· *The Constant Wife* by Somerset Maugham is presented by the MRT, using the same key people as *Candida* did in October. (★60)
· Le Cercle dramatique des anciens du Collège de Montréal forms, led by André Montpetit.

1931

JANUARY

· Rupert Caplan directs Kapek's *R.U.R.* for the MRT. Through the 1940s Caplan will be an influential figure in radio broadcasting in Montreal. (★60)

FEBRUARY
- *La souriante Mme Baudet* by Denys Amiel and André Obey is presented by the MRT in French at Victoria Hall. Martha Allan stars and directs. (★60)

MARCH
- *The Roof* by John Galsworthy is presented by the MRT. (★60)

APRIL
- *Le Rosaire* by André Bisson is produced at le Théâtre Stella.
- The New Orpheum Players, yet another stock company, present Alfred Kempe's *East Lynne* and *What Could the Poor Girl Do?*.
- New managers are announced for the Orpheum and the Princess respectively.

MAY
- Inaugural gala performance of the Canadian Opera Company at one of Montreal's largest downtown cinemas, the Loew's: *Romeo and Juliet* is the chosen opera, supervised by Wilfrid Pelletier.
- Head of the Yiddish Art Theater Maurice Schwartz makes his first of many appearances in Montreal at le Monument-National.

NOVEMBER
- *The Mask and the Face* by Luigi Chiarelli presented by the MRT. (★61)

DECEMBER
- A joint production of the MRT and the Ottawa Drama League. Ottawa does A.A. Milne's *The Truth About Blayds* and MRT C. B. Fernald's *The Cat and the Cherub*. (★61)

1932
JANUARY
- Will Berkett praises the MRT's production of Elmer Rice's *The Adding Machine* in *Canadian Forum*. He adds, however, that "the expressionist technique of the play and treatment so confused or disgusted the conservative fraternity that the company beat

a hasty retreat, and were to be found soon afterwards safely enshrined in davenports and dinner jackets."

APRIL

· Sir Barry Jackson and The Company of British Players presents J.M. Barrie's *Quality Street*, Goldsmith's *She Stoops to Conquer* and *The Barretts of Wimpole Street* by Rudolph Besier. (★42)

· Noted Yiddish actor from New York Maurice Schwartz is at le Monument-National: *Hard to be a Jew* by Sholom Aleichim, Leonid Andreyev's *The Seven Who Were Hanged*, and *God, Man and Devil* by Jacob Gordin.

MAY

· Sir John Martin-Harvey's last visit to Montreal. He offers Leopold Lewis' *The Bells*, a favourite production of Sir Henry Irving, and Frederick Jackson's *The King's Messenger*. (★14)

· The MRT acquires its headquarters on Union Street, including the studio space, an abandoned indoor golf course.

· A touring production of Sheridan's *The School for Scandal* features Ethel Barrymore at His Majesty's. (★17)

· MRT workshop productions of six one-act plays are put on at Moyse Hall. Henri Letondal's *L'erreur* is one of them.

NOVEMBER

· *Mon bébé* by Maurice Hennequin opens at le Théâtre Stella.

· The New York Theatre Guild-sponsored *Mourning Becomes Electra* by Eugene O'Neill opens at His Majesty's.

DECEMBER

· Co-produced with the Ottawa Drama League, *Hamlet* is presented by the MRT at McGill's Moyse Hall. The Shakespeare tragedy is directed by the head of the MRT, Martha Allan, and stars the Governor General's son, Viscount Duncannon. (★66–9)

· MRT Studio produces Henri Ghéon's *The Marvelous History of St Bernard*. Cecil West directs. (★62)

1933

JANUARY
· MRT produces one-act plays in French by noted local playwright Léopold Houlé (*Matines et laudes*) and by future influential radio dramatist Robert Choquette (*La grande demande*).

FEBRUARY
· Louis Mulligan directs a Studio production of Frantisek Langer's *Periferie*. (★62)

MARCH
· MRT does a joint production with les Anciens du Gesù of André Obey's *Noé* at la Salle du Gesù. Pacifique Plante assists Martha Allan in the direction. Future play-wright Yvette Mercier-Gouin stars. (★61, 66)
· MRT presents Shakespeare's *Twelfth Night*, first as a Studio production and then in April-May as a major production at Moyse Hall. Edwyn Wayte directs and designs. (★61)

APRIL
· *The Royal Family* by Kaufman and Ferber is presented by the Westmount Dramatic Club at Victoria Hall. Whittaker designs set. (★45)
· The Stella Theatre Company presents Maurice Pagnol's *Marius* at the Imperial Theatre.
· Ian Hay's *Tilly of Bloomsbury* brings the recently retired stock company star Mildred Mitchell back to the stage, courtesy of St Andrew and St Paul's Players at Kildonan Hall.
· A translation of von Hofmannsthal's *Jedermann* presented by the Everyman Players at the Church of the Messiah. Whittaker designs the production for director and pro-ducer, George M. Brewer. The Everyman Players would produce one play a year until 1940. (★21–3)

· New troupes at le National (comédie-burlesque) and at le Théâtre Arcade (troupe Joseph et Marda).

· At le Saint-Denis, Julien Daoust's play *La conscience d'un prêtre* is staged.

MAY

· The MRT presents Yvette Mercier-Gouin's *Ma-Man Sybille*, the first performance of this local playwright's work. Mercier-Gouin acts, produces, and writes plays through the 1950s. Her plays, in particular, were comedies of manners looking closely at upper-class Montreal.

· The MRT School, headed by Filmore Sadler, an American with extensive theatre training, opens.

· The first of Gustave Lamarche's pageant plays, *Jonathas*, is performed at le Collège Bourget. Lucien Desbiens writes in *Le Devoir*: "Une tragédie digne de figurer à côté de celles de Corneille et de Racine." Lamarche would write over thirty-five plays, mainly on spiritual themes, and was influenced by Paul Claudel and Henri Ghéon.

OCTOBER

· Drama and music critic of the *Gazette* Tom Archer has his one-act play *Three Characters in Search of a Plot* produced as an MRT Studio production. (★45, 69–70)

· Ibsen's *Hedda Gabler* is produced by the MRT at Moyse Hall. Martha Allan directs and stars opposite Filmore Sadler. Cecil West designs. (★61)

· *Thespis en panne*, a work by local theatre critic Jean Béraud, is put on by MRT. (★69)

NOVEMBER

· MRT's Studio presents a typical evening of one-act plays, this time written locally: plays include *Problems Have Their People* by Leslie Stone and *Between Two Worlds* by Charles Rittenhouse. (★62)

· MRT does J.B. Priestley's *Dangerous Corner* at Victoria Hall. Professional actor Alan Marshall stars, Martha Allan directs, and A. Guadagni designs. (★72)

DECEMBER

· Another joint Ottawa–Montreal production – Shakespeare's *Romeo and Juliet* performed at Moyse Hall. Rupert Harvey directs and Governor General Bessborough designs. (★61)

1934

JANUARY

· MRT Studio showcases extracts of Eugene O'Neill's *The Hairy Ape*. (★62)
· February Martha Allan directs an MRT production of Gogol's *The Inspector General* at Victoria Hall. Stalwart of local amateur productions Maud Aston stars. (★61)

MARCH

· At le Théâtre Stella, Edouard Pailleron's *Le monde où l'on s'ennuie* opens.
· *A Midsummer Night's Dream* is put on at West Hill High School and directed by Charles Rittenhouse and designed by Herbert Whittaker. This was the first of their many collaborations on Shakespeare's plays. Rittenhouse will direct, act, and produce for the next twenty years and, through his position as Head of English for the Protestant School Board of Greater Montreal, be influential in the flourishing of high school theatricals in the 1940s, 1950s, and 1960s. (★27–8)

APRIL

· *The Holy Grail* by George Brewer is presented by the Everyman Players; Whittaker designs. (★24–5)
· MRT leaves to compete in the second Dominion Drama Festival finals with *All on a Summer's Day* by Martha Allan. (★62)

JUNE

· A major MRT production of Henri Letondal's *Le cheval de course* is put on. Young actor Gratien Gélinas has a leading role.

SEPTEMBER

· Antoinette Giroux takes over management of le Théâtre Stella with mixed success.

· A Studio production by MRT, a ballad play called *Fair Annie*, is designed by Whittaker. (★69)

OCTOBER

· ... *We Mortals*, by Martha Allan, is directed for the MRT Studio by Edwyn Wayte. Whittaker supplies some mask designs. (★69)

NOVEMBER

· The peripatetic MRT presents Ashley Dukes' *The Man with a Load of Mischief* at the ball-room of the Ritz-Carlton; Whittaker designs his first mainstage MRT production. (★70–1)

1935

APRIL

· *La Passion* is produced at le Théâtre Stella.

· Another original play by George Brewer, *The Spanish Miracle*, is presented by the Everyman Players; Whittaker designs. (★25)

· Local playwright Yvette Mercier-Gouin has her *Cocktail* produced at le Théâtre Stella to great acclaim.

MAY

· The MRT presents *The Merry Wives of Windsor*. Gratien Gélinas appears again in an MRT production, this time playing the role of the Dr Caius, the French physician. Whitfield Aston stars as Falstaff. (★61, 150)

JUNE

· Summer fare from MRT – Martha Allan directs and Cecil West designs an adaptation of that old warhorse *Uncle Tom's Cabin* for the ballroom of the Ritz-Carlton. (★61)

NOVEMBER

· The Morris Gest version of S.I. Hsuing's *Lady Precious Stream* is produced by the MRT Studio. Marjorie Brewer stars and Martha Allan directs. (★26)

DECEMBER

· *Romeo and Juliet* is produced at West Hill High School, directed by Rittenhouse and designed by Whittaker. It receives great critical praise. (★28)
· Le Théâtre Stella becomes a movie house.

1936

FEBRUARY

· The YM–YWHA Players produce Shaw's *Dark Lady of the Sonnets*. Whittaker directs. (★117)

MARCH

· The Dominion Drama Festival opens. Montreal companies competing include the Sixteen-Thirty Club with J. William Rogers' *Judge Lynch*, le Théâtre École with *Il était une bergère* by Marcel Lattes, and the MRT with Shaw's *The Dark Lady of the Sonnets*. (★30–1)
· MRT Studio put on Clifford Odets' *Waiting for Lefty*. Marjorie Brewer and Charles Rittenhouse star in a Martha Allan production. (★62)
· The YM–YWHA Players produce Kaufman and Hart's *Once in a Lifetime*. Mada Gage Bolton directs and Whittaker designs. (★117)

MARCH–APRIL

· The Everyman Players remount their *Everyman* at the Church of the Messiah. (★25)

APRIL

· Gratien Gélinas' first professional revue, *Télévise-moi-ça!*, is produced at le Saint-Denis. (★150)

- Henri Letondal's *As-tu vu mes jumelles?* plays at le Théâtre Imperial and is produced by the Barry-Duquesne troupe.
- Jean Béraud's *Initiation au Théâtre* is published, a plea for greater directorial artistry.
- Julien Daoust's *Les fils du Canada* (a scenic evocation of Canada) opens at le National.

MAY

- The New Theatre Group presents Clifford Odets' *Waiting for Lefty* in Victoria Hall. This is the latest of a series of performances put on in Montreal this year.
- Yvette Mercier-Gouin's *Le jeune Dieu* is performed at le Théâtre Imperial.
- Le Théâtre National comes under the leadership of Rose Ouellette (better known as la Poune) and her troupe; the theatre reaches its greatest period of prosperity.

JUNE

- Another summer production of the MRT at the Ritz-Carlton. This time Martha Allan, Filmore Sadler, and John Pratt are involved in Walter Reynolds' *Young England*. (★61)

JULY

- The Brae Manor Theatre is founded by Filmore and Marjorie Sadler in Knowlton, Quebec, and is one of the first successful summer theatres in Canada. Productions with students of the theatre school and experienced or professional actors continue through 1956. (★102–4)

AUGUST

- In the first full-length play put on at Brae Manor, Filmore Sadler directs future professional Robert Goodier and Margaret Sutherland in Clare Kummer's *Her Master's Voice*. (★104)

NOVEMBER

- Shaw's *Arms and the Man* is staged at the YMHA. Ada Span directs; Whittaker designs. (★117)

DECEMBER
· The MRT presents Noel Coward's *Hay Fever*, Martha Allan and Filmore Sadler co-direct and star.

1937
JANUARY
· The New Theatre Group presents *It Can't Happen Here*, an adaptation of a Sinclair Lewis novel by John C. Choffit.

MARCH
· The Barry-Duquesne troupe appears in a play by Henry Deyglun, *Notre maître l'amour.*
· Shakespeare's *The Taming of the Shrew* at West Hill High School is directed by Rittenhouse and designed by Whittaker. (★28–9)
· The Everyman Players produce T.S. Eliot's *Murder in the Cathedral.* (★25)

APRIL
· La Troupe la Poune is at le National and present *Cupidons de l'amour, L'enfant du péché,* and *Y' en a pas comme la Poune.*
· Jacob Prager's *The Water Carrier* stars Maurice Schwartz at le Monument-National.
· Three Montreal troupes compete at the DDF: the MRT presents *Eleventh Hour* by local writer Joseph Schull; la Renaissance Théâtrale presents *L'absolution* by José German and Emmanuel Bercier; the Sun Life Players show Maeterlinck's *Interior.*

MAY
· Sir George Williams College performs *The Playboy of the Western World.* The director, Douglass Burns Clarke, becomes an important theatre practioner and educator in Montreal.
· Père Émile Legault forms les Compagnons de Saint-Laurent for the production of religious drama. This troupe becomes one of the most influential in Canada. (★153)

NOVEMBER

• Les Compagnons show Ghéon's *La bergère au pays des loups* at le Collège de Saint-Laurent.

• Yvette Mercier-Gouin's latest play, *Un Homme*, opens at His Majesty's, presented by Henri Letondal and under the auspices of Martha Allan and the MRT.

1938

JANUARY

• John Van Druten's *The Distaff Side* is directed by Martha Allan and designed by Cecil West for Victoria Hall. An all-star cast of Montreal actors are featured: Martha Allan, Eleanor Nichol, Roberta Beatty, and Joy Lafleur. (★73)

MARCH

• The first of Gratien Gélinas' spectacularly popular revues (*Fridolinades*), *Fridolinons 38*, is produced at le Monument-National. This annual tradition continues through 1946. Gélinas hired popular actors like Fred Barry and Juliette Beliveau to perform with him. Pacifique Plante, a lawyer who had managed les Anciens du Gesù, was general manager for these revues. (★150–1)

• An adaptation of Pushkin's *Festival in Time of Plague* is presented by the Sixteen-Thirty Club, directed by Herbert Whittaker. Marjorie Brewer wins the Dominion Drama Festival's best actress award. (★32–4)

APRIL

• Le National continues its comedy-burlesque fare: *Au pays de l'amour, Joseph à l'hôpital,* and Henry Kistemaeckers *La blessure.*

• Shaw's *Saint Joan* is presented by the Everyman Players and features Marjorie Brewer. Whittaker designs. (★25, 26, 39)

• Kaufman and Hart's *You Can't Take It With You* reaches His Majesty's in a Sam. H. Harris touring production.

• The New Theatre Group shows Odets' *Awake and Sing* at Victoria Hall.

- Soirée française du MRT at la Salle du Gesù (a DDF fundraiser): *Maldonne* by Arthur Prévost, *Le billet de sweepstake* by Robert Choquette, and *Trio* by Louis Francœur are performed.
- *Les mains rouges* (adapted from radio for stage), an anti-communist, pro-Franco play, is staged uncut at le Monument-National.

MAY

- The DDF Finals opens in Winnipeg and outside Ottawa. Montreal groups performing include the newly formed Mont-Royal Théâtre Français, which wins with Prévost's *Maldonne.* Also competing is *Festival in Time of Plague.* (★33–4)
- Gustave Lamarche's stupendous quasi-medieval play *La défaite de l'enfer* is performed on the mountain of Rigaud before 10,000 spectators.
- Père Legault of les Compagnons receives a grant to study contemporary French drama and leaves for the academic year.

NOVEMBER

- The MRT Studio presents *Uncle Vanya,* designed by Whittaker and directed by Charles Rittenhouse – its Canadian première. (★62–3)
- MRT School of the Theatre produces Sidney Howard's *The Late Christopher Bean*; Filmore Sadler directs. (★61)

DECEMBER

- An ill-timed opening of Gaby Morlay and her company le Théâtre de la Madeleine from Paris in *Victoria Regina.* The company also showed Francis de Crosset's comedy *Il était une fois* at His Majesty's. (★127–8)

1939
JANUARY

- Laurence Housman's *Victoria Regina* with Helen Hayes eclipses Gaby Morlay's version with a lavish production designed by Rex Whistler. (★127–8)

· The MRT presents Wilde's *The Importance of Being Earnest* at Victoria Hall. The third of six mainstage productions of the MRT for 1938–39, all performed at Victoria Hall and all directed by Martha Allan.

FEBRUARY
· Direct from Chicago, Gertrude Lawrence stars in Rachel Crothers' *Susan and God.* (★129)

MARCH
· The North American premiere of Charles Morgan's *The Flashing Stream* is seen at His Majesty's. (★128)
· Herbert Whittaker commissions a play from Janet McPhee based on Sarah Bernhardt's visit to Montreal. *Divinity in Montreal* opens at Channing Hall in a Sixteen-Thirty Club production with Marjorie Brewer as Bernhardt. Betty Taylor wins the award for best actress at the DDF Finals. (★34–5)

MARCH–APRIL
· The Everyman Players present Paul Claudel's *Tidings Brought to Mary* at the Church of the Messiah. (★25)

APRIL
· The New York Yiddish Art Theatre brings Odets' *Awake and Sing* to le Monument-National.
· The MRT presents François Mauriac's *Asmodée*, the professional debut of Yvette Brind'Amour, at Congress Hall.
· Troupe la Poune continues its success with *Faut pas s'en fer* at le National.
· The MRT presents *Aren't We All* by Frederick Lonsdale with ex-Broadway actress Roberta Beatty pinch-hitting as director for Martha Allan. This was the first of Beatty's directorial credits in Montreal. (★73)

MAY
· Noel Coward's *Private Lives* produced by MRT with Joy Lafleur and Cecil West starring.

AUGUST

· Mildred Mitchell makes a guest appearance at the Brae Manor summer theatre in Benn Levy's *Mrs Moonlight*. (★105)

OCTOBER

· Martha Allan, who had served in the First World War, forms a Wartime Entertainment Organization. The MRT would establish a wartime production, *The Tin Hats Review*.

· Les Compagnons present Molière's *Le misanthrope*.

· The touring Colborne and Jones Company presents Colborne's *Charles the King* at His Majesty's. (★128)

NOVEMBER

· Le MRT Français marks Racine's tercentenary with a production of *Les plaideurs* at la Salle Saint-Sulpice.

· The touring Colborne and Jones Company returns to present Shaw's *Geneva*. (★128–9)

· Shaw's *Heartbreak House* is staged by the Sixteeen-Thirty Club at Channing Hall. Whittaker designs and directs. (★38–9)

1940

FEBRUARY

· Chekhov's *The Seagull* presented by the Sixteen-Thirty Club at Channing Hall. Whittaker designs and directs. (★36–8)

MARCH

· Reginald Denham and Edward Percy's *Ladies in Retirement* with Estelle Winwood, Isobel Elsom, and Flora Robson opens at His Majesty's. (★130)

· The Sixteen-Thirty Club's last show, Janet McPhee's *Bus to Nowhere*, is produced at Victoria Hall. Two other original works by local writers – Mada Gage Bolton's *Her Affairs in Order* and John Hoare's *The Shoemakers of Syracuse* – are also put on.

APRIL

· Troupe la Poune continues at le National with *Ma chrysanthème, Dans la tourmente* and *Pour l'honneur d'une femme.*

· Marlowe's *Dr Faustus* is shown by the Everyman Players in the Church of the Messiah – their last production. Whittaker designs. (★25)

· Les Compagnons de Saint-Laurent present Racine's *Britannicus.*

· The MRT presents Ivor Novello's *Fullhouse*, starring Mildred Mitchell.

· Maurice Schwartz and the Yiddish Art Theatre at His Majesty's with a production of *Salvation* by Sholem Asch.

APRIL–MAY

· S.N. Behrman's *No Time for Comedy* stars Katharine Cornell and the Playwrights Company at His Majesty's. (★126–7)

JUNE

· The first performance of the MRT *Tin Hats Review* for civilians is given in the Windsor Hotel ballroom. Staged by Keith Handyside, it stars John Pratt, Robert Goodier, Lionel Murton, and Eileen Clifford.

JULY

· The new Brae Manor Theatre playhouse opens; the company presents *Hay Fever*, starring Martha Allan. (★104)

JULY–AUGUST

· The Lakeshore Summer Theatre opens with Robert Dufresne as president, Douglass Burns Clarke as production manager, and Herbert Whittaker as scenic director. Among the seven plays produced that summer are Emlyn Williams' *Night Must Fall* and Edward Chodorov's *Kind Lady.* (★101–2)

OCTOBER

· Noel Coward's *Tonight at 8:30* at His Majesty's. (★130)

NOVEMBER

· Martha Allan and Cecil West co-direct Marjorie Raven (née Brewer) in an MRT production of Maxwell Anderson's *Mary of Scotland*.

1941
FEBRUARY

· A touring production of Emlyn Williams' *Night Must Fall* comes to His Majesty's. (★131)

APRIL

· A Gala in honour of Julien Daoust's contributions to Montreal's theatre is at le National.

· Yvette Mercier-Gouin's *Le plus bel amour, ou zone libre* is performed at le Théâtre Arcade.

APRIL–MAY

· *The Man Who Came to Dinner* by Kaufman and Hart stars Alexander Woollcott at His Majesty's. (★131)

MAY

· The MRT presents the *Tin Hat Revue of 1941*.

JULY

· The Lakeshore Summer Theatre presents Wilder's *Our Town*, directed by Mildred Mitchell and with Madeleine Sherwood (née Thornton) as Rebecca. (★102)

AUGUST

· The Lakeshore Summer Theatre presents Shaw's *Candida*, directed by Herbert Whittaker. (★102)

OCTOBER

· Filmore Sadler directs George Oppenheimer's *Here Today*, the first MRT mainstage production of the 1941–42 season. This is the first time in MRT history that Martha Allan has not been in the director's chair to open a season.

NOVEMBER

· La Comédie de Montréal (1941–43) is founded and performs at le Monument-National. Its first production is Marc-Gilbert Sauvajon's *L'amant de paille*, starring Jean-Pierre Aumont. The company includes French actors in exile and local Quebec artists.
· *The World We Make* by Sydney Kingsley opens at the YW-YMHA Little Theatre, directed by Ada Span.
· Le Jeune Colombier company is founded (1941–44) by French actors. Their opening production is *La veine d'or*.

1942

FEBRUARY

· Ferber and Kaufman's *The Stage Door* is put on at Victoria Hall by the Westmount Women's Club. Whittaker directs. (★116)

MARCH

· Arrival of European actress Ludmilla Pitoëff. She stars in and directs Paul Claudel's *L'échange* for les Compagnons at l'Ermitage. Legault writes that "elle vibrait comme un violon." (★154)
· La Comédie de Montréal presents *La tragédie de Mayerling*, a play by Quebec writer Jean Despréz.

APRIL

· The MRT presents *Jupiter in Retreat* by Janet McPhee and Herbert Whittaker at Victoria Hall, directed by Charles Rittenhouse and designed by Whittaker. (★38–9)
· Death of Martha Allan at age 47. (★77)

· Henry Deyglun's *Vie de famille – 1942* is produced at la Salle du Gesù.

MAY

· The Negro Theatre Guild's production of Marc Connely's *Green Pastures*, directed by Don Haldane, opens at His Majesty's after first appearing at Victoria Hall. (★122–3)

OCTOBER

· With the help of medieval scholar Gustave Cohen (Sorbonne), les Compagnons de Saint-Laurent stage *Le jeu d'Adam et Eve* and *Le jeu de Robin et Marion* at l'Ermitage.

· Edwyn Wayte directs Julian Thompson's *The Warrior Husbands* at Victoria Hall. Youthful local stars Adelaide Smith and Robert Goodier appear in this MRT production. (★80)

· From Boston comes the touring production of Chodorov and Fields' *My Sister Eileen*. (★131)

NOVEMBER

· Ada Span directs the YW-YMHA in Lillian Hellman's *Watch on the Rhine*.

· Coward's *Private Lives* comes to His Majesty's. (★131)

DECEMBER

· The MRT acquires a permanent theatre on Guy Street. The last Victoria Hall production of the MRT is Miles and Colton's *Nine Pine Street*. Old stock company star Mildred Mitchell directs.

1943

JANUARY

· Having founded l'Équipe, the twenty-year old Pierre Dagenais mounts its first production, Julien Luchaire's *Altitude 3200*, at le Monument-National.

· The MRT moves to Guy Street location and opens with a production of Hellman's *Watch on the Rhine*; Whittaker designs. (★79–80)

· The MRT Studio produces Shakespeare's *Richard II*. Edwyn Wayte directs. (★80)

MARCH

· Sidney Howard's *The Late Christopher Bean* is the next MRT show on Guy Street. Filmore Sadler directs and Whittaker designs. (★80)

APRIL

· Troupe la Poune offers *Grand-mère* and *Saisie arrêt* at le National.
· Troupe d'Arcade presents Hennequin's *Mon bébé* starring Germaine Giroux and Henri Letondal.
· The MRT presents Alexander Afinogenov's *The Distant Point*, designed by Whittaker. Ada Span directs and Adelaide Smith and Charles Lewis star. (★80)
· Ludmilla Pitoëff appears in a French version of *The Doll's House* at l'Ermitage until May 1; again she impresses everyone. (★154)

MAY

· Les Compagnons de Saint-Laurent stage Ghéon's *Le comédien et la grâce*.
· The first Montreal performance of the *Army Show* with Johnny Wayne and Frank Shuster. (★131)

SEPTEMBER

· The first Montreal performance of the troop show *Meet the Navy*. (★131–2)

DECEMBER

· L'Équipe stages *L'homme qui se donnait la comédie* (*Night Must Fall* by Emlyn Williams) at le Monument-National, directed by Dagenais.

1944

MARCH

· The YM-YWHA presents Sherwood's *There Shall Be No Night;* Whittaker directs and designs. (★117–18)
· Edouard Schneider's *L'exaltation* is at le Théâtre Arcade with Marcel Chabrier and veteran actress Antoinette Giroux.

APRIL

· Ruth Draper at His Majesty's with her familiar touring show of character sketches.

· Mercier-Gouin's play *Sous le masque* is produced at le Théâtre Arcade.

· Les Compagnons de Saint-Laurent stage Beaumarchais' *Le barbier de Séville*.

· *Green Yankees* at His Majesty's stars Aaron Lebedeff and Lee Fuchs, celebrated Yiddish comedians.

· Rosanna Seaborn, later noted for her open-air productions of Shakespeare on Mount Royal, directs for the MRT for the first time. Philip Barry's *Hotel Universe* is the play. (★80)

MAY

· Pierre Dagenais brings l'Équipe and Marcel Pagnol's *Marius* to le Monument-National. (★157)

· John Hoare's *The Devil and All* is produced by MRT. Hoare directs and Louis Mulligan designs. (★80)

SEPTEMBER

· Paul Robeson stars in The Theatre Guild's *Othello.* Margaret Webster directs and the production features José Ferrer and Uta Hagen. The touring production reaches His Majesty's.

· J.B. Fagan's *And So To Bed* is directed for the MRT by John Ready. Robert Watt plays Samuel Pepys. (★80)

NOVEMBER

· Les Compagnons present two plays by Jean Cocteau – *Orphée* and *Œdipe-Roi*.

· Mildred Mitchell, now producing director of the MRT, directs herself in Wilde and Eunson's *Guest in the House.* (★80)

1945

JANUARY

· YM-YWHA presents Chekhov's *The Cherry Orchard;* Whittaker designs and directs. (★119)

FEBRUARY

· The Yiddish Art Theatre from New York tours Montreal led by Maurice Schwartz. (★134–5)
· For the MRT Mildred Mitchell directs Whitfield Aston in Paul Osborn's *On Borrowed Time*. (★80)

MARCH

· Roberta Beatty directs Robert Sherwood's *There Shall Be No Night* for the MRT.

APRIL

· The Ballet Russe de Monte Carlo arrives at le Saint-Denis. Repertoire includes *Rodeo*, *Red Poppy*, *Le bourgeois gentilhomme*, and *Les sylphides*.
· Les Compagnons de Saint-Laurent's *Rabelais* or *Picrochole* opens at l'Ermitage.
· Henry Deyglun's annual revue, *Vie de famille – 1945 (L'ombre de mort vivant)*, opens at le Monument-National.

MAY

· Maurice Schwartz and company present *Three Generations* at His Majesty's.
· The Shakespeare Society of Montreal is restarted – its first production is *Much Ado about Nothing* at Moyse Hall, directed by Roberta Beatty, art direction by Herbert Whittaker, produced by Charles Rittenhouse. (★81–3)

AUGUST

· L'Équipe presents a spectacular *Songe d'une nuit d'été* in an outdoor setting at l'Ermitage. (★157)

NOVEMBER

· Les Compagnons present Alfred de Musset's *On ne badine pas avec l'amour*, Obey's *Noé*, and Marivaux's *Le jeu de l'amour et hasard* through the month of November.
· L'Équipe performs Molnar's *Liliom* at la Salle du Gesù.

DECEMBER

- *St Lazare's Pharmacy* by Eddie Dowling, with Gratien Gélinas in the lead opposite Miriam Hopkins, opens at His Majesty's. The production would go on to Chicago but not to New York. (*151)
- The new Canadian Art Theatre led by Joy Thompson stages Ibsen's *Ghosts* at Victoria Hall. Whittaker replaces Thompson as director. (*116)
- La Salle du Gesù is renovated. The space (now including a revolving stage) attracts many companies, including les Compagnons and l'Équipe.

1946

JANUARY

- YM-YWHA produces Thornton Wilder's *The Skin of Our Teeth*; Whittaker designs and directs. (*119–20)
- L'Équipe produces Jean-Paul Sartre's *Huis clos* at la Salle du Gesù. Later Sartre himself will request a special performance of the play and it will be put on at the Windsor Hotel. (*157)

MARCH

- Claude-Henri Grignon's *Un homme et son péché* is remounted for le Monument-National. Séraphin stars.
- L'Université de Montréal presents *Phèdre* with Ludmilla Pitoëff in the lead role. (*154)
- Charles Rittenhouse directs the William Saroyan comedy *The Beautiful People* for the MRT. Hans Berends designs. (*80)

APRIL

- The MRT presents Rodney Ackland's *The Old Ladies* from a story by Hugh Walpole. This is Whittaker's directorial debut for the MRT. (*87–8)
- Les Compagnons shows Shakespeare's *La nuit des rois* (*Twelfth Night*) at la Salle du Gesù; noted artist Alfred Pellan designs.
- Édouard Schnieder's *L'exaltation* enjoys another showing at le Théâtre Arcade; long-time stars Antoinette Giroux and Jeanne Demons appear.

· Bernstein's *La cœur* closes the seventh season of French comedy at le Théâtre Arcade; it is the thirty-second play of the season.

MAY
· The Shakespeare Society of Montreal presents *King Lear* at Moyse Hall, directed by Pierre Dagenais and designed by Whittaker. (★83–6)
· The hundredth production of the MRT is *The Corn Is Green*. Roberta Beatty directs and Doreen Lewis stars. Lewis will take over the post of production director of the MRT from Mildred Mitchell. (★88)
· Jean Vézina's play, *La statue fragile*, opens at le Saint-Denis. Cast includes Jeanne Demons and Antoinette Giroux.

JUNE
· The classic Goldsmith comedy *She Stoops to Conquer* is performed by the MRT. Long-time Montreal performer Maud Aston directs.

AUGUST
· Shaw's *Candida* is produced at the long-running Brae Manor Theatre. Whittaker directs and designs. The production is remounted for the Seigneury Club at Murray Bay in October. (★106–8)

OCTOBER
· MRT opens the season with Thomas Job's *Uncle Harry*, directed by Jean de Savoye. *Tin Hats* and *Meet the Navy* favorites Robert Goodier and Eileen Clifford star.

NOVEMBER
· Les Compagnons de Saint-Laurent present Molière's *Les précieuses ridicules* and *Le médecin malgré lui* at the Chalet at Mount Royal.

NOVEMBER–DECEMBER
· The MRT presents *Asmodée* (*The Intruder*) by François Mauriac, directed by Pierre Dagenais. (★88–9)

DECEMBER

· L'Équipe presents *Le héros et le soldat* (Shaw's *Arms and the Man*), directed and designed by Whittaker. (★157–60)

1947

JANUARY

· The MRT presents Jean Giraudoux's *Amphitryon 38*, directed by Roberta Beatty. The production will be taken to the newly re-constituted Dominion Drama Festival. (★89)

· Wilde's *The Importance of Being Earnest*, directed by John C. Wilson with John Gielgud and Margaret Rutherford, opens at His Majesty's. (★139–40)

· Donald Wolfit brings his company to His Majesty's with a selection of Shakespearean favorites. (★137–8)

FEBRUARY

· Cocteau's *The Eagle Has Two Heads*, with Tallulah Bankhead starring, appears at His Majesty's. (★136)

MARCH

· The MRT presents S.N. Behrman's *Biography*, directed by Whittaker and starring Betty Wilson. (★90)

· Les Compagnons stage Félix Leclerc's (unpublished) *Maluron*, which proves to be a popular success.

APRIL

· Farewell evening for Yvette Brind'Amour and Roger Garceau – *Huis clos* at la Salle de la Légion canadienne; Pierre Dagenais directs.

· Les Compagnons stage Martens and Obey's *Les gueux au paradis* at la Salle du Gesù. Les Compagnons will take another of their productions, *Le médecin malgré lui*, to the DDF Finals in London, Ontario. This production will win top honours, with the troupe recognized as "le groupe théâtral le plus important au Canada tout entier." (★153, 162–3)

· Roberta Beatty directs Rudolph Besier's *The Barretts of Wimpole Street* for the MRT. Eleanor Stuart stars. (★89)

MAY

· The Shakespeare Society of Montreal presents their last production, *Romeo and Juliet*, at Moyse Hall, directed by Charles Rittenhouse and designed by Whittaker. (★86–7)
· Pierre Dagenais directs Armand Salacrou's *Les fiancés du Havre*; Jean Despréz is a guest artist on this production at la Salle du Gesù.
· The MRT presents Maxwell Anderson's *Joan of Lorraine*, directed by Malcolm Morley, with Marjorie Raven (née Brewer) in the lead. (★89)
· Another spectacular production at Rigaud – Gustave Lamarche's biblical drama *Tobie* – requires 160 performers.
· Elisabeth Bergner tours in Martin Vale's *The Two Mrs Carrolls* at His Majesty's. (★135)
· Rodgers and Hammerstein's *Oklahoma!* reaches His Majesty's with a touring production.

JULY

· Rosanna Seaborn Todd initiates large-scale outdoor productions of Shakespeare on Mount Royal: the first production is *A Midsummer Night's Dream*.

AUGUST

· The Brae Manor Theatre presents Thomas's *Charley's Aunt* and Hellman's *The Little Foxes*, both directed by Whittaker. Malcolm Morley's own play, *The Beacon Light,* is directed by Morley and designed by Whittaker. Morley would be an important figure in the development of indigenous professional theatre in Canada (★108–10)

NOVEMBER

· Les Compagnons stage Racine's *Andromaque* at la Salle du Gesù.

1948

JANUARY

- The YM-YWHA presents an all-Yiddish production, *Tzurick Tzu Zein Folk*.
- Eugene O'Neill's *Ah, Wilderness!* is presented by the MRT and directed by Whittaker. (★90–1)
- The Dublin Gate Theatre arrives in Montreal at His Majesty's with Shaw's *John Bull's Other Island*, Denis Johnston's *The Old Lady Says No*, and others.

FEBRUARY

- Pierre Dagenais' play *Le temps de vivre* is presented at le Monument-National and receives a critical drubbing. L'Équipe disbands later in the same year. (★156–7)

MARCH

- The MRT stages three one-act plays by Robertson Davies, including his first one-act play, *Hope Deferred*, under the direction of Reta Wheatley and Dorothy Pfeiffer.
- Norris Houghton directs *Macbeth* with Michael Redgrave and Flora Robson at His Majesty's.

APRIL

- Les Compagnons stage Molière's *Le bourgeois gentilhomme* at la Salle du Gesù.
- The Negro Theatre Guild's *Emperor Jones* by O'Neill is staged at the MRT Guy Street Playhouse with future professional Percy Rodriguez in the lead. (★123–4)
- Herbert Whittaker directs future professional John Colicos in the Commercial High School production of André Obey's *Noah*. (★116)

MAY

- Gratien Gélinas' *Tit-Coq* premiers at le Monument-National; this production is considered a watershed in Québécois theatre. The play would transfer to la Salle du Gesù and an unprecedented run of over two hundred performances. (★152)
- The MRT presents Van Druten's *I Remember Mama* at Moyse Hall, directed by Whittaker. (★91–3)

AUGUST

· The Brae Manor Theatre presents Kaufman and Ferber's *The Royal Family*. A stellar cast includes John Colicos; Whittaker directs. Malcolm Morley directs Sheridan's *The Rivals*, in which Christopher Plummer fills in on an emergency basis. (★112–14)

NOVEMBER

· Les Compagnons go fully professional in a new theatre with a French version of Tennessee Williams' *The Glass Menagerie*.
· Yvette Brind'Amour and Mercedes Palomino found Le Théâtre du Rideau Vert.
· YM-YWHA presents S. Ansky's *The Dybbuk*; Whittaker designs and directs. (★120–2)

DECEMBER

· *Escape Me Never!* by Margaret Kennedy comes to His Majesty's with Elizabeth Bergner in the lead. (★135–6)

1949

FEBRUARY

· Le Théâtre du Rideau Vert's first production, *Les innocents,* a French translation of Lillian Hellman's *The Children's Hour*, opens.
· The Mountain Playhouse opens under the leadership of Joy Thompson. The company will produce summer theatre at the Playhouse on Mount Royal.
· The Negro Theatre Guild's production of *The Emperor Jones* wins the top award at the Western Quebec Regional Drama Festival. Two productions of Whittaker's, *The Dybbuk* and J.B. Priestley's *The Linden Tree,* put on by the Trinity Players, are also entered. (★121–2)

MARCH

· The MRT presents *The Glass Menagerie*, directed by Whittaker, with Amelia Hall, Betty Taylor, and Silvio Narizzano. (★93–5)

APRIL

· La Poune is still performing at le Théâtre Arcade.

· La Société V.L.M. presents Félix Leclerc and Guy Maufette's collection of sketches, *Le p'tit bonheur*, at le Théâtre des Compagnons.

APRIL–MAY
· Les Compagnons stage *Peace* by Aristophanes.

MAY
· J.M. Barrie's *What Every Woman Knows* is offered by the MRT.

JUNE
· Le Théâtre du Rideau Vert's second production, *KMX Labrador* by Jacques Deval, opens.

JULY
· Brae Manor opens for the season with a new stage house designed by Whittaker. (★104)
· Montreal's Music and Drama Festival opens: O'Neill's *The Emperor Jones* (Negro Theatre Guild), Racine's *Phèdre* (Conservatoire Lasalle) and Molière's *Les femmes savantes* (Cours François Rozet) are in the lineup.

OCTOBER
· Theatre critic Eloi de Grandmont's first play, *Un fils à tuer*, opens at la Salle du Gesù.

NOVEMBER
· The MRT stages Somerset Maugham's *The Constant Wife* in celebration of the twentieth anniversary of its founding; long-time contributor to Montreal theatre Louis Mulligan directs.

NOTES

THE STORY SO FAR

1 David Gardner's article in *The Oxford Companion to Canadian Theatre* (OCCT), "Little theatre and amateur theatre," is a convenient and useful survey of the flourishing English-language little theatre activity of the first half of this century. Extensive discussions of the traditions of *les soirées de famille, les cercles,* and other mainifestations of amateur theatrical activity in French Canada and Quebec can also be found in the OCCT (see Gilbert David's "Theatre in Quebec, French") and, most usefully, in Legris, Larrue, Bourassa, and David, eds., *Le théâtre au Québec, 1825–1980.* Apart from another version of *Setting the Stage,* published in *Canadian Drama*; Philip Booth's MA thesis, "The Montreal Repertory Theatre: 1931–1961"; Booth's article in *L'Annuaire théâtral;* and Jonathan Rittenhouse's article *"Herbert Whittaker: A Theatre Life,"* there are very few significant published analyses or discussions of the English-language theatre of Montreal of this era. Such important and celebratory texts as Camerlain and Pavlovic's *Cent ans de théâtre à Montréal photographies,* for example, completely ignore productions from English-language companies.

2 Winter carnival activities were a long tradition in Montreal and Ice Palaces were annually designed and erected on Fletcher's Field just off of Park Avenue and visible from Whittaker's window.

3 Betty Lee's *Love and Whisky* still provides the most complete discussion of the Earl Grey Musical and Dramatic Competitions and the Dominion Drama Festival.

4 The Kean story details can be found in John Ripley's "Shakespeare on the Montreal Stage, 1805–1826" (*Theatre History in Canada* 3 [Spring 1982]: 3–20).

5 The most recent discussions of this famous incident from pre-Conquest Canada can be found in Leonard E. Doucette's *Theatre in French Canada: Laying the Foundations 1606–1867* (Toronto: University of Toronto Press, 1984) and Gilbert David's OCCT article "Theatre in Quebec (French)." This account follows the de la Roche version of events (109).

6 Exactly what did occur in 1693–94 and the motives of the principal players still arouse discussion. Certainly Lieutenant Mareuil was imprisoned for his intention to produce the play. In Doucette's extensive analysis of the controversy (*Theatre in French Canada,* 23–30) he is not convinced of the bribery details and suggests a more complicated integration of the *Le tartuffe* affair with the many and various struggles between church and state for control of the French colony.

7 Doucette (ibid.) and OCCT provide basic information on these performances. Baudoin Burger's *L'activité théâtrale au Québec (1765–1825)* (Montréal: Parti Pris, 1974) provides the fullest discussion.

8 In *The Letters of Charles Dickens, vol. 3, 1842–43*, edited by Madeline House, Graham Storey, and Kathleen Tillotson (Oxford: Clarendon Press, 1974), 234–48, details of Dickens's visit to Montreal and his theatrical performances are carefully discussed. Dickens performed twice in May 1842, once a private performance (May 25) and once a public one (May 28). The editors of the letters suggest that the interlude was written by a Mrs Gore. In the public performance the Poole farce was replaced by Townley's *High Life Below Stairs*.

9 In the anthology *Canada's Lost Plays. Volume One: The Nineteenth Century*, edited by Anton Wagner and Richard Plant (Toronto: CTR Publications, 1978), Sam Scribble's 1865 "local political burlesque," *Dolorsolatio*, is reproduced (54–66).

10 Bernhardt's version of her visit can be found in her *My Double Life: Memoirs of Sarah Bernhardt* (London: Heinemann, 1907, 380–97); the historical reconstruction of her many visits to Canada are in John Hare and Ramon Hathorn's article "Sarah Bernhardt's Visits to Canada: Dates and Repertory" (*Theatre History in Canada* 2 [Fall 1981]: 93–116).

11 Collard's *Montreal Yesterdays: More Stories from All Our Yesterdays* (Montreal: *The Gazette*, 1989) provides the anecdote.

12 Walter Hampden's long career of performing and touring included two productions of *Richelieu*, one of which visited New York in December 1929, the other in May 1934. The *New York Times Directory of the Theater* (*NYTDT*) is a quick and useful source for tracking down once popular but now forgotten theatre artists, playwrights, and plays.

13 *NYTDT* confirms that the first three plays premiered in fall 1934, while the popular revue opened in 1933.

CHAPTER ONE

1 Davies 1975 book lovingly details the activities of Sir John Tresize and Milady.

2 *Oedipus Rex*, along with *Hamlet* and six other plays, was part of Martin-Harvey's 1923–24 tour of Canada. Robert Lawrence's article, "John Martin-Harvey in Canada" provides information concerning the actor's seven tours across Canada (1914–32). Bill Graham's memory piece, "Sir John Martin-Harvey: The Last Imperial Envoy," is an excellent recollection of Sir John and his style of performing from the perspective of a young lad in Winnipeg.

3 Mantell had a long career, mainly touring in the regions, which ended with his death in 1928. See *The Oxford Companion to Theatre* (*OCT*), 4th ed., Phyllis Hartnoll, ed. (Oxford: Oxford University Press, 1983) for fuller details of his life.

4 George Hayes' tall son John – much mourned in 1993 – was later to become a most valued member of the production staff at Ontario's Stratford Festival. In turn John's son, Elliot, proved valuable to that festival as playwright and literary manager before an untimely death one year later.

5 The Keith-Albee circuit was a wholesome or family vaudeville circuit that provided entertainment to many out-of-the-way theatres as well as major centres throughout North America in the first part of this century until the coming of the "talkies."

6 *OCT* tells us that Bransby Williams was a music-hall star as early as 1896 and entertained audiences on stage, radio, and television for half a century with his impersonation skills.

7 *The New Grove Dictionary of Opera* (London: Macmillan, 1992), 49 refers to Vladimir Rosing and an unnamed company that toured North America throughout the 1920s providing opera in English to its audiences.

8 The *New Grove* (ibid.) does note under its San Carlo Opera Company entry that this company had a much longer record of performance (1913–51) than Rosing's troupe. The San Carlo Company made many visits to Montreal over the years.

CHAPTER TWO

1 In the *Encyclopedia of Music in Canada*, 2nd ed., Helmut Kallmann, Gilles Potvin, eds. (Toronto: University of Toronto Press, 1992), the entry for Brewer notes his long-standing commitment to the college from 1903 to his death in 1947.

2 See Edwards' essay "A Playwright from the Canadian Past" in *Theatre History in Canada* for a fuller accounting of Tremayne's career, as well as his entry in *OCCT* on Tremayne.

3 Stephen Mayle, in his *William Van Horne* (Don Mills: Fitzhenry and Whiteside, 1976, 57), refers to the railroad baron's fifty-two-room mansion where El Grecos vied with paintings by Turner, Hogarth, Rembrandt, Goya, and Renoir and valuable ceramics and Japanese pottery were on display.

4 Thomas Archer in *The Gazette*, 23 May 1935, 19, described *The Spanish Miracle* as appearing much like an El Greco picture and wrote that "the real triumph lies in the staging and the costuming which are often exceedingly beautiful."

5 See Patrick Neilson's article, "Charles Burkett Rittenhouse" for a complete assessment of Rittenhouse's career.

6 On 12 December 1935, 11, Archer wrote, "What is quite possibly the best production of a Shakespeare play done here in the last ten years was seen at the West Hill School Thursday."

7 At the end of the nineteenth century actor and director William Poel established the Elizabethan Stage Society which was committed to performing the plays of Shakespeare and his contemporaries in open playing spaces similar to the theatres of Shakespeare's age. His influence on early twentieth-century productions of Shakespeare was significant.

8 Stikeman's review can be found in the 19 March 1937 edition of the *McGill Daily.*

9 See Bernhardt, *My Double Life: Memoirs of Sarah Bernhardt* (London: Heineman, 1907), and Hare and Hathorn, "Sarah Bernhardt's Visits to Canada: Dates and Repertory" (*Theatre History in Canada* 2 [Fall 1981]: 93–116).

10 Coverage of Littlewood's adjudicator's remarks can be found in *The Gazette,* 15 April 1939, 19, and 17 April 1939, 1, 9.

11 The Montreal Museum of Fine Arts 1991 exhibition catalogue *The Architecture of Edward and W.S. Maxwell* provides full details of the brothers many architectural achievements. See pages 179–82 for a photo and description of the Church of the Messiah.

CHAPTER THREE

1 Peter Briggs' article in *Canadian Drama*, "Sir Barry Vincent Jackson and the Canadian Theatre," notes the company's appearance in fall 1931 and spring 1932. The OCT chronicles Jackson's establishment of his Repertory Theatre in 1913 and his influence on theatrical production throughout the 1930s.

2 Eric McLean was music critic for *The Montreal Daily Star* and *The Gazette* from 1950–90.

3 The Westmount Dramatic Club produced the play for one night only (!), 8 April 1933.

4 Morgan-Powell's *Memories That Live* has many essays on visiting professional performers, including one on Sarah Bernhardt.

5 On 12 March 1949, 23, Morgan-Powell wrote: "For several years past Mr. Whittaker has been writing comments on plays and motion pictures that have been

characterized by critical acumen often enlivened by a mordant wit … He has written a great deal to encourage the development of Canadian talent and has taken an active part in the direction of performances by amateur organizations here."

CHAPTER FOUR

1 *New York Times Directory of the Theatre* (*NYTDT*) supplies the information that Cornell first performed for the Players in November 1916 in a play called *Bushido*.

2 C.W.E. Bigsby's *A Critical Introduction to Twentieth-Century American Drama. Volume One: 1900–1940* (Cambridge: Cambridge University Press, 1982) provides a clear overview of these American developments.

3 These plays premiered in New York in 1921 and 1922 and subsequently toured North America.

4 Kenneth Macgowan's book/report of theatrical activities (professional, amateur, and educational) in the US, *Footlights across America: Towards a National Theater* (New York: Harcourt, Brace, 1929), includes much information about the burgeoning little theatre movement and drama in education.

5 Sir Montagu became chairman of the Allan Steamship Line in 1909 and retired in 1912. Thomas E. Appleton's *Ravenscrag: The Allan Royal Mail Line* (Toronto: McLelland and Stewart, 1974) describes many interesting details of the Allan family's business affairs.

6 Whittaker's entry on Martha Allan in *OCCT* gives another précis of Allan's many achievements. Obituaries for the forty-seven-year old Allan in *The Montreal Daily Star, The Gazette, Le Devoir,* and *Le Canada* on 6 April 1942 detail her accomplishments as producer, director, actress, and writer, including receipt of the Canadian Drama Award in 1935.

7 In Toby Gordon Ryan's memoir *Stage Left Canadian Theatre in the Thirties* (90), Rose Kashtan, a leader of the New Theatre Group in Montreal, also recalls the same MRT production. She, too, was shocked: "The first shock was to see Edna, wife of the striking taxi driver, dressed in a beautiful English tweed skirt and a very lovely silk blouse."

8 *Cue*, the official organ of the MRT from December 1930, included detailed descriptions of local theatrical activities in the 1930s and 1940s. Unfortunately, no complete run of the magazine exists.

9 The performance was another one-night affair, 1 November 1938. J. Douglas Clayton's *Theatre History in Canada* article "Bears and Beavers" notes that this *Vanya* appeared a good thirteen years before the play's next production in 1951.

10 Howard Fink's *OCCT* entry, "Radio Drama in English," offers the most useful and concise overview of the development of English-language broadcasting in Montreal.

11 Mario Duliani's comments were printed in *Le Petit Journal*, 9 March 1952.

12 Edward Gordon Craig (1872–1966) was one of the century's most influential set designers and stage theorists.

13 One of which, *The Eighth Square*, the Sixteen-Thirty Club entered into the Western Quebec Regional Festival under Charles Rittenhouse's direction with Marjorie Brewer as its victim of euthanasia.

14 Whittaker's *OCCT* entry on Eleanor Stuart notes her presence in the first Stratford, Ontario, company in 1953 and her influential teaching position as voice instructor when the National Theatre School opened in 1961.

15 Fink's *OCCT* entry, "Radio Drama in English," sketches in some details of Caplan's work and influence.

16 *NYTDT* gives information about nineteen New York productions in which Roberta Beatty appeared from 1921–35, including a 1929 version of *Sherlock Holmes*.

CHAPTER FIVE

1 See Booth's "Archives du théâtre de langue anglaise à Montréal" for further discussion of the provenance of the MRT collection.

2 In *Renown at Stratford* (Toronto: Clarke, Irwin and Company, 1953), 6, Guthrie wrote: "It has long been my opinion that there will be no drastic improvement in Shakespearean production until we revert to the sort of theatre for which the plays

were written; a building in which the stage is designed to conform to the conventions of the Elizabethan stage, with certain permanent architectural features, such as a balcony and a trap; and without the facilities of the proscenium stage, where illusionary effects are prepared as a surprise behind a curtain."

3 Archer's review appeared 18 May 1945, 3.

4 Both *Gazette* and *Star* reviews (26 May 1948) admired the large scale of the production but also noted the difficulty in maintaining consistency in the acting.

5 His most famous directorial credit is probably the 1966 *Georgy Girl*.

6 Whittaker's "A Critic's Farewell" appeared 12 March 1949, 22.

CHAPTER SIX

1 Whittaker's *OCCT* entry on Brae Manor provides a good overview of this summer theatre. In the National Archives Mr and Mrs F. Sadler Collection (MG30 D152), scrapbooks filled with programs and notices supply a complete record of Brae Manor's productions and activities.

2 Whittaker's review appeared 13 July 1940, 4.

3 A notice in *The Herald*, 8 April 1949, 20, informs us that Whittaker designed the new "stage house," providing Brae Manor with an ample $25' \times 45'$ stage.

4 Whittaker's review appeared 9 August 1947, 18.

CHAPTER SEVEN

1 *OCCT* provides more information in Whittaker's entries on Norma Springford and the Mountain Playhouse.

2 Thomas Archer's review of 15 January 1946, 3, is positive: "This is a remarkably good performance. Here and there it is a little over-anxious a little eager to keep things going brightly at all costs, but, aside from these occasional explosions of superfluous energy, the Little Theatre can take to itself an immense amount of credit for a genuine achievement in the art."

3 The review appeared 22 November 1948, 6.

4 See the 22 February 1949, 6, *Gazette* notice for the festival performance of *The Linden Tree.*

5 See articles in *The Gazette* for reports of the adjudicator's after-show remarks, 25 February 1949, 6; for a report of his final festival decisions see 28 February 1949, 7.

6 Whittaker's review of the production appeared 8 May 1942, 2.

7 Whittaker's review of the first performance of the play appeared 12 April 1948, 6.

8 See *The Gazette,* 28 February 1949, 7, for a complete report of these comments.

CHAPTER EIGHT

1 The Ballet Russe made frequent stops at Montreal including February 1941, October 1941, and October 1942.

2 The production of *Geneva* eventually made a January 1940 visit to the Henry Miller Theater in New York, after its tour of Canada.

3 The OCCT entry by Ross Stuart on Earle Grey discusses the career this Dublin-born actor had in Canada, including starting his own Shakespeare festival which ran from the 1940s into the 1950s.

4 Patrick O'Neill's entry on *The Dumbells* in OCCT notes that the group had a long-lasting stage life – it continued in one form or another from 1917 to 1933.

5 Patrick O'Neill's entry on *The Navy Show* for OCCT discusses the *Meet the Navy* show.

6 Three photos of the Chinatown events appeared on page 11 of *The Gazette*, 3 September 1945. An accompanying article described the celebratory lion dances, Peking opera, and open-air dance.

7 The ecstatic review appeared 28 January 1947, 6.

8 The *Encyclopedia of Music in Canada* (Helmut Kallmann and Gilles Potvin, eds., Toronto: University of Toronto Press, 1992) entry for the booking agency asserts that Koudriavtzeff was president and general director of the company from 1943–76 and organized at least 147 Canadian tours of foreign artists.

9 However, Her Majesty's disappeared only after the Civic Auditorium Whittaker had championed in his final article for *The Gazette* in 1949 had finally appeared, with the 1963 completion of Montreal's performance complex, Place des Arts.

CHAPTER NINE

1 Along with Jean Hamelin, Béraud was one of the earliest chroniclers of Quebec's theatre history with his *350 ans de théâtre au Canada français*.

2 These were stars of local burlesque, revues, and stock theatre companies who performed at such venues as le Théâtre National and le Théâtre Stella.

3 Comprehensive details of Gélinas' early career can be found in Anne-Marie Sicotte's *Gratien Gélinas. Tome 1, 1909–56*.

4 *The Globe and Mail*, 9 January 1951, 1: "It will be a long time before Canadian theatre experiences an evening as full of excitement as last night, when Toronto welcomed Gratien Gélinas and his play, *Ti-Coq*, at the Royal Alexandra … What the distinguished first-night audience saw was a strong, almost ugly drama, wrenched out of the native soil of Quebec by a man who understands his people well … This forthright drama has been set down with immense craftmanship by Mr. Gélinas, the brilliant revue artist and actor turned playwright. There is surely dramatic structure here, rarely wavering from an intensity which holds its audience alive to the problem proposed. It starts out, however, as a comedy, drawing a great deal of laughter from the scenes of army and family life, before it plunges into a tragic dilemma … Mr. Gélinas has given his play a magnificently expert production … with a maximum of professional skill."

5 There are many useful and interesting assessments of père Legault's and les Compagnons' contribution to Quebec and Canadian theatre history. The most comprehensive is Anne Caron's *Le père Legault et le théâtre au Québec*.

6 A most recent assessment of Dagenais and l'Équipe is Jean-Cléo Godin's insightful article "L'Équipe (1942–1948) de Pierre Dagenais."

AFTERWORD

1 Critical response to the production can be found in *The Gazette*, 13 August 1953, 11, and *The Montreal Daily Star*, 13 August 1953, 30–1.

2 In Montreal le Théâtre du Rideau Vert (1948) and le Théâtre du Nouveau Monde (1951) were newly formed professional theatre companies organized to produce major productions of mainstream legitimate drama. The extraordinary professional success of local performer Gratien Gélinas with his *Tit-Coq* (252 performances) and its English translation *Ti-Coq* (121 performances) from 1948 to 1951 also provides an example of local professionalism. The flagship English-language theatre company, the Montreal Repertory Theatre, only decided to become fully professional in 1956. It closed five years later.

3 See Bryden's cogent prefatory essay, particularly page xviii.

4 See my article "Herbert Whittaker: A Theatre Life."

5 See "Herbert Whittaker, Reporting from the Front," Wagner, *Establishing Our Boundaries*, 215–33.

6 Maria Tippett's *Making Culture: English-Canadian Institutions and the Arts before the Massey Commission* (Toronto: University of Toronto Press, 1990) provides an excellent analysis of the cultural atmosphere of mid-century Canada. The Massey-Lévesque Report eventually led to the creation of the Canada Council in 1957.

7 Not one of the local English-language theatre companies mentioned in the book still exists. Of the hundreds of English-speaking Montrealers referred to in the book, only Griffith Brewer still lives and works in theatre there.

8 This section on the 1920s, 1930s, and 1940s in Montreal owes a great deal to the following, each of which provides close analysis of Montreal during this period: John A. Dickinson and Brian Young, *A Short History of Quebec*, 2nd ed. (Toronto: Copp Clark Pitman, 1993), 195–290; Paul-André Linteau, *Histoire de Montréal depuis la Confédération* (Montreal: Les Éditions du Boréal, 1992), 283–403; Donald Kerr, Deryck W. Holdsworth, Susan L. Laskin, and Geoffrey J. Matthews, *Historical Atlas of*

Canada. Vol. 3. *Addressing the Twentieth Century, 1891–1961* (Toronto: University of Toronto Press, 1990); Margaret W. Westley, *Remembrance of Grandeur: The Anglo-Protestant Elite of Montreal 1900–1950* (Montreal: Libre Expression, 1990), 129–296; William Weintraub, *City Unique: Montreal Days and Nights in the 1940s and '50s*; André-G. Bourassa and Jean-Marc Larrue, *Les nuits de la "Main,"* special issue of *L'Annuaire théâtral* (23, printemps 1998); and Eugene Benson and Leonard W. Conolly, editors, *The Oxford Companion to Canadian Theatre.*

9 Along with providing many details about who was who in Montreal's close-knit financial community, Westley, *Remembrance of Grandeur*, 178, points out that the Exchange had only sixty members. See Dickinson and Young, *A Short History of Quebec*, 212, for further details about the financial elite.

10 Linteau, *Histoire de Montréal*, 373–4 describes Sir Robert Holt, head of the Royal Bank from before the war until 1934, as the dominant financial figure in Montreal. Westley, *Remembrance of Grandeur*, 201–2, also provides an interesting portrait of the differing styles and cliques associated with the two heads of the influential rail companies, Sir Edward Beatty of Canadian Pacific Railways and Sir Henry Thornton of Canadian National Railways.

11 Westley (ibid., 200) quotes an anecdote of a young lawyer dispatched to the Royal Bank in November 1927 with two cheques each worth about $45 million, and needed to keep the bank from being bankrupt. Dickinson and Young, *A Short History of Quebec*, 212–13, discusses the financial assets of Sun Life.

12 Westley, *Remembrance of Grandeur*, 158, refers to that important text of the Montreal elite – *Dau's Blue Book* – which in its 1928 edition lists well over one hundred clubs effectively restricted to anglo-Protestants. She also notes (159) the continuing significant role played by the militia in Montreal's social calendar, particularly the Black Watch and its sponsorship of varied social activities.

13 By the end of the 1920s the cinema chain Consolidated Theatres controlled all four commercially viable spaces for English-language performance: the Gayety, the Orpheum, the Princess, and His Majesty's.

14 Franklin Graham's personal, anecdotal, and quirky *Histrionic Montreal* (Montreal: Lovell and Co., 1902), 295–9, provides details about the theatre's gala opening.

15 Dane Lanken's *Montreal Movie Palaces: Great Theatres in the Golden Era 1884–1938* (Waterloo, ON: Penumbra, 1983) offers the most complete overview of these theatres.

16 The Historic Theatre Trust's 1995 *Bulletin* is completely devoted to the subject of atmospheric theatres in Canada and includes interesting information about their history.

17 See Dickinson and Young, *A Short History of Quebec*, 250–4, for a more detailed assessment of the Taschereau government.

18 Linteau, *Histoire de Montréal*, 218–25, describes the battles concerning municipal hygiene, and plate 32 of the *Historical Atlas*, "New Approaches to Diseases and Public Dependency" by Lynne Marks, offers details of health initiatives across Canada. Terry Copp's *The Anatomy of Poverty: The Conditions of the Working Class in Montreal, 1897–1929* (Toronto: McClelland and Stewart, 1974) also offers many details of Montreal's public health in chapters and 7.

19 Plate 38 of the *Historical Atlas,* "Organized Labour" by Gregory S. Kealey and Douglas Cruikshank, graphically indicates the extraordinary rise in Catholic unions in the 1920s. Dickinson and Young, *A Short History of Quebec*, 221–5, suggests that the stereotypical description of Quebec as having avoided union ferment is incorrect as there were strike events throughout the decade.

20 Plate 37 of the *Historical Atlas*, "Working Worlds" by Lynne Marks, provides a picture of the national workforce in 1921. Dickinson and Young, *A Short History of Quebec*, 217–21, discusses women and work, noting that by 1921 women made up more than 25 percent of Montreal's paid workforce.

21 Linteau, *Histoire de Montréal*, 313–32, provides full analysis of the demographic change in Montreal and description of the city's many communities. Tables 12.1 and 12.2 offer data about population increase and ethnic composition, respectively.

22 See Jean-Cléo Godin's overview article "Julien Daoust: dramaturge 1866–1943"for a complete understanding of his importance to Montreal's cultural development.

23 See Chantal Hébert's *Le burlesque au Québec* for a thorough and scholarly analysis of popular forms of entertainment.

24 Alonzo Le Blanc's informative edited version of the play has a full discussion of the story and play's fascinating history.

25 Linteau, *Histoire de Montréal*, 321–2, and Dickinson and Young, *A Short History of Quebec*, 241, 286, discuss Groulx's intellectual influence.

26 See Jean Laflamme and Rémi Tourangeau's *L'Église et le théâtre au Québec* for details on this phenomenon.

27 The article on Tremayne and references to Caplan in the article on radio drama in English for the *Oxford Companion* give some idea of these professionals' activities in Montreal and the United States.

28 *The Gazette* (9 February 1920, 3) makes brief mention of the two-week gross for the production – $58,000.

29 Plate 55 of the *Historical Atlas*, "Metropolitan Dominance" by Gunter Gad, demonstrates Toronto's evolving control of Canada's economy.

30 See Dickinson and Young, *A Short History of Quebec*, 250.

31 Plate 45 in the *Historical Atlas*, "Workers' Responses" by Gregory S. Kealey and Douglas Cruikshank, provides information of union activity. Plate 40, "Economic Crisis" by Elizabeth and Gerald Bloomfield, Deryck W. Holdsworth, and Murdo MacPherson, and plate 41, "The Impact of the Depression on People" by Deryck W. Holdsworth and Murdo MacPherson, demonstrate the devastating decline in Canada's economy from 1929–32 and its minimal and tentative prewar recovery.

32 Dickinson and Young, *A Short History of Quebec*, 280–3, discusses the "Duplesssis Phenomenon," his rise to power, and first term of office.

33 Dickinson and Young (ibid., 285–6) assesses the conflicts in Quebec's Catholic Church between conservatism and modernism.

34 See *The Gazette* article "The Little Theatre" (23 November 1929, 10). The writer (J.L.S.) makes reference to the recently published report by Kenneth Macgowan about little theatre development in the United States and Canada.

35 Full details of the meeting were carried in *The Gazette,* 25 November 1929, 5. Chapters 2 and 3 of Booth's MA thesis offer the most comprehensive assessment of Martha Allan's achievements with the MRT.

36 While Whittaker's entry on the Montreal Repertory Theatre in the *Oxford Companion* is a useful synthesis, again the most comprehensive source for details about the MRT can be found in Booth's MA thesis.

37 Westley, *Remembrance of Grandeur,* 231, describes this particular cultural conflict.

38 Betty Lee's *Love and Whisky* gives a book-length account of the many theatrical and political events surrounding the Dominion Drama Festival.

39 Domination in the production, distribution, and exhibition aspects of the motion picture industry by Americans did lead in the early years of the economic crash to a comprehensive Department of Labour investigation into the monopolistic practices of the industry in Canada. The final report, completed in 1931, pointed out the obvious, that a monopoly situation existed in Canada. No action was taken. Manjunath Pendakur's *Canadian Dreams and American Control* (Toronto: Garamond Press, 1988), 56–91, offers a compelling analysis of the motion picture industry at that time.

40 Tippett's *Making Culture,* 80, provides details about the origins of the network.

41 Dickinson and Young, *A Short History of Quebec,* 227, generally discusses the cultural effect of radio on Quebec culture. Renée Legris in her article "La radiodramaturgie québécoise" provides a wealth of contextual assessment of radio's influence in Quebec culture as does Madeleine Greffard's "Le théâtre à la radio."

42 The *Oxford Companion*'s articles on le Théâtre Stella, Fred Barry, and Theatre in Quebec (French) give some further details of this theatre's history. A complete discussion of Mercier-Gouin's significance in Montreal culture, with a special emphasis on *Cocktail* can be found in Christyl Verdun's article "Une voix féminine précoce au théâtre québécois."

43 The most recent assessment of this period of Montreal theatre is Jean-Marc Larrue's "Le théâtre au Québec entre 1930 et 1950."

44 Anne-Marie Sicotte's *Gratien Gélinas* provides a complete, almost day-by-day biography of Gélinas and his theatrical activities.

45 See Gilbert David's article in the *Oxford Companion*, "Theatre in Quebec (French)."

46 Gilbert David's article, "L'offensive du théâtre théocentrique," notes the significant impact of religious thought on the development of Quebec theatre throughout the 1930s and 1940s.

47 In the 1940s les Compagnons published their own bulletin, *Les cahiers des Compagnons* (1944–47), with many essays on the purpose and meaning of theatre.

48 Toby Gordon Ryan's *Stage Left,* 86–107, offers some first-hand accounts of the New Theatre Group's activities in Montreal.

49 In *City Unique* Weintraub evocatively recreates the activities surrounding the monarchs' visit in the first seventeen pages of his history of Montreal's cultures.

50 Plate 48 in the *Historical Atlas*, "The Home Front in the Second World War" by Christopher A. Sharpe and Lynne Marks, notes the nearly 73,000 Montrealers employed in the war industries.

51 Weintraub, *City Unique*, 50–2, provides full details of these wartime tensions.

52 Dickinson and Young, *A Short History of Quebec*, 283–7, analyses these developments, the precursors to the Quiet Revolution of the 1960s.

53 Plate 48 in the *Historical Atlas* demonstrates the increasingly dominant role of the federal government during the war years. Dickinson and Young, *A Short History of Quebec*, 280, details the legislative initiatives of the federal government.

54 Dickinson and Young (ibid., 282–3) notes the initiatives of the provincial government.

55 See Plate 55 in the *Historical Atlas* for a graphic presentation.

56 Weintraub, *City Unique*, and Bourassa and Larrue in *Les nuits de la "Main"* give full details of the various forms of nightlife that flourished in Montreal.

57 Weintraub, *City Unique*, 116–20, proffers all the dirt.

58 Sicotte's book on Gélinas (233–303) describes all the details of the *Tit-Coq* success story.

59 A quote from Arthur Laurendeau writing for *L'Action nationale* in March–April 1949 to celebrate the 150th performance of *Tit-Coq* (cited in Sicotte, *Gratien Gélinas*, 245).

SELECTED BIBLIOGRAPHY OF ARTICLES
AND BOOKS PERTAINING TO THEATRE
IN MONTREAL, 1920–1949

Full bibliographical information for those texts referred to in *Setting the Stage* that do not appear in this selected bibliography is provided in the notes.

Anonymous. "Auditoria, professional theatre, civic theatre." *The Arts in Montreal, Report of a Survey of Montreal's Artistic Resources.* Montreal: Junior League of Montreal, 1956.

– "Brae Manor Theatre: A Success Story." *Curtain Call* 12 (April 1941): 6.

– "Discussion: histoire du théâtre amateur et professionnel/ History of English Canadian Amateur and Professional Theatre." *Canadian Drama* 1 (Fall 1975): 68–75.

– "Little Theatre Activities across Canada." *Curtain Call* 9 (Oct. 1937): 22–3.

– "Montreal Repertory Theatre." *World Premieres Mondiales* 16 (March 1961): 3.

– "Perspectives sur les Compagnons de Saint-Laurent." *Le recueil* 17 (Jan. 1946).

– "Troupe from Canada." *Newsweek*, 23 Dec. 1946, 84.

Archer, Thomas. "'Hamlet' by the MRT." *Saturday Night*, 7 Jan. 1933, 6.

– "Little Theatre Work in Montreal." *Saturday Night*, 7 Jan. 1933.

– "The Montreal Season." *Saturday Night*, 3 June 1933, 6.

– "Montreal Theatre." *Saturday Night*, 22 April 1933, 15.

– "The MRT in Montreal." *Saturday Night*, 3 Dec. 1932, 25.

Aubry, Suzanne. *Le théâtre au Québec. L'émergence d'une dramatique nationale.* Montreal: Centre québécois de l'Institut international du théâtre, 1983.

Auteuil, Georges-Henri d'. "Le théâtre de 1930 à 1945." In Pierre de Grandpré, ed., *Histoire de la littérature française du Québec (1900–45),* vol. 2, 295–305. Montreal: Beauchemin, 1968.

– "Le théâtre de 1945 à nos jours." In Pierre de Grandpré, ed., *Histoire de la littérature française du Québec*, vol. 4, 181–234. Montreal: Beauchemin, 1969.

Ball, John, and Richard Plant, eds. *Bibliography of Theatre History in Canada: The Beginning through 1984.* Toronto: ECW Press, 1993.

Beauchamp-Forget, Jacques. "*Radio et théâtre en 1948,*" introduction by Pierre Pagé. *L'Annuaire théâtral* 9 (Spring 1991): 37–52.

Beauchamp-Rank, Hélène. "Histoire du théâtre amateur et professionel au Québec." *L'Art dramatique canadien* 1 (Fall 1975): 56–9.

Beaugrand-Champagne, Guy. "L'histoire des Compagnons." *Jeunesse canadienne* 13 (Dec. 1948): 19–24.

Beaulieu, Paul. "Réflexions sur *l'Échange.*" *La relève* 4 (June 1938): 7.

Beaulne, Guy. *Notre théâtre, conscience d'un peuple.* Quebec: Ministère des Affaires culturelles, 1967.

– "La radio au service du théâtre." *L'Annuaire théâtral* 9 (Spring 1991): 121–36.

Benson, Eugene, and Leonard W. Conolly, eds. *The Oxford Companion to Canadian Theatre.* Toronto: Oxford University Press, 1989.

Béraud, Jean. "Pour un théâtre national." *Initiation à l'art dramatique*, 183–227. Montreal: Les Éditions Variétés, 1936.

– Béraud, Jean, Léon Francke, and Marcel Valois. *Variations sur trois thèmes: le théâtre, le cinéma, la musique.* Montreal: Éditions Fernand Pilon, 1946.

– *350 ans de théâtre au Canada français. Encyclopédie du Canada français*, vol. 1. Montreal: Le Cercle du livre de France, 1958.

– "L'ancien théâtre Stella." *Theatre* 2 (May 1965): 53–5.

Bisson, Margaret Mary. "Le théâtre français à Montréal, 1878–1931." Master's thesis, McGill University, 1932.

Boivin-Allaire, Émilia. *Têtes de femmes.* Québec, Éditions de l'Équinoxe, 1963.

Bolduc, Yves. "Gratien Gélinas." In Wyczynski, Julien, and Beauchamp-Rank, eds., *Le théâtre canadien-français.*

Bolster, Charles. "Shakespeare dans le théâtre québécois." In Wyczynski, Julien, and Beauchamp-Rank, eds., *Le théâtre canadien-français.*

Bolton, Mada Gage. "The Lakeshore Summer Theatre." *Curtain Call* 12 (Oct. 1940): 5–6.

Booth, Philip J. "The Montreal Repertory Theatre: 1930–1961 – A History and Handlist of Productions." Master's thesis, McGill University, 1989.

– "Le Montreal Repertory Theatre et les théâtres d'art." *L'Annuaire théâtral* 13 (Spring-Fall 1993): 59–74.

– "Les archives du théâtre de langue anglaise à Montréal." *L'Annuaire théâtral* 17 (Spring 1995): 53–62.

Bourassa, André-G. "Vers la modernité de la scène québécoise: les contrecourants, 1905–1951." *Pratiques théâtrales* 13 (Fall 1981): 3–26.

– "Vers la modernité de la scène québécoise (II): les contrecourants, 1901–1951." *Pratiques théâtrales* 14–15 (Fall-Winter 1982): 3–31.

– "La Salle de l'Ermitage." In Benson and Conolly, eds., *The Oxford Companion to Canadian Theatre.*

– "La Salle du Gesù." In Benson and Conolly, eds., *The Oxford Companion to Canadian Theatre.*

– "Premières modernités (1930–1965)." In Legris, Larrue, Bourassa, and David, eds., *Le théâtre au Québec, 1825–1980.*

– "La Salle du Gesù, 1865–1995: une pièce d'archives." *L'Annuaire théâtral* 17 (Spring 1995): 17–26.

Bourassa, André-G., and Jean-Marc Larrue. "Le Monument-National (1893–1923): trente ans de théâtre dans la Salle Ludger-Duvernay." *L'Annuaire théâtral* 10 (Fall 1991): 69–102.

– *Les nuits de la "Main": cent ans de spectacles sur le boulevard Saint-Laurent (1891–1991).* Montreal: VLB éditeur, 1993.

Briggs, Peter. "Sir Barry Vincent Jackson and the Canadian Theatre." *Canadian Drama* 6 (Fall 1982): 242–55.

Bruchési, Jean. "L'œuvre du Montreal Repertory Theatre." *La revue moderne* 14 (March 1933).

Brunet, Berthelot. *Histoire de la littérature canadienne-française.* Montreal: L'Arbre, 1946.

Bryden, Ronald, and Boyd Neil, eds. *Whittaker's Theatre.* Greenbank, Ont.: The Whittaker Project, 1985.

Burkett, Will. "Community Drama in Montreal." *Canadian Forum* 12 (June 1932): 358–9.

Camerlain, Lorraine, and Diane Pavlovic. *Cent ans de théâtre à Montréal photographies.* Montreal: Éditions des Cahiers de théâtre Jeu, 1988.

Caron, Anne. *Le père Legault et le théâtre au Québec.* Montreal: Fides, 1978.

Carrier, Denis. "Le Théâtre National." In Benson and Conolly, eds., *The Oxford Companion to Canadian Theatre.*

Clairoux, Jacques M. "Le vaudeville au Québec 1900–1930." *Les cahiers de la Société d'histoire du théâtre du Québec* 8 (June 1992): 3–64.

Clayton, J. Douglas. "Bears and Beavers: Canadian Stage Productions of Russian Plays." *Theatre History in Canada* 3 (Fall 1982): 149–63.

Coleman, Francis A. "The Theatre in Canada: Les Compagnons." *Theatre Arts* 30 (July 1946): 391–2.

Compagnon, Un. "Vers un théâtre authentique: 'Le Misanthrope' de Molière." *Le Laurentien* 11 (Nov. 1939): 6.

Comte, Gustave. "Le Monument-National revient aux Canadiens." *La Patrie*, 23 August 1923, 14.

Corriveau, Jeanne. "Le théâtre collégial au Québec. L'apport de Gustave Lamarche." In Wyczynski, Julien, and Beauchamp-Rank, eds., *Le théâtre canadien-français.*

Conolly, Leonard W., ed. *Theatrical Touring and Founding in North America.* Westport, Conn.: Greenwood Press, 1982.

Cotnam, Jacques. *Le théâtre québécois: instrument de contestation sociale et politique.* Montreal: Fides, 1976.

Cunningham, Joyce. "L'ancien théâtre Stella 1930–1936." *Jeu* 6 (Summer-Fall 1977): 62–79.

D'Auteuil, Georges-Henri. "Le théâtre de 1930 à 1945." In Pierre de Grandpré, ed., *Histoire de la littérature française du Québec*, vol. 4. Montreal: Beauchemin, 1973.

Dagenais, Pierre. ... *et je suis resté au Québec*. Montreal: Éditions *La Presse*, 1974.

– "Pierre Dagenais." In Wyczynski, Julien, and Beauchamp-Rank, eds., *Le théâtre canadien-français*.

David, Gilbert. "Theatre in Quebec (French)." In Benson and Conolly, eds., *The Oxford Companion to Canadian Theatre*.

– "Les Compagnons de Saint-Laurent." In Benson and Conolly, eds., *The Oxford Companion to Canadian Theatre*.

– "Léopold Houlé." In Benson and Conolly, eds., *The Oxford Companion to Canadian Theatre*.

– "Signaux contradictoires d'un théâtre renaissant." *L'Annuaire théâtral* 23 (Spring 1998): 11–18.

– "L'offensive du théâtre théocentrique." *L'Annuaire théâtral* 23 (Spring 1998): 38–52.

Davies, Robertson. "Mixed Grill: Touring Fare in Canada, 1920–35." In L.W. Conolly, ed., *Theatrical Touring and Founding in North America*.

Day, Pierre. *Une histoire de La Bolduc – Légendes et turlutes*. Montreal: VLB éditeur, 1992.

Demchinsky, Bryan. *Montreal: Then and Now*. Montreal: *The Gazette*, 1985.

Deschamps, Marcel. *Dossier en théâtre québécois de 1935 à nos jours*. Quebec: Département des études canadiennes, Université Laval, 1970.

Desmarchais, Rex. "Les Compagnons de Saint-Laurent." *L'école canadienne* 18 (Jan. 1943): 197–9.

Doat, Ian. *Anthologie du théâtre québécois 1606–1970*. Quebec: Éditions la liberté, 1973.

Duliani, Mario. *La fortune vient en parlant*. Montreal: Éditions Fernand Pilon, 1948.

Doucette, Leonard E. "Theatre, French-Language." *The Canadian Encyclopedia*. Edmonton: Hurtig, 1985.

– "Drama in French." In Benson and Conolly, eds., *The Oxford Companion to Canadian Theatre.*

Duval, Étienne-F. *Le jeu de l'histoire et de la société dans le théâtre québécois 1900–1950.* Trois-Rivières: Université du Québec à Trois-Rivières, 1981.

Edwards, Murray D. "A Playwright from the Canadian Past: W.A. Tremayne (1864–1939)." *Theatre History in Canada* 3 (Spring 1982): 43–50.

– "William A. Tremayne." In Benson and Conolly, eds., *The Oxford Companion to Canadian Theatre.*

Fink, Howard. "Canadian Radio Drama and the Radio Drama Project." *Canadian Theatre Review* 36 (1982): 12–22

– "Radio Drama, English Language." *The Canadian Encyclopedia.* Edmonton: Hurtig, 1985.

– "Radio Drama in English." In Benson and Conolly, eds., *The Oxford Companion to Canadian Theatre.*

Fink, Howard, and Brian Morrison. *Canadian National Theatre on the Air – 1925–1961.* Toronto: University of Toronto Press, 1983.

Forsyth, Louise. "Drama in French. 1900 to 1948." In *The Oxford Companion to Canadian Literature.* Toronto: Oxford University Press, 1983.

Fortin, Marcel. "Les artisans des jeux scéniques et le mouvement associatif québécois." *L'Annuaire théâtral* 10 (Fall 1991): 21–32.

Fournier, Marcel. *L'entrée dans la modernité. Science, culture et société au Québec.* Montreal: Éditions Saint-Martin, 1986.

Gagnon, Gilles. "Le théâtre des Compagnons de Saint-Laurent." *Culture* 30 (1969): 129–45.

Gardner, David. "Little Theatre and Amateur Theatre." In Benson and Conolly, eds., *The Oxford Companion to Canadian Theatre.*

– "Little Theatre Movement." *The Canadian Encyclopedia.* Edmonton: Hurtig, 1985.

Gascon, Jean. "Le théâtre comme façon de vivre." *Société royale du Canada/Présentations* 33 (4th quarter 1978).

Gélinas, Gratien. *Les Fridolinades, 1938–40, 1941–42, 1943–44, 1945–46.* 4 vol. Montreal: Quinze, 1980–88.

— "Pour un théâtre national et populaire." *Amérique française* 1 (April-June 1949): 32–42.

— "Pour une littérature théâtrale." *La nouvelle relève* 6 (Dec. 1947): 17–22.

— "Un théâtre national et populaire." *L'action universitaire* 15 (April 1949): 30–9.

Germain, Jean-Claude. "À quel moment faudrait-il situer la naissance du théâtre québécois." *Jeu* 13, 1 (1979): 19–25.

Gibbon, John Murray. *Our Old Montreal.* Toronto: McClelland and Stewart, 1947.

Gobin, Pierre. "Les années difficiles: crises et renaissances des théâtres à Montréal 1929–1945." *Histoire du théâtre au Canada* 1 (Fall 1980): 124–34.

Godin, Jean-Cléo, and Laurent Mailhot. *Le théâtre québécois.* Montreal: Hurtubise HMH, 1970.

Godin, Jean-Cléo. "Foreign Touring Companies and the Founding of Theatres in Quebec, 1880–1900 and 1930–1950." In L.W. Conolly, ed., *Theatrical Touring and Founding in America.*

— "Julien Daoust: dramaturge 1866–1943." *Histoire du théâtre au Canada* 4 (Fall 1983): 113–20.

— "Henry Deyglun." In Benson and Conolly, eds., *The Oxford Companion to Canadian Theatre.*

— "Olivier Guimond." In Benson and Conolly, eds., *The Oxford Companion to Canadian Theatre.*

— "L'Équipe (1942–1948) de Pierre Dagenais." *L'Annuaire théâtral* 23 (Spring 1998): 74–89.

Gold, Muriel. "A Study of Three Montreal Children's Theatres." Master's thesis, McGill University, 1972.

Goulet, Charles. *Sur la scène et dans la coulisse.* Quebec: Ministère des Affaires culturelles, 1981.

Graham, Bill. "Sir John Martin-Harvey: The Last Imperial Envoy." *Theatre History in Canada* 14 (Spring 1993): 90–103.

Grimaldi, Jean. *Jean Grimaldi présente*. Montreal: René Ferron Éditeur, 1973.

Grandmont, Eloi de. "Marius." *Le Devoir*, 16 May 1944, 4.

Greffard, Madeleine. "Le théâtre à la radio: un facteur de légitimation et de redéfinition." *L'Annuaire théâtral* 23 (Spring 1998): 53–73.

Greffard, Madeleine, and Jean-Guy Sabourin. *Le théâtre québécois*. Montreal: Éditions du Boréal, 1997.

Hamelin, Jean. *Le théâtre au Canada français*. Quebec: Ministère des Affaires culturelles, 1964.

– *Le renouveau du théâtre au Canada français*. Montreal: Éditions du jour, 1962.

Hare, John E. "Bibliographie du théâtre canadien-français." In Wyczynski, Julien, and Beachamp-Rank, eds., *Le théâtre canadien-français*.

– "Le théâtre professionnel à Montréal de 1898 à 1937." In Wyczynski, Julien, and Beauchamp-Rank, eds., *Le théâtre canadien-français*.

– "Le théâtre québécois des origines à 1930." In René Dionne, ed., *Québécois et sa littérature,* 216–41. Sherbrooke: Naaman, 1984.

– "Samuel Morgan-Powell." In Benson and Conolly, eds., *The Oxford Companion to Canadian Theatre*.

Harvie, Jennifer, and Ric Knowles. "Herbert Whittaker, Reporting from the Front." In Wagner, ed., *Establishing Our Boundaries*.

Hébert, Chantal. *Le burlesque au Québec: un divertissement populaire*. Montreal: Hurtubise HMH, 1981.

– *Le burlesque québécois et américain*. Quebec: Presses de l'Université Laval, 1989.

– "Burlesque (Quebec)." In Benson and Conolly, eds., *The Oxford Companion to Canadian Theatre*.

Houle, Jean-Pierre. "Les Compagnons." *Action universitaire* 12 (Dec. 1945): 20–2.

Houlé, Léopold. *L'histoire du théâtre au Canada: pour un retour aux classiques*. Montreal: Fides, 1945.

Jubinville, Yves. "La traversée du désert. Lecture discursive des *Cahiers des Compagnons* (1944–1947)," *L'Annuaire théâtral* 23 (spring 1998): 90–106.

Kidd, Ross. "Théâtre et action populaire au Canada." *Offensives* 2 (Sept.-Dec. 1981).

Laflamme, Jean, and Rémi Tourangeau. *L'Église et le théâtre au Québec.* Montreal: Fides, 1979.

Laframboise, Phillipe. *Fred Barry, père du théâtre canadien d'expression française et doyen des artistes du Québec (1887–1964).* Montreal: Chez l'auteur, 1965.

– *La Poune.* Montreal: Éditions Héritage, 1978.

La France, Micheline. *Denise Pelletier ou la folie du théâtre.* Montreal: Éditions Scriptomedia, 1979.

Lamarche, Gustave. *Textes et discussions.* Montreal: Éditions de l'Action nationale, 1969.

Lamonde, Yvan, and Esther Trepanier, eds., *L'avènement de la modernité culturelle au Québec.* Quebec: Institut québécois de recherche sur la culture, 1986.

Larrue, Jean-Marc. *Le monument inattendu: le Monument-National de Montréal, 1893–1993.* Montreal: Hurtubise HMH, 1993.

– *Le théâtre yiddish à Montréal – Yiddish Theatre in Montreal.* Montreal: Jeu, 1996.

– "Le théâtre au Québec entre 1930 et 1950: les années charnières." *L'Annuaire théâtral* 23 (Spring 1998): 19–37.

Laurence, Gérard. "Radio Drama, French-Language." *The Canadian Encyclopedia.* Edmonton: Hurtig, 1985.

Laurendeau, André. "À propos de Fridolin et d'art populaire." *L'Action catholique,* 30 Jan. 1941.

Laurent, Edouard. "Tit-Coq, un conscrit qui passera à l'histoire." *Culture* 9 (Dec. 1948): 378–83.

Laurion, Gaston. "L'au-revoir des Compagnons." *L'Action nationale* 29 (June 1947): 483–5.

Lavoie, Pierre. *Pour suivre le théâtre au Québec. Les ressources documentaires.* Quebec: Institut québécois de recherche sur la culture, 1985.

Lawrence, Robert G. "Touring Stars and Companies (British)." In Benson and Conolly, eds., *The Oxford Companion to Canadian Theatre.*

– "John Martin-Harvey in Canada." *Canadian Drama* 6 (Fall 1980): 234–41.

LeBlanc, Alonzo. "La tradition théâtrale à Québec (1790–1973)." In Wyczynski, Julien, and Beauchamp-Rank, eds., *Le théâtre canadien-français.*

– "Aurore, l'enfant martyre." In Benson and Conolly, eds., *The Oxford Companion to Canadian Theatre.*

– "Fred Barry." In Benson and Conolly, eds., *The Oxford Companion to Canadian Theatre.*

– "Le Monument-National." In Benson and Conolly, eds., *The Oxford Companion to Canadian Theatre.*

– "The Cross-Fertilization of Cultures in Quebec Theater." In Donahue, Joseph I. Jr., and Jonathan M. Weiss, eds., *Essays on Modern Quebec Theater.* East Lansing: Michigan State University Press, 1995.

Lee, Betty. *Love and Whisky: The Story of the Dominion Drama Festival.* Toronto: McClelland and Stewart, 1973.

Legault, Émile. *Confidences.* Montreal: Fides, 1955.

– "Quelques notes sur les Compagnons de Saint-Laurent (1937–1952)." In Wyczynski, Julien, and Beauchamp-Rank, eds., *Le théâtre canadien-français.*

– "Perspectives sur les Compagnons." *Relations* 5 (Oct. 1945): 272–3.

– "Le théâtre immortel." *Théâtre Canada* 1 (Jan.-Feb. 1951): 3–4.

– "Théâtre populaire." *L'Action nationale* 11 (June 1938): 514–21.

– "Le théâtre qu'il nous faut." *Amérique française* 2 (June 1943): 27–35.

LeGrand, Albert. "Avec les Compagnons à l'Ermitage." *Relations* 2 (Dec. 1942): 331–2.

Legris, Renée. "Radio Drama in Quebec." In Benson and Conolly, eds., *The Oxford Companion to Canadian Theatre.*

– "La radiodramaturgie québécoise. Quelques perspectives historiques." *L'Annuaire théâtral* 9 (Spring 1991): 23–36.

Legris, Renée, Jean-Marc Larrue, André-G. Bourassa, and Gilbert David, eds. *Le théâtre au Québec, 1825–1980: Repères et perspectives.* Montreal: VLB éditeur, 1988.

Legris, Renée, and Pierre Pagé. "Le théâtre à la radio et à la télévision au Québec." In Wyczynski, Julien, and Beauchamp-Rank, eds., *Le théâtre canadien-français.*

Leroux, Normand. "Yvette Brind'Amour." In Benson and Conolly, eds., *The Oxford Companion to Canadian Theatre*.

– "Le Théâtre Stella." In Benson and Conolly, eds., *The Oxford Companion to Canadian Theatre*.

MacPhail, Sir Andrew. "The Montreal Repertory Theatre Inc." *Theatre Arts Monthly* 16 (July 1932): 566–7.

Mailhot, Laurent. "Le théâtre québécois jusqu'en 1945." *Revue de l'Université d'Ottawa* 49 (Jan.-April 1979): 59–62.

Mailhot, Laurent, and Doris-Michel Montpetit. *Monologues québécois 1890–1980*. Montreal: Fides, 1981.

Malouin, Serge. "Les Compagnons de Saint-Laurent." Ph.D. diss. Sherbrooke: Université de Sherbrooke, 1968.

Marquis, G. E. "La statistique de théâtres dans la province du Québec," *Mon magazine* 3 (Jan. 1929): 8.

Moore, James Mavor. "History of English Canadian Amateur and Professional Theatre." *Canadian Drama* 1 (Fall 1975): 66–7.

Morgan-Powell, Samuel. *Memories That Live*. Toronto: Macmillan, 1929.

N., M.E. "MRT Anniversary." *Saturday Night* 65 (Dec. 1949): 19.

Nardocchio, Elaine. *Theatre in Quebec: A Cultural Reflection*. Toronto: Canadian Theatre Review Publications, 1982.

Neilson, Patrick. "Charles Burkett Rittenhouse: Theatrical Avocations and Affiliations 1925–76." *Theatre History in Canada* 4 (Spring 1983): 73–92.

Noiseux-Gurik, Renée. "Laure Cabana: pionnière du métier de costumier." *Histoire du théâtre au Canada* 8 (Spring 1987): 36–48.

– "À la recherche des peintres scéniques du Monument-National." *Les cahiers de la Société d'histoire du théâtre du Québec* 1 (Sept. 1990): 5–23.

Normand, Jacques. *Les nuits de Montréal*. Montreal: Éditions *La Presse*, 1974.

O'Neill, Patrick B. "The Dumbells." In Benson and Conolly, eds., *The Oxford Companion to Canadian Theatre*.

– "The Navy Show." In Benson and Conolly, eds., *The Oxford Companion to Canadian Theatre.*

Pagé, Pierre. "Le théâtre de répertoire international à *Radio Collège* (1941–1956)." *L'Annuaire théâtral* 12 (Fall 1992): 53–87.

Pagé, Raymond. "De la scène à la radio: le *Jeu de la Voyagère.*" *L'Annuaire théâtral* 10 (Fall 1991): 45–54.

Pageau, René. *Gustave Lamarche, poète dramatique.* Quebec: Les Éditions Garneau, 1976).

Palmieri, Joseph Archambault. *Mes souvenirs de théâtre.* Montreal: Éditions de l'Étoile, 1944.

Parabolier. "Mouvement du théâtre canadien." *Carnets viatoriens* 7 (April 1942): 134

Parent, Jean-Marie. "Les Compagnons de Saint-Laurent." *L'Action nationale* 6 (Feb. 1938): 162–6.

Pétrie, Juliette, and Jean Leclerc. *Quand on revoit tout ça! Le burlesque au Québec 1914–1960.* Montreal: Les Éditions Juliette Pétrie, 1977.

Petitjean, Léon, and Henri Rollin. *Aurore, l'enfant martyre,* edited by Alonzo Le Blanc. Montreal: VLB éditeur, 1982.

Prévost, Robert. *Que sont-ils devenus?* Montreal: Éditions Princeps, 1939.

Primeau, Marguerite-A. "Gratien Gélinas et le théâtre populaire au Canada français." In William H. New, ed., *Dramatists in Canada, Selected Essays.* Vancouver: University of British Columbia Press, 1972.

Rabinovitch, Israel. "Yiddish Theatre in Montreal," 2: 166–71. Montreal: *Canadian Jewish Year Book, 1940–41.*

Raymond, Marcel. "*L'échange* chez les Compagnons de Saint-Laurent." *La nouvelle relève* 1 (Feb. 1942): 366–71.

Rickett, Olla. "The French-speaking Theatre of Montreal, 1937–1963." Ph.D. diss. Cornell University, 1964.

Rinfret, Edouard G. *Le théâtre canadien d'expression française: répertoire analytique des origines à nos jours,* vols. 1–4. Montreal: Leméac, 1975–78.

Ripley, John. "Gratien Gélinas." In Benson and Conolly, eds., *The Oxford Companion to Canadian Theatre.*

– "Her Majesty's Theatre (Montreal)." In Benson and Conolly, eds., *The Oxford Companion to Canadian Theatre.*

– "*Tit-Coq.*" In Benson and Conolly, eds., *The Oxford Companion to Canadian Theatre.*

Rittenhouse, Charles. "Montreal Experiences Theatre Renaissance." *Saturday Night* 62 (Sept. 1946): 23.

Rittenhouse, Jonathan. "Herbert Whittaker: A Theatre Life." *Theatre History in Canada* 3 (Spring 1982): 51–78.

– "Theatre in Quebec (English)." In Benson and Conolly, eds., *The Oxford Companion to Canadian Theatre.*

– "Charles Rittenhouse." In Benson and Conolly, eds., *The Oxford Companion to Canadian Theatre.*

– "Herbert Whittaker." In Benson and Conolly, eds., *The Oxford Companion to Canadian Theatre.*

Robert, Guy. *Aspects de la littérature québécoise.* Montreal: Beauchemin, 1970.

Russell, D. W. "Le théâtre de langue française au Canada avant 1945." *L'Art dramatique canadien* 7 (Spring 1981): 1–2.

Ryan, Toby Gordon. *Stage Left: Canadian Theatre in the Thirties: A Memoir.* Toronto: CTR Publications, 1981.

Sandrow, Nahma. *Vagabond Stars – A World History of Yiddish Theater.* New York: Limelight Editions, 1986.

Saumart, Ingrid. *La vie extraordinaire de Jean Despréz.* Montreal: Les Éditions du Jour, 1965.

Sicotte, Anne-Marie. *Gratien Gélinas: Le ferveur et le doute. Tome I, 1909–56.* Montreal: Éditions Québec/Amerique, 1995.

Stuart, Ross. "Earle Grey." In Benson and Conolly, eds., *The Oxford Companion to Canadian Theatre.*

Tait, Michael. "Drama and Theatre 1920–1960." In Carl F. Clinck, ed., *Literary History of Canada 1920–1960,* vol. 2. Toronto: University of Toronto Press, 1976.

Tougas, Gerard. *Histoire de la littérature canadienne-française.* Paris: Presses universitaires de France, 1967.

Tourangeau, Rémi. "L'église et le théâtre au Québec ou l'apparent paradoxe du clergé," *L'Art dramatique canadien* 7 (Spring 1981): 19–28.

Usmiani, Renate. *Gratien Gélinas.* Toronto: Gage, 1977.

Verduyn, Christl. "Une voix précoce au théâtre québécois: *Cocktail* (1935) d'Yvette Ollivier Mercier-Gouin." *Histoire du théâtre au Canada* 11 (Spring 1990): 48–58.

Wagner, Anton, ed. *Establishing Our Boundaries: English-Canadian Theatre Criticism.* Toronto: University of Toronto Press, 1999.

– "Theatre and National Identity, French Canadian Political Theatre, 1606–1971." *Alive* 31 (1973): 17–21.

– "Nationalism and the French-Canadian Drama." *Canadian Theatre Review* 1 (Winter 1974): 22–7.

Weintraub, William. *City Unique: Montreal Days and Nights in the 1940s and '50s.* Toronto: McClelland and Stewart, 1996.

Whittaker, Herbert. "Fridolin Our Star." *Canadian Review of Music and Art* 5 (Feb. 1946): 11–13.

– "Shakespeare in Canada before 1953." In *Shakespeare Seminar, Stratford, Ont. Stratford Papers on Shakespeare,* 71–89. Toronto: Gage, 1964.

– "The Theatre." In *Illustrated Library of the World and Its Peoples: Canada.* New York: Greystone Press, 1967–68.

– "Canada – Theatre." In *Encyclopedia Americana,* 5: 435–7. Toronto: Americana Corporation of Canada, 1970.

– *Whittaker's Theatre. A Critic Looks at Stages in Canada and Thereabouts.* Edited by Ronald Bryden and Boyd Neil. Greenbank, Ont.: The Whittaker Project, 1985.

– "Whittaker's Montreal: A Theatrical Autobiography, 1910–49," edited and with an introduction by Rota Herzberg Lister. *Canadian Drama* 12 (Fall 1986): 233–331.

—   "Martha Allan." In Benson and Conolly, eds., *The Oxford Companion to Canadian Theatre.*

—   "Brae Manor Theatre." In Benson and Conolly, eds., *The Oxford Companion to Canadian Theatre.*

—   "Pierre Dagenais." In Benson and Conolly, eds., *The Oxford Companion to Canadian Theatre.*

—   "Dominion Drama Festival." In Benson and Conolly, eds., *The Oxford Companion to Canadian Theatre.*

—   "L'Équipe." In Benson and Conolly, eds., *The Oxford Companion to Canadian Theatre.*

—   "Montreal Repertory Theatre." In Benson and Conolly, eds., *The Oxford Companion to Canadian Theatre.*

—   "Mountain Playhouse." In Benson and Conolly, eds., *The Oxford Companion to Canadian Theatre.*

—   "Orpheum Theatre (Montreal)." In Benson and Conolly, eds., *The Oxford Companion to Canadian Theatre.*

—   "Norma Springford." In Benson and Conolly, eds., *The Oxford Companion to Canadian Theatre.*

—   "Eleanor Stuart." In Benson and Conolly, eds., *The Oxford Companion to Canadian Theatre.*

Woods, Alan. "Touring Stars and Companies (American)." In Benson and Conolly, eds., *The Oxford Companion to Canadian Theatre.*

Wyczynski, Paul, Bernard Julien, and Hélène Beauchamp-Rank, eds. *Le théâtre canadien-français.* Vol. 5 in *Archives des lettres canadiennes.* Montreal: Fides, 1976.

INDEX